Travel Lessons

Your personal guide to better travel

Travel Lessons

Your personal guide to better travel

Glenn Schmidt

HenschelHAUS Publishing, Inc.
Milwaukee, Wisconsin

Photographs provided by the author unless otherwise noted.
Cover Photo: Amsterdam in Winter.

Published by HenschelHAUS Publishing, Inc.
www.henschelHAUSbooks.com
Milwaukee, Wisconsin

ISBN: 978159598-993-2
LCCN: 2024937850

Printed in the United States of America.

Travel Lessons
Your personal guide to better travel

Table of Contents: The Travel Curriculum

Introduction

In this photo I'm sitting at a café table alone on the Left Bank in Paris. It's 2004 and you can see a coffee cup, the remnants of a croissant and an International Herald Tribune spread out in front of me, its contents so clear as to be readable. I'm smiling, perhaps laughing, at my friend, Curt Christensen, who is fiddling with the settings of his 3D camera. An unusual bit of bygone technology, it's a relic of the 1960s, and is also known as a stereo camera. Curt loves his toys.

With similar technology to the venerable View-Master kids' toy, the camera never really caught on, mainly because you need special equipment to view the photos. I have literally seen this photo only once. Virtually no one else except Curt has ever seen it.

Fast forward a mere 18 years. I'm at a table at the Hofbräuhaus in Munich. I'm not just looking at the camera, I'm laughing uproariously as I force my friend Bob Lehmann to toast my gigantic mug of beer with what looks like a shot glass by comparison.

By the time we left the table, I had edited the photo and posted it on Facebook. By the time my friends in America got up in the morning, they knew exactly how much fun I was having 5,000 miles away. By the next day, hundreds of people had seen it, often sharing their own stories of Munich and beer.

There's something else about the two photos. I can see it in my face. If you're a traveler, you probably could see it too. There's a certain smugness—let's call it self-satisfaction, in my expression. If you travel the way I do—without a safety net—you've even had the same expression on your face.

On the other hand, if you've traveled on some kind of group tour, you've passed people like us as you struggled to keep up with the woman holding the red-checkered flag who controls your movements. You've glanced our way, wondering why we feel sorry for you. After all, you're in Paris too. You're at the Hofbräuhaus. You're traveling.

Here's the difference. You made one decision to get to this point. Which tour to take. We've made dozens, if not hundreds, of decisions to get here. You've invested money. We've invested ourselves.

I won't explain this any further. If you are content on the tour bus, I wish you happy and safe travels. You can put down this book now.

But if you want more out of travel, this book is for you. It will take you to places you've never seen and help you look at common travel problems as opportunities.

I'm a teacher. I've spent my entire adult life in the classroom creating lesson plans. It's second nature to me. I do what I've always done: study the topic, select what's important, provide some context then design a lesson plan targeting my chosen audience.

Learning travel lessons is a different matter. My teacher is usually experience, an often unsympathetic and disorganized one. She offers no grades for a job well done but plenty of sanctions for one done poorly.

I'm also a trade union leader, with experience on the national and international level. The first piece you'll read is a journey inward. Confessing that I'm a dog is about as introspective as I get. The rest of the book is much more concerned with helping you see the world through a different lens, one that brings everything closer.

Since World War II, we have been living in the Golden Age of Travel. The Cold War couldn't kill it. Neither could terrorism, epidemics or regional wars. Nor could an abused climate striking back with hurricanes, fires, floods and extreme heat. This era has now been joined by the Golden Age of Communications. You can take family and friends with you and they won't have to leave home.

You can be a tourist and take moderate advantage of these concurrent 21st century trends. Or you can be a traveler and take full advantage. Read on.

I am a border collie

Well, not literally. After all I'm not a dog—I'm a cat person really. But I've known from a young age what I am. I take sheep and move them from one place to another, keep them safe, keep them doing what they need to do.

When I was about ten years old, I was a baseball fanatic. With the baby boom years, there were kids in almost every house on the block. I was the guy who organized the baseball games. My early sheepdog instincts required me to knock on every door and get every kid—boy kid, at least—out on the baseball diamond we had carved out of the fields behind the drive-in movie theater.

I cared that I played well, made those diving catches at shortstop and eventually was able to hit the ball over the wall into the drive-in stalls and maybe clank one off the speakers. But what drove me were those whistles, inaudible to others, that directed me to take the herd from a condition of chaos to that of a smooth-running organism, brought together by innings, baselines, and arcane rules.

One year the local park and rec department expanded its kids' softball league out to nearby Bluffview Park, so we fielded an expansion team. We went 0-22 that first year. One bright spot was that I made the all-star team. It took only a little luster off that accomplishment when I found out they had to pick two people from each team and that my friend Pete actually deserved it.

Anyway, I hated losing, so I went out recruiting the following year. I managed to secure all-stars at every position and we fielded a winning team. In fact, I accumulated so many good players that I ended up sitting on the bench during games. That didn't bother me nearly as much as the evil coach who was hired by park and rec. He put me on a leash. He didn't acknowledge that it was my flock out there and insisted it was his job to arrange the players in the field, and he didn't need any help doing it. It didn't go well.

Naturally I selected a career with the most border-collie characteristics: teacher. Not just any teacher; I was a special education teacher. I specialized in the most reluctant sheep, the black sheep, the lame sheep and those in the way of the herd. I used all the tools of a border collie in his prime. Some of the lambs needed a gentle nudge or a sympathetic nuzzle, others a sharp bark or a threatening glare.

Some had parents who had done their best to prepare them for life in the flock; others had parents who mainly concerned themselves with eating grass and defecating in the same patch.

I found that participating in the teachers' union gave me even greater opportunities to use my skills. I was elected president of a 500-member flock, many of whom exhibited non-flockish behavior (and seemed very proud of it). By that time, I knew how to recognize and work together with other border collies. We focused mainly on keeping the herd safe and leading it to more fertile pastures.

Many of the individual sheep in the sheep union didn't know or care who was controlling the herd as long as they stayed warm and dry and safe. Others were very aware—dare I say "woke" sheep, and understood and appreciated the work of the dogs. Still others pretended to be border collies but actually were wolves with a taste for mutton.

Through it all I never gave much thought to who was blowing the whistle. I was no different than the sheep who were being sheepish. I was doing what border collies do. Was it God on the other end of the whistle? Genetics? The media? Politicians? I don't know. I'm just a border collie.

I've spent much of my life traveling, going to exotic places such as Japan, New Zealand, Machu Picchu, Cape Town, the English Lake District, and my favorite, Paris. I am writing this overlooking the Bay of Naples in Sorrento.

I have a unique traveling style. I assemble a flock—10 for this trip through Italy, 22 for a Caribbean cruise last January, 23 when we walked across England. I select the particular fields to visit, usually by collaborating with the sheep themselves, accommodating their fraying wool and my graying fur.

I know I can't keep doing this forever. Counting sheep makes me tired. But I'm a border collie and that's what we do.

Tourist vs Traveler

Name a tour company that gives Americans tours of places in America. Can't come up with one? You've never been on one? That's because Americans don't travel that way here. So it's always mystified me why they think they have to travel that way in Europe. Seriously, it's not that different.

Here are the three reasons that surface when I ask.

1. I don't have much time and I want to see as much as possible.
2. I can't speak the language and don't understand their culture.
3. I want someone more qualified than me to make travel decisions.

Here's my response.

Time

Let's say Paris is your destination. Every year, the French seek out the best baguette in the city, to be served to the president all year at the Elysee Palace. This year it's Au Levain des Pyrenees bakery, located at 44, rue des Pyrenees. You can grab a loaf on your way to see rock singer Jim Morrison's grave at Pére-Lachaise Cemetery.

Neither of those places will be on your tour. You'll certainly be able to check off the Arc de Triomphe from your list, but so what? Watching Paris traffic defeat a shiny monument from the window of a bus isn't as much fun as you'd think. The bread is a better investment. So is the cemetery. Get rid of your check-off list. It's not bingo.

Language and Culture

When you walk into a shop in Paris, turn to the clerk, and say, "Bonjour." If you do not adhere to this ritual, the clerk may not even agree to sell you that nice scarf you picked out. In France, the customer is NOT always right. Protocol is. What's the worst thing that happens if you don't know that rule? An uncomfortable experience that gives you a story to tell when you get home. And you buy a different scarf.

As for language, the world is so different from even a decade ago. English isn't quite everywhere, but it's never far from you when you need it. If a woman from Portugal meets a man from Germany in France, which language do they speak? Yours. Not only that, your phone keeps finding new ways to connect people who speak different languages. Practice using Google Translate and your confidence will soar.

Travel choices

Many people prefer to leave the planning to others. I understand. But how on earth did you manage that Grand Canyon trip with the family? Or the four days in Las Vegas with friends? You did a little bit of research and booked it online. Or if it was too complicated, you had your local travel agent do it.

San Diego is about 2,000 miles from my house. Dublin, Ireland is about 3,600 miles. When I go to either one, I prepare the same way. I get the latest Frommer's or Rick Steves guidebook, check TripAdvisor for hotels and restaurants, and wrestle with Google Flights for an affordable and convenient ride there.

You could possibly make a case that a tour is your best bet for your first time in Europe. My wife and I took a cheap Globus tour shortly after we were married. We had a great time. But all our trips since then have been independent—and better.

There are many places in the world where I would be likely to book a package tour. Europe isn't one of them. I will occasionally defer to local guides for short, specialized tours. The beaches of Normandy are mostly just beaches without some way to recall the war. My Paris tour of Hemingway's favorite bars and cafes would have been much less rewarding without an experienced guide.

Here are some admittedly biased, and occasionally snarky, comparisons of tourists and travelers.

A tourist waits in the rain at 7:15 am on a dreary morning so she can board the bus for another day on the road.

A traveler gets up at 7:15 am to close the balcony doors because the crashing surf is keeping her awake.

A tourist flies Draconian Airlines to Europe with a five-hour layover in Haiti because that's what the tour company had in inventory.

A traveler pays attention to the airline "metal" when he books flights. If he buys a United ticket, he tries to stay on United airplanes because it makes booking seats easier.

A tourist visits his seventh church in three days because it's on the tour.

A traveler sits in a sidewalk café sipping a glass of local wine and munching on a croque monsieur (the French version of a grilled ham and cheese sandwich).

A tourist puts a pillow over her head to muffle her partner's snoring in their little hotel room.

A traveler hands her partner his pillow and pushes him out to their villa's spacious living room couch.

A tourist eats in the hotel's dingy dining room because it's included in the tour.

A traveler gets recommendations for three kabob restaurants near the hotel and chooses the one with the most succulent slabs of meat in the window.

A tourist explores a town selected because it will accommodate the tour bus.

A traveler detours to an American cemetery to visit her uncle who died in WWII.

A tourist puts up with the strangers with him on a trip because he really has no choice.

A traveler puts up with friends and family on a trip because he really has no choice.

A tourist can't hear the church choir practicing because the guide is babbling in her headset about where they're going to meet.

A traveler goes to Sunday services with the locals.

A tourist thinks it's beyond his ability to drive a car on the left-hand side of the road even though he's been driving since he was 16.

A traveler is only temporarily flummoxed when he has to downshift with his left hand.

A tourist pays $4500 apiece for seven days on the Rhine River.

A traveler pays $4500 for an entire four-bedroom boat for seven days on the canals of Burgundy.

Assumptions

The above couplets make a very important assumption: You are healthy and have sufficient physical resources to overcome minor problems without a safety net. (And so are your travel mates). If you do have mobility issues or other health limitations, there are tour companies geared to different needs. The aforementioned Globus, for example, has "Adventure Travel for Seniors."

Cruises often contain a high percentage of travelers who are compromised in some way but are still able to enjoy travel. I recall walking the length of a cruise ship and finding a mobility scooter parked outside the door of about a third of the cabins. (Keep in mind that the newest ships are about the length of three American football fields.) Cruises also make a good choice for passengers who have good days and bad days with health issues. On bad days they can stay on board and still be comfortable, entertained, fed, and cared for while more mobile cabin mates climb pyramids on shore.

One thing to watch for, especially when traveling with older family members, is cognitive difficulties. We took Mom around the world with us until she was in her upper eighties. Physically, she was fine. Cognitively, she seemed to have lost the ability to make decisions efficiently. We were constantly rescuing her from the bike lanes in Copenhagen because she didn't perceive the danger.

One last couplet:
> A tourist makes the most of being able to see the world.
> A traveler makes the most of being able to see the world.
> It's all good.

Chapter I - History

A Look Back

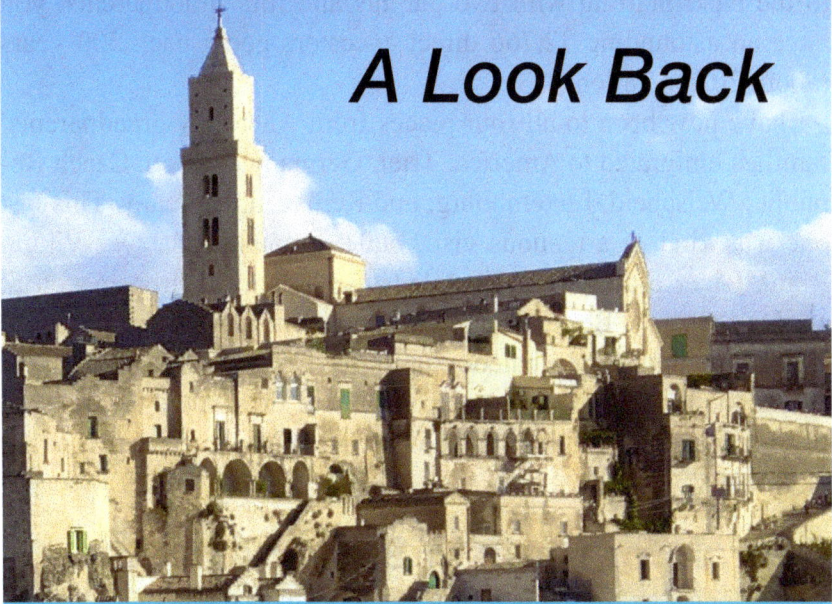

Matera, Italy

When you're young, you tend to group all the generations in front of you as the old people in your life. When you're middle-aged, you're busy worrying about the next generation, which is becoming less dependent on you, and the older generation, which is becoming more dependent. You don't have time to think about your place in the larger cycles of time and family. Finally, when you're older, you have the time and distance to look back to see where you fit in the generational lineage.

Executing a lesson plan

If you are reading this book in the Japanese, French or Klingon versions, you won't recognize the beauty of the English phrase, "executing a lesson plan." Normally, the word "execute" means to implement. Less commonly, it means to kill.

A teacher must be ready to do either one with a given lesson plan. Weather, sickness, schedule changes and a thousand other factors can impact even the best plans.

So it is with travel plans. At the beginning of each chapter we will examine pivotal points where planning meets reality. Safe to say that reality usually wins.

My friend, Debbie's, experience with Sicily, and mine with Luxembourg, may stimulate your search for your own connections to the past. Starting with two parents and four grandparents, you have an astounding 32,766 direct ancestors going back 500 years (about 20 generations).

I have now been to all four places from where my grandparents' families emigrated to America: Trier, Germany; Trebon, Czech Republic; Welscheid, Luxembourg; and Remagen, Germany. This last one was kind of a tenuous visit, but I'm counting it. Our Viking Rhine River cruise was scheduled to motor through Remagen at about 10:30 pm. Because an engine problem slowed the boat to a crawl, I waited on my balcony until about 2:30 in the morning to take a fuzzy picture of the town. I'm sure that would sound a lot like whining to the ancestors who braved an Atlantic crossing in the mid-1800s.

Search for roots in Sicily pays off

It's a long way from Sun Prairie, Wisconsin to southern Italy. With friends Debbie and Steve Meyer, my wife and I embarked on a 16-day October journey that spanned thousands of miles and encompassed more than 100 years. In the discussion below, I play the veteran traveler and travel planner who has been to about 50 countries, and Debbie plays the rookie, on just her second trip overseas. Her quickness to comprehend the art of independent foreign travel with just a little guidance sets the tone for this book.

Q. Debbie, this trip was partly about finding your roots in Sicily. Did you find them?

Debbie: Absolutely. I set out in search of the village of Santo Stefano, on the northern coast of Sicily where my grandfather, Ignazio Gagliano, grew up. My goal was to wander through the same streets he knew so well as a young boy. I wanted to breathe in the sea air and take in the views of the Mediterranean where he once fished with his father and brothers. With the aid of a family biography, I was able to find not only his village, but also the small mountaintop church where he was baptized in 1888. It was an incredible moment I will always cherish.

Glenn: I love getting off the tourist path. While we were having lunch in Santo Stefano, the townspeople would wander past, giving us the kind of curious glances you never get where tourists congregate. It took us a half hour to drive to the mountaintop above Santo Stefano where Debbie's grandfather's church was. I can't imagine how long it took them 130 years ago. They had certainly built the church as close to heaven as they could get.

Q. Describe the planning process that went into your trip.

Debbie: I am a project-oriented person, and completely threw myself into helping with the planning of this trip. Once Glenn gave me a list of potential locations, I enjoyed hours of previewing accommodations, places of interest and local restaurants. I also delved into learning to speak Italian, so I could communicate basic needs, get directions and, of course, order from delis or restaurants. I also familiarized myself with euros and the cultural differences we might encounter.

Glenn: We flew United direct from Chicago to Rome, about 8.5 hours. On the way home, we also flew direct, clearing customs at O'Hare then flying to Madison. I put a lot of time into choosing the hotels and apartments we rented, with an emphasis on location. The Borgobeltrani Hotel in Trani, on the Adriatic coast, was so central that athletes in the annual Night Run pounded away under our balcony for what seemed like hours. The hotel was ranked number one by TripAdvisor, my most indispensable tool in selecting the places. Debbie turned out to be a natural at travel planning. As a direct result of her research, we spent a delightful afternoon of wine tasting at the Gambino Winery on Mount Etna.

Q. Your itinerary took you to Rome, Sorrento, Taormina (Sicily), Venice, Matera, Trani, and Bari. Which one impressed you the most?

Debbie: Sorry, can't pick just one. Rome was incredible and larger than life in so many ways. Sorrento and the Almafi Coast were breathtaking. But if I had to be specific about the most impressive areas we visited, I would include the ruins of Pompeii, the ancient Greek amphitheater in Taormina, and the *stunning cavernous mountain village of Matera, which is where both The Passion of the Christ* and the new James Bond movie were filmed.

Glenn: Matera. The pictures I saw ahead of time didn't do justice to the ancient jumble of caves, rock, and mystery. It looked like an MC Escher print, with stairways to nowhere and impossible passages. Our maps and GPS units were useless. I had to ask three different inhabitants to direct us to the main square.

Q. Did all your many transportation connections work out? What did and didn't?

Debbie: Yes, most of the time. However, some presented more of a challenge than our group would have liked. Our scheduled five-hour train ride from Naples to Taormina, Sicily started well as we successfully rendezvoused with another Sun Prairie couple, Brion and Cathy Pagel. But it stretched into a ten-hour trip due to an earthquake in the outlying area. On the plus side, when our train arrived at the tip of the Italian boot, they took the train cars apart, loaded them onto a ferry, then reassembled the train across the bay.

Glenn: Our unexpectedly late arrival at the train station in Taormina, Sicily was greeted by darkness, a driving rain, and an empty taxi stand. Finding one lonely taxi van, we packed the whole group into it for the short ride up the mountainside. The next day, we rented cars. I hate that part of travel, but both times we did it, it turned out well. At the Avis office two blocks from our Taormina hotel, I assumed command of an imposing Mercedes station wagon with a standard transmission. Steve was a little reticent about driving at first, but I never drove another mile once he slid behind the wheel two hours later.

Q. Debbie's husband, Steve, promised he'd eat his way through Italy. How'd that work out?

Debbie: He was a pretty happy guy. Seriously, how can you have a bad meal in Italy? We made it a point to seek out restaurants that the locals enjoyed as often as possible. One of the things I discovered is that most restaurants offer house red and white wines that are both delicious and inexpensive. Steve loves fresh seafood, and in Italy, it's plentiful. He claimed he had the best mussels he's ever tasted when we dined in Trani. Crusty bread is another favorite food group of Steve's. One morning in Matera, three of us made a run to a local bakery. It was bread heaven, filled with the fragrance of mountains of freshly baked breads and rolls. We returned to our apartment with several loaves of crusty local perfection, which Steve enjoyed immensely with his morning cappuccino.

Steve: Once I ordered a pasta course with sea urchin and octopus, which our waiter nervously accepted. After we had eagerly polished it off, he shared with us that this was the dish most often sent back to the kitchen by foreigners. He was obviously very proud of the food he served and truly happy when we enjoyed our meal. Debbie ate her own way around the country. Her goal was to eat a cannoli every day she was there. Every. Single. Day. And she did.

Glenn: I've never eaten better on a trip. In Sorrento, we ate at a restaurant that made us feel like we were in a terrarium. Steve had gotten a tip from a taxi driver that a fish called *pezzogna* was the thing to order. It wasn't on the menu. When Steve asked the waiter about it, they were suddenly best friends and the waiter started bringing us dead fish to look at before their transformation in the kitchen.

Q. What were your basic costs for the trip? Did you add any luxuries?

Debbie: We stayed at a combination of hotels and rented apartments. I was surprised at how reasonably priced accommodations were in Italy. We focused on three-or four-star properties, usually in the center of town. The hotels provided wonderful European-style breakfasts. Midafternoon we stopped for a beverage of choice and a snack, which curbed our appetites until our late dinner. If we splurged on anything, it was probably our dinners. As foodies, we wanted to try new foods and wines, and did so at every opportunity.

Glenn: I'm a sucker for splurging on a great view. The top floor, three-bedroom apartment we rented through Booking.com in Sorrento had a deck overlooking the magnificent Bay of Naples with Mount Vesuvius looming over it. Each bedroom cost $132 per night when we broke it down, so maybe it doesn't qualify as a splurge, especially considering that the hotel down the street with the same view charged about $500 per night for a room. You can buy a cheap tour for a few thousand dollars, but you probably won't end up in front of your grandfather's church on top of a mountain.

Q. Looking back, what would you change?

Debbie: This trip was an incredible experience. However, if I were to do it over again, I would probably visit fewer places and stay longer in each one. We only had one day in Rome and a few hours in Venice between flights. I could easily spend a few weeks simply romping through the hills and valleys of Sicily.

Glenn: Europe's cheap airlines entice you into doing unusual things, such as the Venice stopover Debbie mentioned. I've been to Venice before and the best time to experience it is in the morning before the crowds come and, in the evening, when the reflections give it a magical touch. Instead, we mainly fought the midday crowds at St. Mark's Square (before the most recent flooding) and tried to avoid getting lost (although getting lost is the point of Venice).

Postscript: Three years later, Debbie was confident enough in her abilities to lead her own group of family members on a similar tour. Lessons learned.

Reclaiming Luxembourg ancestry

" Don't we have some ancestors from Luxembourg?" The voice on the phone was that of my younger brother, Bob. Usually laconic and often needling, his voice was instead eager and excited.

"A bunch of them," I answered confidently, although I was equally sure I couldn't name a single one. "What's up?"

"I just read an article in the paper about reclaiming our Luxembourg citizenship," he said. "But we're running out of time."

Quickly he summarized the *La Crosse Tribune* article for me. A judge in Luxembourg found that citizens who left there in the 1800s had had their citizenship illegally taken away from them. A subsequent law issued by Parliament gave the descendants of those affected ten years to reclaim citizenship. The window would close in December 2018. (The closing date was later extended due to COVID and other factors). We appeared to be eligible.

So began a two-year odyssey to achieve dual citizenship with our native USA and our ancestral Luxembourg.

First we tracked down a genealogy of our mother's side of the family, which a relative had compiled two decades ago. There I found my grandmother's parents, Maria Feyen and Wilhelm Zanter, from Welscheid, Luxembourg.

I asked my 88-year-old mother about them. "You mean Grandpa Bill?" she asked. She remembered him coming to live with them when he was an old man. Born in 1853, he died in 1944 and is buried in St. Joseph, a small town just outside La Crosse, Wisconsin.

With ancestors in place, we contacted the Luxembourg American Cultural Society (LACS) and set up a meeting at their national headquarters, which just happened to be in little Belgium, Wisconsin, located between Sheboygan and Milwaukee. There we were told that about 80,000 emigrants from Luxembourg had come to America in the 1800s. Their descendants accounted for about two and a half million Americans today, slightly less than 1% of the US population.

We signed up for their extensive two-part process for reclaiming citizenship. The first part would be to confirm our eligibility (through Grandpa Bill) and the second part to confirm our own status, including an FBI background check. LACS would translate everything into the mandatory French.

At this point, most people ask, "What good is citizenship in Luxembourg?" There are three benefits that are evident, besides the obvious one of connecting with your past:

1. You can get a Luxembourg passport and vote in European elections.
2. Depending on your residency status, you may qualify for free health care in one of the 27 European Union countries.
3. Your grandchildren (and their descendants) will have European citizenship in their favor if they apply to college in Europe (Great Britain is excluded because of Brexit.) Higher education in Europe is much less expensive than the US.

The last step of the process is showing up at City Hall (Hôtel de Ville) in Luxembourg City to sign the papers. If you want citizenship to be passed on, the first generation (me) and second generation (my son) both must be there in person. The third generation (grandkids) do not.

While successful completion of the process assures citizenship, a Luxembourg/EU passport still needs to be obtained. Luxembourg has embassies or consulates in three US cities: New York, San Francisco and Washington, DC. You have to go to one of those cities (or back to Luxembourg) after your citizenship has been confirmed in order to get a passport.

My brother and I and our wives took a preliminary trip to Luxembourg in April 2017. There we found a beautiful, affluent and cosmopolitan place nearly identical in size to Dane County, Wisconsin, where I live. Modern Luxembourg is about a thousand square miles inhabited by a little more than half a million people.

On our next trip, a year later, we brought our families. We rented a five-bedroom home for a month just across the Luxembourg/Belgium border near Bastogne. The four weeks of the month were subdivided roughly into four phases: friends of mine; my brother and his family; my wife and family; my sister and her family.

Each week featured a drive into Luxembourg City with relatives where I found a regular parking spot under City Hall. Successive family members presented their papers to an official at City Hall who met with them for about 15 minutes. Since the papers had already been vetted by the Cultural Center back in Wisconsin, we encountered no problems and were issued citizenship shortly after we got back to the US.

Word spread among my 88 first cousins about what we were doing. At last count, about 40 descendants of Grandpa Bill have become dual citizens.

As of this writing, the citizenship window has remained open. While you can attempt to negotiate the process by yourself, your French had better be good and your genealogical research abilities even better. Contact LACS (www.lacs.lu) for (paid) assistance if you want the easiest route.

Ancestors are closer than they appear

I have a twin cousin, Rita. We are not close.

Her father, Bernie, could not have been very close to his sister, Arlene, either, with a 19-year gap in their ages. Arlene (my mom) was the youngest in a family of 14. She and Bernie's wife Kate shared adjoining hospital rooms seven decades ago while they had babies, a highly usual event in my Catholic family.

In 1949, Rita and I became grandchildren numbers 55 and 56 for Peter and Mary (Zanter) Hundt. (I'm not sure which of us was first). Keep that Zanter name in mind. It's important for our purposes. Anyway, they would go on to have another 32 grand kids, for a total of 88. I'm guessing the thrill of grandparenting was mostly gone by the time Rita and I came along, and I wasn't close to them either.

I didn't see Rita at my mother's funeral in La Crosse two years ago (and didn't expect to) where my most memorable contact with a relative was Father Bob (grandchild #13), who had presided over the burial. I asked him if he had been to Vatican City lately. The priest, a rabid Republican who had lived in Rome for several years and got on well with previous (conservative) Vatican regimes, replied acerbically, "There's nobody there I want to see."

Rita grew up on a farm in Middle Ridge, a pretty piece of Appalachia in the hills above La Crosse. My family had a small, unproductive farm not far from hers outside St. Joseph Ridge, the next ridge over. We moved into La Crosse when I was five after my very young father shrewdly deduced how physically hard farming was and bought a tavern in La Crosse with money borrowed from his father. We became city kids.

Rita and her large family (13 kids) stayed with the land. Our paths did cross briefly for four years at Aquinas, the Catholic high school in La Crosse, where I don't believe we ever even had a class together. She married the high school quarterback—one of the nicest guys in class—and settled into being a Republican in the Milwaukee suburbs while I became a public school teacher and Democrat in the Madison suburbs.

If we've had a dozen conversations in our entire lives, I'd be hard-pressed to say what they were about.

Last week, Rita called me. Her daughter wanted to become a citizen of Luxembourg.

Cousin Rita was just the latest member of the family tree to look for her roots in Europe. Like the rest of us, she needed to prove her connection to the original Zanter family from Welscheid, Luxembourg. She needed the birth certificate of Grandpa Bill's daughter Mary, who happened to be our grandmother.

Rita tried the County of La Crosse, but they referred her to the archives office in Madison which told her the record she sought did not exist.

So it was in a bit of desperation that Rita called me. She emphasized her own lack of personal interest in Luxembourg, but that her globetrotting daughter was adamant, and Rita was doing her best to help.

I went through my files and concluded that I didn't have the birth certificate. I called my sister (grandchild #50), who is usually highly reliable about such things. She didn't have it either.

I called my brother (grandchild #64) who usually is not. He told me a story I had forgotten. We had run into the same roadblock as Rita four years ago. No birth certificate. But my brother had discovered a workaround: You could substitute a Certificate of Baptism.

The Catholic Diocese of La Crosse archives such things at its headquarters on the south side of La Crosse. My brother contacted Father Bob, who has an office there. He personally retrieved the document we needed. My brother recommended that Rita do the same thing.

This should not be difficult. Father Bob is Rita's brother.

Swing tunes in winter

Scattered around the bar, knots of women with purchased blonde hair and earned wrinkles wait expectantly. They are dressed up like it's church night on 6th Avenue in Scottsdale. My mom and I unobtrusively grab the last two vacant bar stools.

A bartender not much younger than the clientele, cleavage exposed and re-exposed, takes our order and slides beers our way, her mobility challenged by the awkward configuration of the bar and the awkward configuration of herself.

A large room across from us has tables for drinking and behind us a partially obscured dining room features tablecloths, lit candles, and vases of flowers.

After a second drink, we get seated at a table adjacent to the stage. It's 9:00 and time for Jimmy Snowden to do his thing, a tribute to the fifties and before.

Jimmy starts the show singing with his back to the audience, fiddling with dials and levers on the elaborate karaoke equipment that will be his band for the night. Crooning "I get no kick from champagne," he finally turns to face us, an average-sized man in black dress pants and a loose-fitting Hawaiian shirt that's not tucked in. His one distinctive feature is an old fedora tipped at a rakish angle. For the crowd filtering onto the dance floor, it's not Frank Sinatra, but it will do.

A completely disinterested waiter finally materializes about five songs into Jimmy's set. As the night goes on, our hunger will fade to match the waiter's interest level.

We speculate about the dancers. Men materialize in what had at first seemed to be an ancient sorority reunion. One, a Don Rickles look-alike, demonstrates agility more than his physique and less than his years would suggest. His previous life as a CEO no doubt presaged his crisp dance floor decisions.

Up on the stage, Jimmy continues to sleepwalk his way through his song list—until he comes to *My Way*. No more fiddling with the dials or slouching nonchalantly, Jimmy grips the microphone like a baseball player with two strikes.

I nudge my mom and she stops fuming about the absent waiter long enough to notice a transformed Jimmy. His eyes mist over and emotion sends a visible shudder down his Hawaiian shirt. When he proclaims that *the record shows he took the blows* we erupt into spontaneous applause.

Not quite finished, he appreciatively looks our way, audibly thanks us—the only time in the set that he has acknowledged an audience member—and gives us the thumbs-up sign.

Jimmy sets the machine on automatic and climbs off the stage as our waiter finally sloughs our way with food as tired as he is.

Dancing continues without Jimmy on stage. A woman with southwestern art panels built into her skirt shares the floor with a man dancing alone with his cane. Joining them are several couples, men in khakis, women in dresses or smart pants. One woman, dressed down in jeans, hadn't gotten the message on what to wear. She doesn't care. Incongruously, a televised basketball game reflects in the mirror behind her.

With effort we track down our waiter, who has aged considerably, pay the bill and include a pointedly small tip.

Seeing us get up, Jimmy leans down to shake hands with both of us, thanks us for coming, and means it.

To get us out of the dining area, we have to exit through the dance area. I physically move aside a man grimly concentrating on his dancing. Despite the smooth wood floor, I feel like I'm in a swamp as the dancers sway around us like cattails in the breeze.

Outside a real breeze hits us, cool for Scottsdale in spring. Not as cool as swing tunes in winter.

Arthur Frommer: There at the creation

The highlight of my string of stories for *Isthmus*, a Madison weekly, was meeting and interviewing a personal hero, Arthur Frommer, who created the guidebook format still in standard use today. His guidebooks started as little more than pamphlets aimed at post-World War II American soldiers stationed in Europe (especially Germany) and looking for a little R&R.

"I would have stayed with friends…" lamented Arthur Frommer, whose book Europe on $5 a Day helped launch the era of modern mass travel. But here he was, the budget travelers' hero, in the most elegant hotel room in Madison, a top-floor suite at the Inn on the Park overlooking the State Capitol.

The room was courtesy of his hosts, the women of the Madison Civics Club, a venerable organization started in 1913 as an outgrowth of the suffragette movement. Frommer (rhymes with "Homer") followed in the footsteps of such illustrious Civics Club speakers as Eleanor Roosevelt and Alex Hailey. He was in Madison to talk to club members about "New Ideas in Travel."

Frommer's brand of budget travel was no longer new, a fact made clear prior to the luncheon when a gray-haired man in his sixties told the 58-year-old Frommer, "I used to read your book when I was a student."

Originally published by Stars and Stripes, Frommer's first book achieved civilian status in 1956 as *Europe on $5 a Day* (the '89 edition allotted $30 per day, while the most recent edition demands $85 a day).

On this day, however, Frommer was more interested in showing off what appeared to be a travelers' *Whole Earth Catalog* called *Arthur Frommer's New World of Travel.*

It served as a starting point for the packed audience of about 700. His speech, as custom-tailored as his Hong Kong suit, covered such topics as cruises, health spas, Elderhostel programs (now called Road Scholar), charters and foreign health care.

After more than three decades of proselytizing for budget travel, Frommer remained a believer—although he acknowledged that budget travel could be just as senseless as travel by the rich. People who merely want to view dead physical structures should stay home and look at pictures, he believes.

After his speech, Frommer answered more than a dozen questions from the audience, and his opinions flowed freely: The ban on travel to Cuba and other countries was "one of the great outrages of our times;" AARP does good political work but "their travel program is an abomination;" no he wouldn't go to Guatemala at this time; yes, you'll usually save money by buying a package (but you'll get an artificial experience).

Later, packing in his hotel room, he offered even sharper opinions: Americans are mal-educated about history, particularly the Middle Ages (unfairly called the Dark Ages in this country); a world currency would be wonderful; the impending 1992 European unification won't have much effect on travel other than lowering inter-European air fares; European roads, trains and public buildings are in much better shape than in the US because Europeans are willing to tax themselves adequately; Reagan's yearly budgetary attack on Amtrak is "loony"—we could become the only developed nation on earth without a train system; and no, you shouldn't take the kids to Europe. "My daughter has been to every country and remembers nothing," he warned. (Pauline went on to become a guidebook writer and president of his travel company.)

Frommer paused to grimace at his lone suitcase, a small brown, soft-sided piece. It was full, and he had things left over. He repacked it. He probably packs luggage in his dreams. Next week Frommer will be on Long Island, in San Juan, Puerto Rico, and in West Berlin.

Does he ever get a vacation? Yes, this year he'll spend it traveling. He's going to France, his favorite destination. (He wants to work on his French).

On his third attempt at packing his recalcitrant suitcase, he managed to zip it up three-fourths of the way, stand it on its side, then stuff the remaining items ruthlessly into the opening.

Some things just don't get any easier, even with practice.

Chapter 2 - Psychology
Thinking it Through

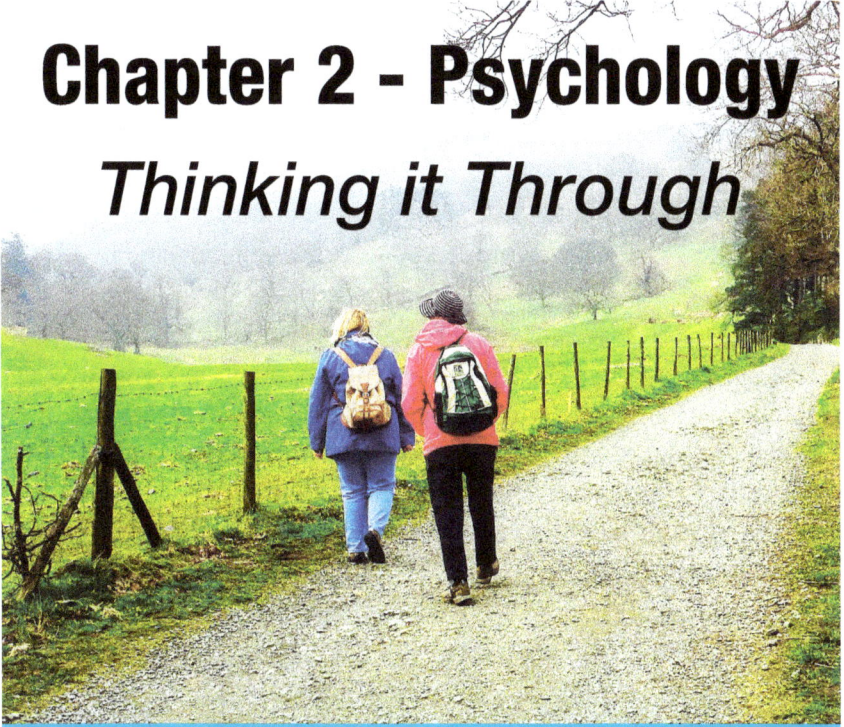

English Lake District

Turning a flight change into gold

I found a message from United Airlines in the morning email. My trip from Madison, Wisconsin to Faro, Portugal six weeks from now had undergone a flight change.

I wasn't entirely surprised. With three segments in each direction, change was more likely than not.

Because three of my six flight segments were on Lufthansa, there was a good chance United had nothing to do with the change. And from what I read in the news,

The giggling guard

I made a TSA officer laugh going through security in Miami. Normally, that's a complete no no, but I couldn't help it.

Four of us were about to go through the scanner. The first guy said, "I have a pacemaker." He was directed to another line.

The next person said, "I have an artificial hip." She too was directed away from the scanner.

The third said, "I have a new knee," and was sent to follow the other two.

I stepped up and chortled, "All original body parts!" and hopped into the scanner past a giggling guard.

Lufthansa was dealing with their continuing operational issues by cancelling 30,000 flights (including, as we discovered, one of mine).

The rebooking details turned out to be way more bizarre than I expected. Instead of changing planes twice to get to Portugal, Lufthansa wanted me to change planes three times, including a situation where I had just 20 minutes to get off one plane and board the next one.

My reaction to the message probably wasn't what you'd expect. I was absolutely delighted. Why? A flight change instigated by the airline is a "get out of jail free" card. You can play it to get out of bad schedules, crummy seats, out-of-the-way airports, and a variety of other travel maladies.

I already knew I had my own mistake to correct. I left myself just 50 minutes to connect with my flight to Munich from O'Hare. I had convinced myself it was OK because United's international flights don't leave from the distant international terminal, but I knew I still had to change terminals and jog through United's strange lighted tunnel to get to my gate, all while dragging three other old guys with me.

Before I called United, I researched the flights I wanted, looking at the fine print to see if the flight was "United metal" or "Lufthansa metal." What's painted on the plane means more than you think. Schedulers have only a limited ability to manipulate flights and seats on partner airlines.

Finally, when I had my ducks all lined up and ready to swim, I called United. After 12 minutes on hold, I was greeted by a young woman with a manageable Asian accent. We'll call her Angel.

Angel was the ditsiest agent I had ever encountered on an airline call. She was probably quite new, very enthusiastic, and delightful company for the next 45 minutes. She was not, however, a master of scheduling details.

It took a long time to explain to her that I wanted just one change. I wanted to fly from Chicago to Frankfurt instead of Chicago to Munich. Why? Because Lufthansa already had me going to Portugal from Frankfurt, and we didn't want to mess with Lufthansa. They had enough problems.

Angel rarely put me on hold while she pounded away on her computer. I could hear her singing pop songs in the background.

After a few verses and an occasional conversation with a superior, she'd come back on the line and bubble happily, "Are you still there, Mr. Glenn?"

Eventually, I got the change I wanted, the flight to Frankfurt. Angel emailed it to me and sent my brother's change in a separate file. Mine was OK, but when I opened his, she still had him going to Munich.

More songs. More conversations with the boss and finally we were set. I asked about seats, and she agreed to assign them. I had researched three sets of seats that I knew were available. The first group was in "premium economy," the second was in "preferred" and the third was in regular economy. I knew first class was out of reach.

When I asked for the premium economy seats, Angel murmured, "Oooh, those are expensive," but she agreed to ask her boss. I'm sure he discovered what I already knew: a block of about 80 seats in that class was completely empty five weeks away from flying. He consented, and I didn't have to settle for the backup seats. When I checked later, our seats were going for an additional $262 apiece.

What about my problem with the 50-minute plane change? The new flight gave me 70 minutes to change in Chicago, so I could breathe just a little easier.

The changes only cost me one extra hour of total travel time. Instead of getting into Faro at 1:30, I'll be there at 2:30. As an unexpected bonus, we are now on the same plane (with Lufthansa painted on it) as the friend we were going to meet in Portugal.

Of course, there's still five weeks left for more surprises.

Trip recap: Everything worked except we missed the last flight from Chicago to Madison. Lufthansa took its sweet time in getting the plane off the ground on the return from Frankfurt, so we got into O'Hare an hour late. That left only a half hour to get through customs, collect (and rebook) luggage, change terminals, go back through security and get to our gate. Not enough time.

United put us on standby for a full plane an hour and a half later. Luckily, there were just enough no-shows for all four of us to board. Our luggage made it too—except for my brother's, which had somehow made it onto our original flight and had to be retrieved from United's storage closet.

Lesson: Leave more time between flights.

Want to make your community better? Get out of town.

Picture yourself in a sleepy Italian town. It's around supper time and the ancient streets are nearly empty, the uneven cobblestones still warm from another day in the sun. You pass vine-ringed doorways and little piazzas with tiny cars parked askew. Gradually you find yourself surrounded by Italians of all ages just meandering past the local church and through the main square. You have joined *la passeggiata,* the nightly stroll that allows old folks to check in on each other, young people to check each other out, and everyone else to check their social priorities in a world that moves too fast.

Now picture bringing this tradition back to your hometown.

The more you travel, the more you realize how rich the world is when it comes to enhancing everyday experiences of social interactions, transportation, food, health, and commerce. Often deceptively small in implementing, such enhancements enrich a culture and provide meaning and reflection for your travels. Packing them up and bringing them home with you isn't always practical, but you shouldn't rule it out. Here are some ideas worth bringing home.

"Fell walking," the Brits call it. In Wisconsin, we would call it "hiking the bluffs," although that presents a somewhat misleading picture of the terrain. Grandad's Bluff in La Crosse rises to about 600 feet, while Scafell Pike in the Lake District eclipses 3,000 feet. On a good day in England (any day above freezing, or less), you'll encounter an astounding array of appropriately dressed Brits scaring the oblivious and ubiquitous sheep on the fells as they use cross-country ski poles to propel themselves up well-marked trails (the hikers, not the sheep).

Countries often build infrastructure to suit such fundamental human activities as walking and running.

In Switzerland, you'll find Alpine hiking trails meandering from hut to hut, offering rustic overnights amid meadows and glaciers. The northern part of Spain provides permanent infrastructure support for the Way of St. James (*Camino de Santiago*), a pilgrimage of hundreds of miles that was already well-established when St. Francis of Assisi walked it a thousand years ago. I walked all 74 miles of Hadrian's Wall, which loosely marks the border between England and Scotland. The Romans engineered it almost 2,000 years ago.

Infrastructures don't have to be permanent but should use the geographic gifts nature has bestowed. I often accompany my brother in his quest to run marathons all over the world (See Chapter 4). In London, we put on almost as much mileage as he did just by walking around the Buckingham Palace security perimeter to get to our hotel. Many of the 26 marathon miles in Aukland, New Zealand parallel the ocean. Stockholm delivers an urban running experience that channeled us into catching the subway home—when we finally found it. Rio de Janiero flaunts its famed beaches for its marathon party.

I love going to Lodi, Wisconsin and taking the car ferry across the Wisconsin River. Such quirky additions to the transportation grid put communities that foster them on the map. I think of Lodi every time I cross Lake Windermere in northern England, which boasts a car ferry identical to the Wisconsin version.

I once took a cruise that stopped in Naples, Italy. We rode the local train to Pompeii and then went on to Sorrento. We were going to take the train back to Naples when we discovered a passenger ferry sailing along the coast right back to our port and took that instead. I doubt that the Italians saw the two modes of transportation as competitive. They were just different experiences.

Train and ferry service that Europeans take for granted as a necessary part of 21st-century transportation are woefully lacking in the car-rich US. More than 2,000 trains per day glide through Zurich station in Switzerland. My local Amtrak station in Columbus hosts two lumbering passenger trains per day, with plans to double that total next year. Woo-hoo. People in Japan, China and all of Western Europe laugh at our "high-speed" trains going a pitiful 100 mph. I used an app called Speed Box to figure out how fast we were going on France's TGV train. It got up to 185 mph. I know Japan's Bullet train can go even faster, but I rode it before such an app was available.

Here's something big to bring home: Luxembourg has made all public transportation free in the entire country. Don't try to purchase tickets on buses, trams, or trains. Just get on. Two blocks from our hotel in Luxembourg City, we found the bus stop we wanted. We waited for about 10 minutes to take a comfortable 25-minute ride to

Junglinster, La Crosse's sister city, where we ate supper at a local restaurant. The ride was easy, safe, social, and free.

Farmers' markets are a tradition many towns have brought back from the old country. I always try to hit a few of them when I'm overseas. They bring together tourists and locals, offer fresh and exotic foods, and open windows on a culture. Many have advanced far beyond simply selling produce. Others consist of just a few trucks showing up on certain days of the week.

I love the *poffertjes* you find at the Albert Cuypstraat market in Amsterdam. These decadent half-dollar-sized pancakes resemble the beignets that make New Orleans so memorable. A friend of mine just encountered them on the streets of Antwerp, Belgium, so perhaps they are migrating.

La Boqueria Market on La Rambla in Barcelona, Spain, anchors that city. The tantalizing smells from a huge variety of fresh, prepared or on-the-go foods draws you in to this sprawling show.

While known more for its antiques than its food market, Portobello Road in London features an exquisite location in the Notting Hill area. Last time I was there, we dived into a fish and chips restaurant to celebrate my friend, Paul's, purchase of a beret.

If you want entertainment with your food, try the Feria de San Telmo in Buenos Aires. You might even get a free tango lesson. It was quite chilly when I visited it on a reverse-season day, so we ducked into a restaurant on-site that specialized in churros and rich hot chocolate. We were buzzed up on sugar the rest of the day.

To avoid harsh weather, you can try an inside market. France is rich with them. On the west end of the country, we experienced the huge Rennes market that delivered on my favorite produce: French breakfast radishes (slender, with white tips). In Burgundy, on the other side of France, we provisioned our canal boat from Auxerre's spacious indoor market. On this continent, Madison, Wisconsin is hoping to open its own indoor market next year.

What about bringing money home? Well, that rarely happens. How about money technology? I ate at a local US restaurant last week and paid the bill using the credit card reader the waiter brought to our table. Of course I did. Why has it taken so long to make this technology common in the US? It's been the norm in Europe for at least 10 years.

How about outdoor dining? Long a delightful staple of life in agreeable climates, eating outside came to America on the wings of the pandemic. It may now be leaving through the kitchen door, past the car up on blocks and pigeons feasting on stale bread. I think that's too bad. The experiment countered American dining expectations and encountered disagreeable weather, while scoring a few notable successes. Mostly the tables have left the median, suggesting that not every innovation translates.

Here are a few things I would urge you not to bring home.

Coffee practices. Three things not to like about European coffee: Never getting a refill for free; paying for a three-ounce cup that's only half-full; standing while drinking it (mostly Italy). The coffee itself is generally very good, except for French roast (where French is a synonym for "burnt"). During my caffeine-free days, I pretty much gave up on finding decaf. Waiters in French cafes act like you just slapped them across the face when you ask for it. They won't even lie to you the way American waiters do. On the other hand, you can sit at a wonderful sidewalk café all afternoon with your single cup of espresso.

Air conditioning. Let me rephrase that: Lack of A/C. The older I get, the more I want, no *need*, to have the air around me not trying to kill me. When it hit 108 degrees on the Villaine River in France, we docked our canal boat in the town of Redon. We found the town's only air conditioner at the harbor's movie theater, which mercifully had a café attached to it. There we spent our time until the murderous heat wave moved on.

Paying for a toilet. What kind of savages are these people? It's not just the 50 pence or 2 zlotys you might have to pay. At a moment when time is typically not your friend, you must: 1. Sort through your change from 3 countries; 2. Identify the correct coinage; 3. Go into battle with a coin machine designed by Picasso during his Cubist period; and 4. Enter the correct bathroom. The international giggles I got as I exited the women's room at a Hungarian rest stop suggest that number 4 should not be taken for granted (especially if you're looking for number two).

Finally, what if travel isn't on your itinerary? How can you bring the world to you? I highly recommend a free app for your phone called Radio Garden. It features an interactive map offering live ra-

dio stations from all over the world. Lately I've been listening to
Radio Bruaysis, from a little French town near the English Channel.
Music and talk are in French (not as common as you think on French
radio). It makes me feel like I'm sitting in the breakfast garden of a
little three-star hotel under huge plane trees while I'm finishing off
a second chocolate croissant.

The broken traveler

I spend a lot of time putting together combinations of travelers who
might keep things interesting. It usually turns out well, but not
always. See if you know some of these travelers. Some are mildly
amusing; others are big-time annoying. The success of your trip will
often depend on how well you negotiate travel styles so everyone
comes out ahead.

Those to avoid

The option taker

This traveler is all in—until he isn't. Somewhere along the
way he gets a better offer and bails out, leaving you with few
options.

Royalty

They question your decisions but refuse to get involved in the
decision-making process. Any resultant discomfort caused by your
bad decisions was clearly aimed at them.

The broken traveler

She can't climb up steps because of her heart and can't climb
down because of her knees. And she's joined you on an Alpine Adventure. Her lips keep writing checks that her body can't cash.

The fish out of water

She's the one dancing by herself at the Captain's Dinner. She
wishes she were on some other kind of trip (with some other people). "I thought you invited her."

The single-interest traveler

You don't share it. But there you are, looking at another Etruscan crypt. Looks a lot like the last one.

The disparager

Nothing is ever as good as it is back home. That cute hotel? "I've stayed in inner city Ramadas with nicer rooms." That homemade breakfast at your B&B? "What the hell were they thinking to put baked beans on my plate for breakfast?" That world-class museum? "I think the madonnas in all those paintings should have turned down the pasta course more often." One of you should have stayed home.

I gotta be me

This clueless traveler blows through cultural stop signs without even seeing them, leaving a wake of astonished looks, closed doors and frustrated companions (which they also don't see). Performing for a camera invisible to the rest of us, the only subject they see in the lens is themselves, and it's awesome.

Travelers to seek out

The Renaissance man

Sure, he'll be arguing with your guide at Macchu Picchu about construction methods, but he's interested in everything and is constantly in learning mode.

The culture vulture

You never would have seen the amazing catacombs of Rome without him.

The foodie

Tired of fighting your way through foreign menus? Let the foodie order for you. You'll like it. Promise.

The shape shifter

When she's in Italy, her hand gestures get more pronounced. In France, she wears the prettiest scarf. When she's in Germany, she disciplines your posture. You always feel like you're traveling with a local.

The good traveler

In my experience, nearly everybody else fits into this category. The good traveler is appreciative, considerate, curious, friendly, and helpful. If you didn't see yourself in any other category, you belong here.

Travel opposites

What happens when travel styles clash? Often things work out to the benefit of both sides, expanding travel experiences in new ways. Other times resentment and misunderstanding take much of the joy out of travel.

The living vs the dead

Those on the dead side can't get enough of old churches, museums, abandoned castles, and stone circles. They are endlessly fascinated by the creations of those long gone.

Those on the living side revel in sidewalk cafes, street performers, the miracles of modern transport, and fellow travelers' opinions on social media.

When these folks travel together, the dead adherents keep wondering why their opposites insist on trudging through the street market instead of sifting through the ruined 19th-century abbey on the edge of town. The live adherents wonder why their opposites never get hungry.

Planners vs spontaneous travelers

The planner has had the details of every hotel room, train ride and pub crawl nailed down since last November. Most of the experiences have been paid for already. He's even planned the travel "surprises" you'll encounter.

The spontaneous traveler alights in Venice in August and says, "Maybe we should find a place to stay tonight." They've never been on Yelp and always believe, "We'll find a place to eat along the way," even if it's the Albanian food truck the local health authorities have yet to apprehend.

When the two travel together, the planner usually wins and the spontaneous traveler chafes at his/her friends' inflexibility, cursing them for making travel so inconveniently comfortable.

Watchers vs movers

Movers only feel part of the scene if they're moving through it. Watchers need a stationary place to hover above it all to get the whole picture.

Putting them on a boat, bus, train, or cab usually works for both. Making the watcher go look for the mover works for neither.

Rich vs poor

There is a surprisingly narrow comfort range when it comes to the economics of travel. If you travel with someone whose tastes are more upscale than yours, you will feel like your ATM card has sprung a serious and continuing leak.

On the other hand, if you are traveling with folks who'd rather walk three miles through the wharf district instead of taking an Uber, you'll end the trip feeling like you traveled by boxcar and slept in a refugee camp.

A cruise is a partial solution to that dilemma, in that you can all eat in the same restaurant while some retire to their inside cabin and the others to their Captain's Suite.

This problem rarely surfaces when families travel together. Witness this exchange that I had with my son when we took his family to Europe: "Don't worry, Dad; money's no object." "You mean my money, don't you?" "Yes, I do."

"Nothing to report?" 12 months of harrowing flights.

What does it take to remember a flight? They all fall into the "nothing to report" category unless something goes wrong, right? I guarantee you'll remember your flight if it makes a forced landing in Newfoundland, if the passenger next to you dies and you have to divert to Fargo, or you spend the night on the cold floors of O'Hare Airport. No, I haven't experienced any of those. Yet.

I flew from Madison to Washington, DC about 50 times between 2000 and 2009 when I was on the National Education Association Board of Directors. I remember just one of those flights. It was in the fall of 2001. I was booked on one of the first flights to take off after the five-day, post-911 grounding of all planes. I remember boarding.

There were eight crew members for just five passengers. "Sit any-where you want," they told us, gesturing at an array of about 120 empty seats. As we approached Reagan National Airport in Wash-ington, we could see the still-smoldering wing of the Pentagon that had been gashed by the hijacked plane.

I have flown quite a bit in the past year. That I can remember nearly every flight is not a testament to my superb memory or de-tailed notes. I assure you, I have neither. Rather it is a function of an airline system that is still not back to what we thought of as "nor-mal" before the pandemic. As will become clear below, it's not just a US problem; it's worldwide.

Below are my recollections of a year's worth of flights, July 2022 through June 2023. You'll find the "nothing to report" catego-ry quite thin. Bear with me; I flew on 31 different airplanes on seven different airlines.

July 9, 2022
Madison to Zurich on American

We would have missed our connecting flight in Philadelphia if it hadn't been for my friend Steve. The Madison flight was delayed almost two hours. When we finally arrived in Philadelphia, it looked hopeless. We had to change terminals and then sprint about a half mile to the gate. Old people don't sprint well. Steve flagged down an attendant in a golf cart who burrowed through pedestrian traffic to get us there as gate agents were beckoning furiously to us in front of the closing doors.

July 14, 2022
Geneva, Switzerland to Rennes, France on EasyJet

We have a train attendant to thank for not missing this flight. We had taken the Glacier Express from St. Moritz to Zermatt and got to know a nice woman who worked in our railcar. A few days later, we were standing on an empty Zermatt train platform bleary-eyed at about 5:30 am when we ran into her. She asked where we were going. When we told her Geneva Airport, she said, "Why don't you just board that train?" pointing at a train on the next platform that was ready to pull out. I regarded it as a "ghost train" because it didn't appear in any of the schedules I had for our Swiss

Rail passes. We got on and arrived in Geneva 45 minutes earlier than scheduled. Good thing, because normal security lines were an hour long. Fellow travelers, Matt and Kathy got separated from us and didn't know that our upgraded EasyJet ticket entitled us to jump the line. They made it through the queue just as we were starting to board.

July 24, 2022
Nantes, France to Madrid, Spain on Iberia

I was recovering from some kind of virus (not COVID) that made travel an ordeal. I remember the terminal in Nantes and the long walk through the Madrid terminal even if I don't remember the plane ride. My most vivid memory was craving a hard-boiled egg after not eating for two days. Mary Jo had picked one up at the breakfast buffet and generously turned it over to me. When I eagerly cracked it open, it turned out to be raw.

July 26, 2022
Madrid to Madison on Iberia

Another "last one on the plane" story. After an uneventful flight from Madrid, we had to go through Customs in Chicago then wait for our luggage at the international terminal (Terminal 5). When it finally arrived, we had to recheck it for the flight to Madison and take the tram to Terminal 1. That all takes time. We were running out of it when we had to go through security again. Good thing we have TSA Precheck, right? Unfortunately, it was printed on all our tickets except for Kris's. She and I had to go through the long regular lines with the kids and dogs. Steve and Debbie were waiting on the plane when Kris and I became the final passengers to board.

September 18, 2022
Chicago to Glasgow, Scotland on Icelandair

All Icelandair flights to Europe stop in Reykjavik. Our departing flight from there to Glasgow was an hour late but it didn't really matter because our plans in Great Britain were flexible. Upon arrival, we hadn't even reached the Customs desk when we were told to stop right where we were. The guards didn't say another word and we stayed stopped. Finally, I noticed a small television. The queen's funeral was being televised and we were experiencing five minutes of country-wide silence.

September 29, 2022
London to Chicago on Icelandair

Our flight was again delayed in Reykjavik. Then it got weird. From across the concourse, I watched a uniformed woman approach Colleen, one of our least experienced travelers, and engage her in conversation. I rushed over, deflected her away from Colleen, and volunteered myself for what appeared to be a Security catch-and-release. They took me to the windowless room, made me empty my carryon and turn on my laptop. Then they checked me for residue (drugs? gunpowder?). After a half hour, they released me into the wild.

December 7, 2022
Madison to Amsterdam on United

This deserves a "nothing to report" grade even though we only had about an hour to make our tight connection at O'Hare. It helps that United's international flights leave from Terminal 1 instead of the remote international Terminal 5.

December 14, 2022
Luxembourg to Chicago on Lufthansa

Plane trip from Hell. The hour-long delay in Luxembourg was just enough to make us miss our connection in Munich. We rebooked on an afternoon flight to Chicago then watched as the weather deteriorated and phalanxes of snowplows descended on the airport. By the time night fell, we were at the only gate in our terminal with the lights on. One by one, passengers gave up until there were only about 100 hopeful souls left. A break in the storm rewarded that hope and we finally boarded. Once we reached altitude, Fred and I each claimed an empty row of middle seats and stretched out for a three-hour nap. Our midnight arrival in Chicago was greeted by even worse weather conditions. Since flights to Madison were distant memories at that hour, Fred's wife heroically drove the 118 miles from Stoughton, Wisconsin to O'Hare to pick us up. We then drove through snow and ice back to Wisconsin. I arrived home exhausted and hallucinating at 3:00 am.

January 27
Madison to Chicago on United
    Nothing to report.

January 28
Chicago to Bonaire, Netherlands Antilles on United
    We were supposed to be on a flight to Panama for a nine-day Panama Canal cruise. Kris's untimely dental emergency grounded us. I calculated that we could catch the ship three days later on the tiny island of Bonaire, just off the coast of Venezuela. When we were changing planes in Houston, United announced a 45-minute delay to wait for some Denver passengers. "Since we only fly to Bonaire once a week, we thought we'd better wait," the United rep told us. I didn't realize how lucky we were to secure a flight on the right day.

February 4
Panama City to Chicago on American
    We got to the Panama airport four hours early then suffered through a two-hour delay, causing us to miss our Miami to Chicago connection. American offered us one seat on the midnight flight. "Won't that be a little crowded for my wife and me?" I asked, not innocently enough. "You have gold status," he replied, ignoring my snark. "By the time you get to your gate, they'll have a seat for both of you." And so they did. I pushed it. "Do you have an aisle seat?" I asked. "Yes, but you won't be able to sit by your wife." "It's OK. We've been together for an entire week." I sat on the aisle. Our 2:30 am arrival at O'Hare found us completely prepared. We crossed the street to the Hilton Hotel and went right to our reserved room, opening the door with my phone.

February 5
Chicago to Madison on American
    Nothing to report.

April 11, 2023
Madison to Faro, Portugal on United and Lufthansa

It doesn't always have to be something bad that causes you to remember a flight. I remember this one because we were in excellent premium economy seats that we hadn't paid for. Lufthansa had completely messed up our flights, scheduling us into an MC Escher set of steps that couldn't be connected. I called the airline and used the opportunity to rework our itinerary and our seats into a best-case scenario that netted the four of us $1,000 in seat upgrades. Chicago to Frankfurt was on time, but the next flight to Faro was delayed by an hour, mildly inconveniencing my cousin, who was picking us up.

April 19, 2023
Faro, Portugal to Luxembourg City on LuxAir

Ring the bell again! Imagine my shock when Luxembourg's national carrier broke out a full meal for us on a three-hour midday flight, and it wasn't bad. The one strange thing was they had the old-fashioned movie screens aboard showing vintage Bugs Bunny cartoons for the entire flight.

April 22, 2023
Luxembourg City to Chicago on Lufthansa

The connection in Frankfurt was memorable because of a Lufthansa functionary screaming at us to line up correctly to board the plane. Of course, even normal announcements in German sound like notification that they are about to invade the Sudetanland. We should have heeded his advice because the plane took off an hour and a half late. Naturally we missed our Chicago to Madison flight. United had two seats for the four of us on a later flight, so my brother and cousin Dave took them. Fred and I waited at the boarding gate with a friendly United attendant for two people who never showed up. You guessed it: We were last ones on the plane.

June 16, 2023
Madison to Amsterdam on Delta

Nothing to report on either Madison to Minneapolis or Minneapolis to Amsterdam. I do wish the Amsterdam airport would get its act together again though. It took two hours to clear customs.

June 29, 2023

Munich to Madison on Delta

Another strange one. Something about my ticket caused problems the entire day. Kris and I were routed through five layers of security at Munich Airport, including a full security sweep just as we reached our gate. The problems followed me across the Atlantic. After we rechecked our bags for the Detroit to Madison flight, we had to go through security again. Piece of cake, right? I've got TSA Pre-check. This time Kris's ticket had it but mine didn't. I snagged a Delta agent and showed him my Global Entry/TSA Pre-check ID. He dutifully typed the number into the system. It REFUSED to print the ticket. So Kris and I followed the kids and dogs to the long regular security lines again. By that time, our flight should have been long gone. A two-hour delay worked in our favor this time and we made the flight.

Chapter 3 - Geography
Interesting places

Santa Cruz, Costa Rica

Oh, Canada

I was in my forties on my way to a fishing trip in Canada with my dad.

Before you start to think, "Ahh, isn't that nice?" I have to tell you, no, it wasn't like that at all. Everything about the trip was kind of one-off.

For starters, my dad wasn't in the van with us. Oh, it was Dad's van alright, but I was sharing it with three of his redneck friends. Dan, the driver, had the largest can of Pabst I had ever seen in the drink

Grace and style in Plovdiv

Kiril, the young Bulgarian we hired to show us around Plovdiv, mentioned that he would be taking part in folk dancing the next day— not for tourists, but for themselves. He invited us to watch.

We diverted from our usual round of shops, ancient artifacts, and restaurants to accept his offer. The dance took place in a large plaza at the end of the pretty, mile-long pedestrian mall in the city's Old Town.

I found it to be a deeply moving experience. Young people executed the steps with strength and purpose, old people with grace and style. Both helped children reap the benefits of an ancient culture.

holder. Dad was flying into some obscure airport in Ontario. We would pick him up there.

My brother had done the trip the previous year and had one piece of advice. "Don't be the last one on the plane." It was an old World War II de Havilland seaplane that held about ten people. The last one aboard had to hold the door shut.

The rednecks in the van were pleasant enough. I already knew that politics were off-limits. (One of the guys was nicknamed "Rush.") After the heavy drinking that lay ahead, I figured no one would ever find my body in the many sloughs and backwaters of the Canadian wilderness.

So we listened to country music stations for most of the six-hour ride. My usual tolerance level for that music at the time was about a half hour, but I decided I'd better extend my vow of silence for the good of the trip, and we proceeded happily through Duluth on up through Thunder Bay.

My dad, always comfortable conducting his business without explanation, was waiting at the airport when we arrived. We added him to the van and stopped for the night at an edge-of-the- wilderness town with exactly one motel and one restaurant.

Conditions on the lake in the morning were a little rough but we managed to take off from the lake's surface heading for Makoki-baton, a fishing lodge deep in the Canadian wilds. We were about halfway there when a line of thunderheads loomed ahead. The pilot wasted no time in turning the plane around.

I don't remember if he recited the classic line about bush pilots: "There are old pilots and there are bold pilots, but there are no old, bold pilots." But it fit.

Anyway, one of the rednecks must have been sleeping during the weather drama and remarked when he saw the motel and restaurant below us, "Hey, we're back in the same place."

The pilot took offense and replied, "You fly the f***ing plane."

Everything was calm about two hours later and we flew through clear weather to land on the water next to the fishing camp dock without incident. No one exited the plane early through the permanently disabled door.

We were not roughing it. The "camp" had five outbuildings for sleeping and a central cabin where meals were prepared for the fishermen (and they were all men). We ate extremely well, with food that occasionally slipped into the gourmet category. (That snails were a food category surprised some of the guys).

For the next three days, we spent eight or ten hours a day in fishing boats, easily eclipsing the total for my entire life. Interestingly, I never shared a boat with my dad. He assigned his friend, Larry, whom I knew and liked, the unenviable task of dealing with a novice fisherman. I was fine with that, but I felt a little sorry for Larry, especially after I snapped the tip off his fishing rod.

The best part of the trip was a shore lunch. We pulled our boats up onto a nearby island at midday and using an open fire, the camp staff prepared a meal consisting exclusively of freshly caught northern pike and fried potatoes. To this day, I remember it as one of the best-tasting meals I've ever had.

The drinking proceeded as planned every night and I mostly retired to my room to read, a choice my dad had never really comprehended.

But it was a good trip anyway. We had the camp pack up our fish (with strict limits on quantity) and reversed the transportation process until we returned to the van. This time, my dad stayed with us. Instead of hardcore country music, he retrieved some bootleg polka tapes from the glove box and proceeded to play them for the next three hours.

I finally broke my vow of silence on complaining and said, "I hear there's some pretty good country stations in this area." The rednecks all enthusiastically supported my suggestion.

About ten years later, I unraveled the mystery of why my dad flew to Canada while the rest of us drove. I discovered you can't get into Canada if you have a DUI on your record. Because my dad, a confirmed alcoholic, had been caught twice driving drunk, he wasn't welcome there.

If you want to know how seriously Canadians take this policy, consider that George W. Bush, when he became president, had to get special dispensation from the Canadian government just to go there to meet with the Prime Minister. Bush's offense had been in his youth, but the law is the law. (Current laws allow for requesting "special entry permission" or a lapse of ten years since your transgression. Multiple offenses are still quite problematic).

Flying into a small Ontario town was a workaround for Dad. My guess is that computer access to international records had yet to come to that backwater airport yet, or a well-placed hundred-dollar bill made my dad's entry an easy one-off for the border guard.

Not a bad day in San Francisco

We're in a squad car, Jerry and I, somewhere between Fisherman's Wharf and the Golden Gate Bridge. It hasn't been a very good day.

We're in search of Piper Laurie. She's starring in a play about Zelda Fitzgerald called "The Last Flapper."

From the other side of the police car's wire mesh barrier, a policeman calls to us, "Are you from San Francisco?"

"Wisconsin," we reply, simultaneously.

"What do you think of when you think of Wisconsin, Rick?" he says to his partner.

"Cheese," he answers himself before Rick has a chance to speak.

We are looking for the Cowell Theater at Fort Mason. The play is scheduled to start at 8:00 p.m. It is 7:50. Our police officers aren't sure where it is either.

"What do you think of when you think of San Francisco? our driver asks us, chuckling.

"The Golden Gate," I say.

"Cable cars," Jerry adds.

"That's very diplomatic of you," the officer replies.

The policemen had found us on a deadend street about a halfmile from our destination. They offered us a lift. We accepted.

In a remote area of Fort Mason, we find the theater. We thank our benefactors, jump out of the squad car, and head for the ticket office. Well, I jump out of the car. Jerry's ankles have been pinned together by some device to control criminals. The police giggle before releasing Jerry from his backseat prison.

The box office is closed.

We approach a man who is busily moving trunks and boxes.

"We'd like to see Piper Laurie," I say.

He stops, takes out a printed card and says, "How about on the 12th in Santa Rosa?" He nods at a sign indicating a schedule change. The evening performance had become a matinee. Piper Laurie is gone.

Jerry and I survey the scene. Apart from the movers, the fort is all but deserted, save for a few bodies floating like moths around the single light of an adjacent building. We walk over there.

"Welcome to the wharf meeting," a woman of indeterminate age says ominously as we approach. We nod, slink into the building, and climb a flight of stairs to the men's room. A homeless man shuffles out of a stall with all his worldly possessions and quickly evaporates.

We are about to go back downstairs when we hear a Bach choir. We follow the sound down a few empty hallways. As we approach the doorway, the singing stops. We leave.

Three men are now huddled outside the building entrance under the single light.

"How can we get to Fisherman's Wharf?" Jerry asks them. One giggles. Another stares. The third suggests a cab. We look around. Not a single moving vehicle is evident.

It hasn't been a good day. We had spent the morning at a conference featuring a failed demonstration and a keynote speaker who first insulted us, then swore at us. The afternoon was spent slogging through heavy rain on a shopping excursion to the Embarcadero Center. It was, of course, closed.

Our twomile cabfree walk from Fort Mason to Fisherman's Wharf leaves us hungry. We see a familiar sign and duck into Alioto's, a fixture on the wharf. After our second bottle of Devil Mountain Railroad, a local brew, our food finds us. Butter is making steaming trails down the sides of my exquisitely prepared filet of sole. I'm having a hard time remembering who Piper Laurie is.

Outside, the lights of the Golden Gate Bridge shine above the masts of boats moored in the harbor. I break off a chunk of sourdough bread, pour a little more Railroad, and contemplate the luminous harbor scene.

It's pretty hard to have a bad day in San Francisco.

Roland, keeper of the keys

We were scanning a menu in front of an Italian restaurant in Stockholm when two men came out. The older man said something in Swedish to me, and as Americans do everywhere, I responded in English.

It turned out that his English was excellent. "You must try this place," he said, remarking several times that the owner was "very clever."

We talked for about five minutes before I asked him about the huge set of keys hanging on his belt. No ordinary keys, they were vintage, bolt-in-the-lock type keys that represented the apex of security one or two centuries ago.

"We will surely take the recommendation of a man who holds all the keys to the city," I said.

He didn't exactly explain the keys, but he did give me his card. It announced him as "Senior Advisor, Keeper of Documents, Maps and Prints" for a Swedish company. His name was Roland.

Scouting restaurants that afternoon, I had to keep my brother in mind. I knew he wanted to do his usual "carbo-loading" since he was running in the Stockholm Marathon the next day.

Unfortunately, the three restaurants on my Trip Advisor-researched list were all handicapped in some way. The first one we looked at was too expensive, even in this expensive town. The second, a French restaurant, was rejected because it was too, well, French.

The third preferred to keep itself hidden from us. While searching for it we found this place, Ristorante Serwito. Finishing our talk with Roland, we descended a steep hill several blocks to return to our hotel.

Further research on Trip Advisor showed Serwito to be rated 561 out of 1939 restaurants in Stockholm. Booking it online failed, so I had the woman at the hotel's front desk call for us. We had gotten to know her quite well as we spent most of the hours from 10:00 am until 2:00 pm (that's 3:00 am to 7:00 am body time) waiting to be issued room keys so we could sleep off some jet lag.

At 7:30, we showed up to claim our supper reservation. I told the owner that his place came highly recommended and showed him Roland's business card. My vague hope was to demonstrate that we weren't just monolingual American tourists taking a break from fast food.

His reaction was inscrutable. He looked at the card, nodded and said, "Oh, Roland," and escorted us to our table.

He gave us menus written in two languages: Swedish and Italian. We studied them with intensity, getting minimal assistance from our overworked waiter. (He disappeared briefly into the kitchen to find out what kind of fish was used in a pasta dish: monkfish).

It didn't matter. The food turned out to be outstanding. All of it. Each dish that flew out of the kitchen looked more impressive than the last. I had a small steak with a muffin-shaped accompaniment that turned out to be potatoes. Turning the prosaic into the exotic.

I can only say *"tack själv!"* to Roland, keeper of the keys, for recommending a very clever place.

Bulgaria beguiles

Five of us took a side trip from Belgium to Plovdiv, Bulgaria as summer approached.

Why Plovdiv? I went on SkyScanner.com to see where Ryan Air, the bare-bones Irish airline, would fly me for the least money. I had never heard of Plovdiv, but found out later that it was Europe's 2019 Capital of Culture. About thirty bucks is all Ryan Air wanted for the two-and-a-half-hour flight from Charleroi (Belgium).

Ryan Air does everything it can to produce cheap fares. It flies from one badly located airport to another at inconvenient times, discouraging luggage of any kind, providing no extras and limiting interactions with you, the customer, whenever it can.

Ryan Air is Europe's "stairwell airline." When the plane you are waiting for lands, you are herded down at least two flights of cold, marginally clean metal and concrete stairs to stand and wait. If you are in the front of the line, you will be able to watch your plane taxi to a designated spot on the tarmac and disgorge passengers down stairs on both the front and the back of the Boeing 737-800.

As soon as the last passenger is off, they unbolt your door, and the stairwell people rush the plane—from both ends. Anyone with a carryon of any size tosses it on a rolling luggage platform to be claimed at the end of the flight—at the carousel, not planeside as on most airlines.

Because we were arriving in Bulgaria late in the day, we had arranged with our hotel for two cabs to transport us into the city. We stayed at the Hotel Evmolpia, a friendly place located on the edge of Old Town.

Bulgaria traces its ancient lineage back to the Romans then back further to Thrace, several centuries before Christ. You have probably heard of Spartacus, the man who led a slave revolt. He was Thracian.

We found this out on an excellent all-day tour with Private Guide Bulgaria. Cost was about $60 apiece and our tour guide, Kiril, was exceptional and spoke excellent English. In fact, Kiril was so good that when we ran into him a day or two later (he lived in Plovdiv), we talked him into another half-day tour before dropping us off at the airport.

With more than 300,000 people, Plovdiv is not small, but the local action focuses mostly on Old Town, where an attractive mix of shops and endless sidewalk cafes winds its way along a two-mile pedestrian mall.

Our dollar was powerful in Plovdiv and bought plenty of *Lev*, the local currency (exchange rate: 58 US cents equaled one Lev). We ate delicious three-course meals at sidewalk cafes or spectacular hillside restaurants for about 10 American dollars. I especially liked Rahat Tepe, just up the hill from our hotel. The commanding view of Plovdiv from the terrace was best accompanied by *Kamenitza* (Communist) beer and some local sausage and potatoes.

After three days, we returned to the Plovdiv airport ready to take another $30 flight, this time to Bergamo, Italy. We saw a military helicopter fly overhead but didn't hear it crash. Ambulances and other emergency vehicles soon descended on the scene where two were killed and another was injured.

Our already-late flight was delayed for two more hours and we ended up landing in Bergamo after midnight. We weren't sure our hotel transportation would be waiting at the airport for us, but they were, with a new Mercedes van. We found out later that the hotel didn't even charge us for it.

The next morning we explored the city, taking the tram up to see Bergamo's Old Town. With another Wisconsin passenger joining us, we bought tickets at the station then grabbed an ancient train to Lecco. There we changed to a beautiful new European model even as a sudden summer rainstorm took us by surprise.

We spent two nights in Varenna, a phenomenally beautiful place on Lake Como. Our home was a quirky Air BnB property exactly 60 uneven steps up from the shoreline. Our biggest accomplishment was taking the lake ferry, then a bus, to a historical plaque from the closing days of World War II. In front of an iron gate in Mezzegra, the Italian strongman, Benito Mussolini, was executed by country-men who had had enough of his attacks on unions, the press, opposition politicians, and democratic institutions. The Italians avoid using his name by putting "April 1945" on the signs leading to the historical site.

We completed our trifecta of Ryan Air flights the next day after an early-morning van to Bergamo Airport, a brief but intense battle over one of our tickets, and a quick flight back to Charleroi, Belgium. The three flights in six days cost $90.

Last-minute Costa Rica

I only knew of two volcanoes in Costa Rica. I found out there are 67 in this Central American country about the size of West Virginia. At 5,479 feet, Arenal is less than half the height of Irazu, the tallest of the volcanoes.

Nevertheless, it looked pretty imposing from our perch at the Arenal Observatory Lodge, less than two miles from the volcano. Arenal last erupted in 1968, destroying a nearby town, but it's been quiet for the last 10 years. On the day we were there in January 2020, it was both quiet and shy, only exposing its summit on brief occasions as cloud cover shielded it from view.

We had a delicious lunch surrounded by floor-to-ceiling windows at the Observatory's restaurant, El Jilguero. If you go there, try to time it so you arrive before noon when a park ranger sets out food for the local wildlife. We paid about $12 apiece to get into Arenal Volcano National Park, where the observatory and restaurant are located, but that also gave us access to some delightful walking trails.

If we had been staying longer, the Observatory's lodge, the only hotel located inside the park, would have been a great choice. Instead, we stayed for just a single night in the nearby town of Fortuna at Hotel Villas Vilma where 78 American dollars bought a clean and quirky room in half of a colorful cottage.

Flights

We flew into Liberia, Costa Rica's lesser-known international airport, because of its location in Guanacaste, the northwest part of Costa Rica notable for good restaurants, hotels, and beaches.

Getting to Liberia from the American Midwest challenged the three couples involved. My wife and I flew from Madison, Wisconsin on American frequent flyer miles with a brief stop in Dallas. Travel times on the return trip didn't match up quite as well, so we had to overnight in a Dallas airport hotel.

Brion and Cathy, the second couple, flew Delta from Milwaukee, also on accumulated miles, with a layover in Atlanta.

My brother and his wife flew Sun Country direct to Liberia from Minneapolis. The trip was a little over five hours long and cost about $350.

Getting Around

Don't expect to drive the countryside at anywhere near the speed of US roads. The ones we traveled were good, but the many curves, small towns, and occasional mountains conspired to keep our rented SUVs pace to a minimum.

Several times, especially near the beaches, the good blacktop roads were replaced by rutted gravel tracks that re-configured the joints in our bodies and slowed our vehicle to a crawl.

We didn't find parking to be a problem, even in some of the busy beach towns, but parking rules seemed to be at a minimum and somewhat random to our North American eyes.

Accommodations

The trip was a last-minute decision, so our choices of accommodations were somewhat limited. I've used both Air BnB and VRBO with considerable success over the years, so I was pleased to see that each of them had some inventory. While the prices of a few of the VRBO properties appeared to have been reduced for last-minute buyers, some of the Air BnB choices approached fire-sale prices. The deal on a two-bedroom condo at The Oaks (yes, it's written in English), near the seaside town of Tamarindo, was too good to pass up. For $705 dollars we secured a week in a large two-bedroom condo at a beautiful gated resort with four swimming pools. The guests seemed to us to be evenly divided between Spanish and English speakers.

My brother and his wife, who were in Costa Rica a week longer than we were, went in a different direction. They spent a week near the Arenal Volcano at The Springs Resort and Spa and a week near Tamarindo at the JW Marriott, located right on the Pacific Ocean. Each of these sprawling properties was beautiful and remote. And expensive. The per night cost was between $300 and $400.

Money

The exchange rate for Costa Rican *colones* was 567 per US dollar when we were there. I had read that American dollars were acceptable throughout the country (but that change returned would be in *colones*). It turned out to be true for me. I had brought quite a few fives, tens, and twenties with me in US money and used them in small transactions. For larger ones (such as restaurant bills), I used credit cards and had them run the transactions in local currency.

Eating

Grocery stores are a great window on other cultures. Three supermarkets were within 10 minutes of our condo. Having a full kitchen meant we didn't have to eat in restaurants for every meal. One night we cooked brats out by the pool and another we made spaghetti. We also bought freshly roasted Costa Rican coffee that was among the best coffee I've ever had. The Sun Burst coffee roaster near the Liberia Airport produced particularly tasty coffee, specially packed to bring home as a much-appreciated souvenir.

Our best restaurant meal was at Coco Loco on Playa Flamingo (Flamingo Beach). I carefully devoured the delicious whole red snapper while the sun relentlessly pursued the horizon. The temperature may have been ninety and the sand about the same, but a nice breeze and some beach umbrellas kept us quite comfortable until the night engulfed us.

Easy

The rewards are many and the drawbacks are few in Costa Rica. I got by on my college Spanish. I didn't hit anything with the car (despite the Costa Rican tendency to walk, stand, and do unpredictable things right next to the roadway). And I found exploring out-of-the-way places to be nearly always productive and surprising.

What more can you ask when you are escaping winter?

Tuscany, before it was cool

This trip to Tuscany, Venice, and Lake Como in 2001 became the template for dozens of other trips that I researched and organized, trips we subsequently dubbed "Tour de Glenns." I took eight teacher friends during our summer break. It's a little dated in such things as technology (we rented an early cell phone), money (this was just before the euro), travelers' checks and house rentals (found in a small ad in a magazine). Otherwise it holds up well and sounds like a trip I'd like to join.

July 26

The grand expedition finally lifted off. Except for Fullmers. They were in Thailand and would join us in Italy. I had already called Thailand twice today, forgetting that Robert Fullmer is not the same as Bob Fullmer to a Thai desk clerk.

I called Bob at about 10:30 this morning (which was about 10:30 p.m. in Jomtien, Thailand). Bob was sleeping.

"How are things going there?" I asked.

"Good," said Bob, "except that Peggy couldn't sleep. I didn't have a problem though, at least until now."

I called Bob to share the number of the European cell phone Barb finally secured from Hertz.

I ran into two other participants, Mary Bell and Anna, at the International Concourse at O'Hare while they were waiting for their SwissAir flight to Milan. We had a drink, then separated. The eight travelers were flying on five different airlines.

Austrian Air could spoil you for other airlines. I only flew it because my frequent flyer miles forced me to bypass United for one of its partners. My wife Kris had different flights that would supposedly have nearly identical arrival and departure times. (I would never do this today.) I was traveling alone.

On boarding we were offered a choice of 8 or 10 European newspapers, many in German. I grabbed an *International Herald Tribune.* The meal, chicken and shrimp with rice, was good, the German wine was better, and the warm bread they passed out was the best of all. They even had a little wedge of Wisconsin cheese.

My seatmate, George, turned out to be the author of Fodor's original guide to Vienna. Nowadays, he covers economics for a British company. He'd lived in Vienna for 35 years and gave me advice on which cafe to visit.

The Astron Hotel was positioned about the length of a bowling alley from the front door of the Vienna airport. A nondescript business hotel, the Astron let me check in early, which was fortunate because jet lag knocked me over the head and made me sleep for a few hours.

I took the airport bus the short 12 miles into Vienna to search for a café. I chose the Deml, George's first choice also. Unfortunately, it was full (outside at least) and I didn't know the protocol for securing a table.

I left and walked the short distance to the Graben, a wide, upscale shopping street with gigantic sidewalk cafes all along its short, elegant length.

I chose the Café del Europe, which was full of people drinking beer or coffee or soda, and not watching the passing crowd. (Most were too busy with their own companions.)

This time I watched the protocol for securing a table. Basically, it was the law of the jungle. When someone gets up, you sprint for the table. As in Germany, sharing tables with strangers is an option.

Shortly after I pounced on a vacant table, it was immediately cleared by a friendly young waiter who spoke some English. I told him what I had come for—Sacher Torte and coffee. I ordered both *"mit schlag"* (with whipped cream). The bill came to about $6.00. It was delicious.

I walked back to the city air terminal for the bus back to my airport hotel. For supper, I tried to find a Vienna sausage and a beer. Although hot dogs were readily available street food downtown, the airport failed to include them as a choice. Of course, it was after 10 by the time my jet-lagged body was hungry. I ended up at an airport food court overlooking a runway where I reluctantly ate a slice of Sbarro pizza washed down with a bottle of good Austrian beer.

July 28

Vienna-Malpensa-Lucca

I found Kris at our designated meeting area at Malpensa Airport fairly quickly, but what followed was about five hours of relative chaos.

I tried to call Barb's cell phone. Unbeknownst to me, the cell phone was not with Barb; it was a few hundred feet from me in the lost luggage area. Barb had unaccountably packed it in her suitcase, which didn't follow her onto her Air France flight after United cancelled.

Luckily, our backup plan worked and I called Barb at her Milan hotel. After retrieving Barb's luggage, Kris and I spent the next 3 1/2 hours waiting for her to pick us up in the van.

The nine-passenger Ford Transit was huge for this area and was a lot like driving a Greyhound bus. Anna and Mary split the four-hour drive to Lucca. The scenery was dramatic. We emerged from one long tunnel after another to be confronted with acrophobic views of buildings and bridges spilling down into the Ligurian Sea.

In those days before VRBO and Air BnB, Americans renting a villa in Europe was pretty exotic. I had found a small ad in one of my travel magazines and called the Virginia phone number. Apparently, the villa was owned by an Italian-American couple who were living in the US but had a place available not far from Florence.

We called our Italian contact, Signora Nora, from the road to let her know we'd be about an hour late getting to the villa. She turned out to be a voluble middle-aged Italian who busily escorted us from room to room in the dark, closed villa. We had arrived in the middle of a wedding at the main villa, so our van was ordered to a parking spot on the lawn by a confused young Italian boy.

We divided up the bedrooms, then four of us set out for some food, which ended up being *gelato* and beer at a little local hangout called Crazy Horse.

July 29
Lucca

I slept until 10:00. In fact, most of us slept in today. We were hungry when we finally got ourselves together and headed for an Italian restaurant just inside the walls across from the tourist office. It was misbranded as an Irish Pub (at least we couldn't find the pub part), but served excellent Italian food from an 18-page menu. My calzone was outstanding.

I took the van from the restaurant alone to retrieve my camera back at the villa. Unfortunately, I forgot the house key. I met the rest of the group at the *duomo* (cathedral) on the other side of Lucca sans camera.

As the day wore on, we became a little worried about supper. We hadn't heard from the chef we had hired through Signora Nora to make a full Italian supper at our house. It was with great anticipation that we followed our noses to the kitchen on our return to find Chef Alberto, embarrassed because he was cooking in just his tee shirt in the steamy kitchen.

What followed was the ultimate Italian meal, an excessive, multi-course circus of offerings: three appetizers (prosciutto and melon, bruschetta with cheese spread and walnut, bruschetta with sardine and tomato); several bottles of white wine; a diamond-shaped pasta; *osso buco* (veal chops) with roasted potatoes; green bean souffle; bread and butter curls; some red wine; and finally, tiramisu for dessert.

July 30
Lucca

Exhausted by all the food, we all slept in late again. We then set out to conquer the walls of Lucca, which are about 60 feet thick and surround the old part of town. We walked about a third of the way around (about 2.5 miles) then cut through town to meet near the cathedral. We changed money at a bank (three and a half minutes for cash, five and a half minutes for travelers' checks). We found ourselves using that method less and less as the trip went on. Once we found that our bankcards worked, we preferred that method as being cheaper, faster, and less dependent upon the capricious schedules of banks.

We made a group trip to the supermarket (which had been closed Sunday and didn't open until 12:30 on Monday). Barb spent a lot of time using her Italian to have cheese and meat cut to order.

Bob and Peggy finally rolled into Lucca about 5:00 p.m. after their Thailand adventure. We went to the railroad station to get them. They were traveling light—luggage was somewhere else on the planet. We had a little picnic for them on the back balcony. Then most of us went back to the RR station (next to it, actually) for *gelato*.

July 31
Pisa, San Giminiano, Siena

We got an early start and took a back road to Pisa, which was less than 20 miles from our villa. We spent two hours, most of it in the hot sun, among the hawkers and gawkers. The Tower, while officially "saved" was not scheduled to allow tourists for another four months. The *duomo* was a big surprise. It had the most ornate interior of any cathedral I've seen yet.

We took more back roads to San Giminiano, a hill town known for its many towers. In our continuous quest to replenish our bodily fluids, we stopped at a sidewalk café on the main street that wound up its narrow path through the town. We had an excellent conversation with a British couple who came to Italy every year.

We labored to the top of a lookout tower, bought a painting done by a local artist, and headed for Siena. We got there more than two hours before our supper reservations. That's a good thing because it took a long time to park and trudge up the hills to the Campo (the place they run the Palio horse race twice a year). Most of us quaffed beers while watching them set up the stage for some event.

The meal at Osteria le Logge, a Frommer recommendation, was excellent. My roast chicken came topped with a huge potato chip.

We took the autostrada home through Florence, getting lost just once.

August 1
Florence

Our reservations at the Uffizzi Gallery were for 9:45 a.m. It was 10:45 by the time we presented ourselves in the museum's reservation area. To our discomfort, the temperature was climbing to 97 degrees.

The harried gatekeeper gave us a 10-minute time out as punishment, then waved us through. The Uffizzi turned out to be a walk-and-gawk kind of museum, with rooms grouped primarily by artist, with few explanations or contexts given in any language.

Massive crowds made the viewing much more of a chore than it should have been.

Dehydrated and suffering from art shock, we made a quick stop in the middle of the Piazza de la Signoria, where a plaque heralded the exact spot where the intense monk, Savonarola, was burned and hanged about 500 years ago. I had just finished a book about him. He wasn't good company.

We commandeered a café table big enough for the six of us (Barb and Jane were going to the museum a different day) right across from Florence's incredible cathedral. Cokes the size of milk cans helped slake our considerable thirst.

The stark interior of the cathedral was a disappointment compared with the busy and ornate exterior. We didn't stay long. We walked several blocks to the Accademia to see Michelangelo's David. He did not disappoint.

David must be viewed from all sides. From the front, he appears relaxed and reticent. From behind, taut ligaments and bulging veins indicate someone ready to do battle. In addition, it becomes clear that the shadow across his shoulder is really a weapon—his sling.

We took a cab to the hotel Barb planned to stay at and found her and Jane refreshed after an afternoon rest.

After a short walk to Ticket Box to purchase opera tickets, we retrieved the van, fought our way out of Florence, and arrived at the villa in time for Chef Alberto.

This time the menu was risotto and a delicate white fish. It wasn't quite as good as the first meal but it made for excellent leftovers.

We lit our mosquito coils and drifted off to our rooms to sleep.

August 2

Cinque Terre

Cinque Terre (five lands) was about an hour away—more if you count the harrowing, curving, mountainous final 15 miles to Monterosso al Mare.

Unfortunately, the heat had followed us and the coastal breeze we had anticipated failed to arrive. The hordes, however, had arrived, as thousands of young people, mostly Italian and German, and some Brits filled the beaches.

Our first decision was the wrong one as we hopped a through train to La Spezia, bypassing the other four coastal towns. By the time we made our way back to Riomaggiore, we had expended about an hour.

After grabbing a sandwich and a Gatorade at the train station café, we split up. Bob, Peggy, and I planned to hike the three-kilometer trail from Riomaggiore to Manarola. We discovered it was closed about halfway, but we walked it anyway up to the construction. It amounted to a flat platform hugging the sheer rocky cliff with spectacular views in three directions and young bodies sunning themselves like little walruses on the rocks below.

My guidebooks had suggested that train and boat service between the towns was frequent. It was not. We were unable to get out of Riomaggiore by foot, by train, by car, or by boat for almost two hours.

Finally, we caught the train to Vernazza, skipping two towns, Manarola and Corniglia. A completely vertical town, Vernazza offered a main pedestrian street that wound down to the sea and a small beach. It had recently been a fishing village but was now, at least in summer, completely taken over by the twenty-something crowd.

Bob, Peggy, and I selected a seaside table and quaffed beer while waiting for the boat to take us back to Monterosso.

Our small launch took only about 10 minutes to return us to where we had started. We docked just ahead of a large ferry that was carrying the rest of our group from Riomaggiore, where they had spent the entire time—most of it hunting for the ferry dock.

We returned to the villa where we swam in the villa's well-appointed and well-hidden pool (We didn't find it until our third day at the villa.) Barb proceeded to make us a tuna salad accompanied by the many leftovers from the previous night's repast.

We ended the evening with a songfest. Mary Bell and I had recently put out an album of angry folk music and were no doubt inspired by the Italian wedding music—except for a schlocky American song (*I Just Called to Say I Love You*), that seemed to be on endless repeat.

August 3
Bagni di Lucca

We left Mary and Anna behind and headed north out of Lucca to Bagni di Lucca. We discovered anew that just because Americans have not heard of a place doesn't mean it's undiscovered. I got the van hung up in a crowded parking lot and had to work for about 10 minutes to free it. We finally found some parking on a sidewalk then did a little exploring. We changed some money at the Bank of Rome, something we had been unable to do in Lucca (the first bank was closed, the second refused to change money, and the third remained invisible).

After refreshments at a sidewalk café, we drove to the Fontaninni factory, famous for its nativity figures. It was August. It was closed. We asked about it at a nearby car repair shop and succeeded in getting Maria Fontaninni's home phone number. We didn't use it.

Barb, relishing her Italian Earth Mother role, again made supper for us. Bob went for a swim again as he did often this week. The rest of us either didn't make time for it or didn't choose to make the quarter-mile trek past Villa Rossi, through the entrance arch, across a country road and next to somebody else's house.

The supper was classic Italian spaghetti, something Barb seemed to be genetically equipped to prepare. It was very good but we ate quickly so we could get to the opera early.

Torre del Lago Puccini was only about a half-hour away. We used Jane's handicapped card to land a close parking spot then spent an hour roaming the pretty lakeside grounds that were splattered with stalls and restaurants.

The opera was very nearly a sellout, perhaps 4,500 people. As we had surmised, the crowd was comprised of mostly Germans and Italians. If there were any other Americans there, we didn't see them.

The featured opera was *Turandot*, Puccini's final one. It was produced on a grand scale. At one point I counted 108 performers on the stage. The setting almost outshone the production. The audience faced the lake. When the program began just after sunset, somebody cued the full moon and it hung suspended on a golden beam over the shimmering lake. A love story at heart, *Turandot* ended happily (except for Lieu, who killed herself), and we all went home fulfilled.

August 4
Lucca to Venice

We vacated the villa punctually Saturday morning. We never did find where to put the trash, but decided it was no longer our problem.

Bad maps and directions meant a little extra van driving in Florence, but our previous experience there helped us find the train station.

We said goodbye to Barb and Jane and the van and spent the next few hours in the station as the day heated up. Finally, the train arrived about 45 minutes late. We had second-class tickets in the smoking car, so it was an uncomfortable three and a half-hour ride on the Eurostar.

After arriving in Venice, we hopped aboard the first available *vaporetto* and cruised the Grand Canal until the Rialto Bridge stop. This proved to be a fairly bad decision because the Rialto is really a big staircase.

After exhausting ourselves dragging our wheeled luggage over the bridge, we confronted our hotel, the Locanda Sturion and its 93 steps to the lobby. It was difficult enough dragging ourselves up, but without elevator or porters, our luggage seemed to increase in weight with each step. To her credit, Kris was accompanying a suitcase that felt like it was filled with stuffed toys. Anna, on the other hand, we are pretty sure was smuggling bars of gold bullion.

We had two rooms, a double for Peggy and Bob, and a quad for Kris, Mary, Anna, and me. Our room, while a little cramped, commanded a great view of the Grand Canal.

For supper, we went around the corner to Ala Madonna. Air conditioning, cold drinking water, and some great food and service made this the best restaurant on our tour.

August 5

Venice

The ornate breakfast room at the Sturion presided over the Grand Canal from its third-floor perch. Cereal, coffee, juice yogurt, and croissants were available from 8:00 until 9:30. After we ate, the hotel arranged for a free water taxi to take us to Art Murano, where they made and sold glass.

There we were assigned a very friendly young keeper whose primary interest was to encourage us to buy expensive pieces of glass, from chandeliers to vases to wine glasses. Mary bought a crystal apple and Anna bought two nice pieces. They were given presents and offered a ride home. The rest of us were let out the back door.

We wandered around the island of Murano for a while looking in little shops and glass factories. (Many shops were closed, either because it was Sunday, or more likely because it was August).

We stopped for a *granite,* one of those intense ice slurpees that Italians favor, then took the *vaporetto* to San Marco.

Bob and I disengaged from the group and after meandering the back streets, found ourselves at the foot of the Accademia bridge at the Restaurant Foscarini, where we had *croque monsieurs* and beer. We got back before our companions and had time for an afternoon nap.

We remained on the island of San Polo when we went out for supper. Frommer's guide suggested Pizza da Sandro. We found it after winding our way through a series of unpromising back streets and canals. All of a sudden, the restaurant appeared alongside shops and other places to eat. No tables were available so we moved to a rude and/or incompetent restaurant nearby that gave us menus, then proceeded to ignore us for about 20 minutes.

We sent Mary back to da Sandro to see if a table had opened up. It had and we had a fine meal there with excellent service. I recommend the huge Viennese Pizza with pieces of hot dogs buried in the cheese. I also had a couple large glasses of Fanta, my new drink of choice in Italy (quite different in flavor and color from the Fanta orange available in the US.)

August 6
Venice

After our hotel breakfast, we shopped our way to San Marco. We stopped at the Kele & Teo Viaggi e Turismo (Rick Steves' travel agency of choice) to buy train tickets, a much more civilized and no more expensive way to secure them. This time, they even promised us a no-smoking car.

Since the line for the cathedral was about two days long, we crossed over to the island of Dorosoduro instead to the Peggy Guggenheim Museum. After 10 days of Madonnas and angels and saints with arrows in them, a good dose of Picasso, Kandinsky, and Jackson Pollack was totally refreshing. So was the museum café where we spent another hour after completing our museum tour.

Our group split up again and Kris, Mary, Peggy, and I rode a *traghetto* across the canal and worked our way back to San Marco. The line for the cathedral had subsided, so we got inside fairly quickly. Entrance was free but there were extra charges for various sights within the cathedral. We each paid for a view of the golden screen, an ornate rectangular box that appeared to have the images of saints stamped into it. I'd tell more but the pay recording behind the screen that described it refused to accept my coin.

I must have been getting museum fatigue because I never did find where St. Mark's remains were, and after a while I didn't care. (I found out later he was under the altar.) I paid to light a candle. When it wouldn't light after three tries, we left and went to Harry's Bar, an old Hemingway haunt. After proper refreshment, we headed back to the canals.

Vaporetto #1 did its best imitation of a city bus stopping at every corner before returning us to the San Silvestro stop. (Not much closer than Rialto but it allowed us to avoid the hectic bridge scene.) That also kept Kris away from temptation. She had already bought one Louis Vuitton piece from African street merchants there. They wanted $70 for a backpack that sold for more than $600 back home. Kris did the bidding herself and got them to move from $70 down to $40.

Since the Bistrot de Venise Restaurant on the island of San Marco was somehow related to the Sturion Hotel, we were eligible for a 10% discount. We divided up into two groups of three to fit the tables available. Mary had stuffed ravioli; Kris and I had roasted and stuffed chicken. We all shared a vegetable platter and the restaurant threw in a little paté in the beginning and tarts at the end. Toss in two beers and a coke and we each paid about $20.

We went back to the hotel to finish Mary's last bottle of white wine from the villa.

August 7
Venice to Varenna

We received a very pleasant surprise when we boarded the train bound for Milan. Our group had the exclusive use of a six-passenger compartment. As a bonus, it was air-conditioned. The three hours passed quickly.

Once in Milan Centrale, we had less than 15 minutes to find the train to Varenna. I found our destination buried in the fine print of the posted schedules and we spotted our train on the next track with time to spare.

The terrain quickly got steeper and more varied and began to look like Switzerland. After an hour and 15 minutes, we disembarked with a handful of other passengers at Varenna, a resort town of 800 permanent residents on the eastern shore of Lake Como.

We ignored three waiting cab drivers because we believed our hotel was very close. I caught up with an older couple walking down the main road, prepared to ask them in French, Spanish, English or Italian where the Hotel Olivedo was. They spoke German. They understood anyway and within minutes we were wheeling our luggage down the road about three blocks to the hotel.

We were met by Signora Laura, a friendly but businesslike woman with a sardonic expression. She directed us to, what else, more stairs, two flights for Kris, Bob, Peggy and me, but three flights for Anna and Mary.

The spartan rooms had wooden floors that creaked—no, sang—when you walked on them. The saving grace was a small balcony that presided over the constantly changing water, sky, and mountains of Lake Como.

Since it was now almost 4:00 and we hadn't eaten since breakfast, we followed the lakeside promenade to a sidewalk café that served ice cream creations as big as footballs. These we ate.

We ate even better a few hours later as we gorged ourselves on the three-course meal that was provided with our rooms out on the hotel terrace.

As we sat at the sidewalk tables outside the hotel, Signora Laura reeled off all the choices of food without benefit of menu. For the first course, she sang about eight choices, including risotto, gnocchi, and dried beef. Main courses consisted of lake fish and lake trout or several kinds of meat, including a delicious cut of veal. Four dessert choices topped off the meal, many with wild blueberries. It was all first-rate.

Bedtime was more problematic because of the noise outside our balcony window. A Mark Knopfler sound-alike was crooning at the restaurant next door. He sang mostly in English, a phenomenon that has taken over much of Italy's radio and public areas. Sad because we really didn't come to Italy to hear the Beatles.

August 8
Varenna

We augmented our continental breakfast on the hotel's terrace with some hot chocolate. Bob and Peggy had slipped away in the early morning hours, so we were down to four—Kris, Anna, Mary Bell and me.

We took the 11-minute ferry ride to Bellagio. We shopped our way up one side of the hill and down another. The shops were pretty upscale and more interesting than the souvenir shops we had been frequenting elsewhere in Italy. Kris found some unique wrapping paper and Anna bought some specially designed pasta.

We drank cappuccino at the Bar Florence (next to the five-star Villa Hotel Serbelloni) and waited while the ticket takers and ferry boat captains returned from their long lunch breaks. (It might look like Switzerland but it's still Italy.)

The return trip to Varenna routed us first across the lake to Menaggio. By chance I was listening to the announcement when we entered the port. I heard the word *"cambia,"* a variant of *"cambio,"* which by now I knew meant change. I also heard the word Varenna. We checked and found out that we needed to transfer to the car ferry that had just pulled in. After switching boats, we watched the passenger ferry go sailing off in the direction of Switzerland, luckily without us.

That afternoon, we watched a brief thunderstorm slash down the mountain, overtake a ferry on the lake, and pound through Varenna. It was dramatic.

We had another great supper on the terrace. We overheard the three people at the next table who turned out to be from Ohio. Their conversation: "At our hotel in Venice someone had written in the guest book, 'Hey, Rick (Steves), why don't you tell us next time that there's 93 steps just to get to the lobby.'"

That had to be the Sturion, I thought.

Sure enough, the Americans recognized us from the previous hotel. Apparently, we were all on the Rick Steves tour of Italy.

August 9
Last day (or not)

"Linate!?" I shrieked as I opened my eyes to see a road sign leading us to Milan's other airport.

"Malpensa," Mary Bell and the driver said in unison as we turned in the right direction for the right airport.

We had been up since 4:00 a.m. saying goodbye to a lightly dressed Signora Laura then driving in the rain and the dark down roads that didn't stay straight for longer than the length of a bus. We were on a $140 taxi ride with Guido, who was no doubt the brother-in-law of either Signora Laura or perhaps the lady from the taxi company.

Guido said nothing. (Well, it was early.) Unfortunately, the exit from the autostrada that would have sent us on a direct route to Malpensa Airport was blocked by an overturned car and flaming warning lights.

After taking the next exit, I watched Guido assume the same haunted and lost demeanor I knew so well from my week of driving. At one point, he even overshot a turn and backed up on the main road.

Nevertheless, we got there unharmed and on time. My Austrian Airlines flight left 40 minutes late, so I made my connection in Vienna just when they were boarding the last group. The 10-hour flight was uneventful. They showed "A Bug's Life" again. (Couldn't one of the flight attendants stop at Blockbuster on the way to the airport?).

My son picked me up an hour early (I waitlisted and got on—with luggage—an earlier United Express flight). He told me Kris was stuck in Italy. The American flight had been cancelled and the whole planeload was bussed to a resort on Lake Maggiore. She tried it again the next morning and ended up getting home about 24 hours later than planned.

New Zealand by sheep

On the tour bus from Te Anau to Dunedin in southern New Zealand, I fell asleep despite the rich scenery. I should have known better than to count sheep. I could never get past about three million before dropping off.

In fact flocks of sheep are ubiquitous on the Southern Island.

New Zealand has 40 million sheep and only 4 million people. Our driver would occasionally taunt them with a honk and a "wake up sheepy" just to see them scamper away.

During November, spring in the southern hemisphere, the most common sight in the green fields was a ewe being trailed by one, or often two, little lambs. Most of the sheep had yet to be shorn, a twice-per-year process that appears temporarily embarrassing for the sheep and is moderately lucrative for the farmer.

We went to a sheep shearing across the lake from Queenstown. The shearer told us the record for shearing by one person was over 300 sheep in one day. He took just a few minutes with electric clippers to remove every strand of wool from his docile victim.

With its glaciers, fjords, and mountains, the Southern Island is very different from the largest city, Auckland, on the Northern Island, where a third of New Zealanders live.

Queenstown, surrounded by lake and mountains, would not be the least bit out of place in Colorado. With its trendy shops, focus on adventure sports for the young (bungee jumping was born here) and night life, it could be Aspen.

We were in New Zealand during the run-up to a national election. The Conservatives were leading Laborites in the polls by about a two-to-one margin. But other parties, such as the Greens and one called ACT, also played a role. We encountered tent cities from the Occupy Wall Street movement in Dunedin and Christchurch. The former group was encamped in a park dead center in the middle of the Octagon, the heart of the city. The city council had ordered it cleared, but the police had refused.

It's difficult to get around New Zealand unless you have a car. Trains are largely limited to the scenic variety, such as the Tranz Alpine express across the top of the Southern Island. The day we took the train was wet and increasingly snowy, especially for late spring, as we ascended to Arthur's Pass.

It's not that easy to get around the country with a car either. The roads are excellent, but there always seems to be a mountain or a lake in your way. Also, traffic is on the left and streets and roads are narrow and twisted by American standards.

One of the standard ways to judge a country is by its bread and wine. New Zealand gets a hit and a miss here. Vineyards producing fine wine have sprouted where sheep and cattle formerly roamed. Bread, on the other hand, generally comes in bland shades of white, great for grilled cheese, but tasteless with anything else.

American and British influences clash here, with the Brits winning most of the battles. Breakfast buffets always featured scrambled eggs, a feature of both countries, but they went on to include fried tomatoes and often baked beans, staples of an English eye-opener. The buffets did avoid the fried ham that the Brits call bacon, but took the meat off the fire prematurely, giving the strips the consistency of watch straps dipped in grease.

In the whole country I saw plenty of animals, but never a pig. Besides the ubiquitous sheep, cattle were quite common. On our way back from a golf course, my brother and I cadged a ride from a farmer who claimed he had 10,000 cows a day to milk. We told him we were from the Dairy State.

Horses were also plentiful, accounting for the more than 70 race-courses in New Zealand. It was not uncommon to be sitting in a pub with most of the televisions tuned to racing. My mom and I spent about an hour in a casino sports book in Auckland betting on races in Australia and New Zealand.

Geographically, New Zealand is slightly smaller than Wisconsin and Illinois combined. In distance terms, it's useful to compare Wisconsin to the North Island and Illinois to the South Island, imagining a treacherous ocean passage between the two states. Not a bad idea, come to think of it.

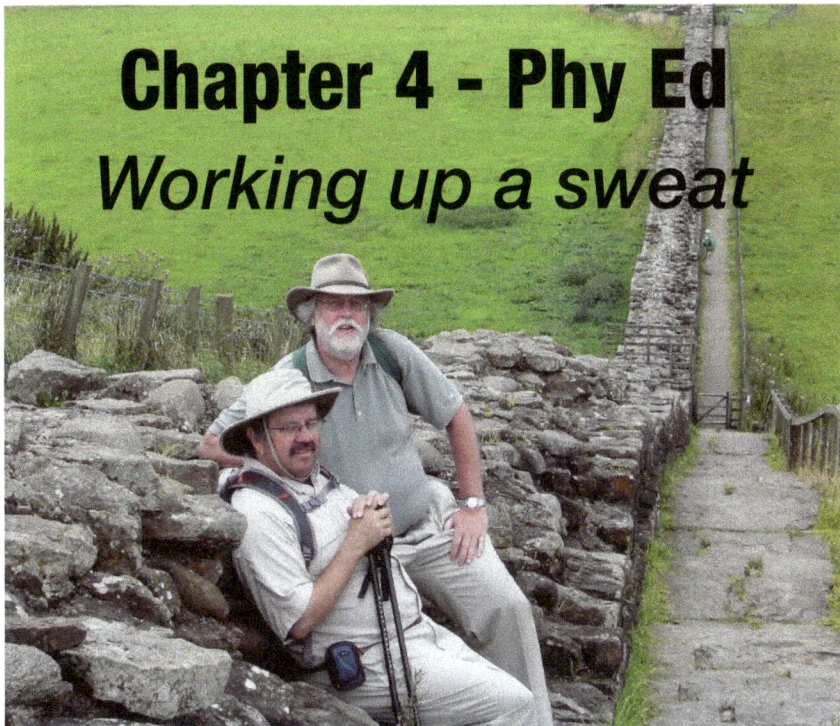

Chapter 4 - Phy Ed
Working up a sweat

Hadrian's Wall, England

Cousins golf in Portugal

"Should we clap if Roger hits it into the water?" I asked my brother.

"That would be bad sportsmanship," he replied.

"So, we should clap?"

"Of course." Guy humor.

Our foursome was standing on the 18th tee of a scenic golf course in Portugal watching the group behind us tee off on the par 3 17th hole with a pond between them and the pin. We were on our 99th and final hole of a week of "cousins golf." We were still having fun.

Common scents in England

We returned to Hadrian's Wall 13 years after we had walked the entire 84 miles. Ingloriously. We were walking up to the Roman fort that sat astride the wall when my wife, Kris, tripped and went down face-first.

The fall drew blood. People at the tourist center provided bandages, patching her up the best they could.

On the previous walk, we only had one fall in seven days. Walking through a wet field on some uneven boards, Julie slipped and fell into the muck.

Her "eau de cow" perfume entitled her to sit alone in the car on the ride home.

We watched as Roger carefully teed up his ball then wasted no time launching a wounded duck toward a watery landing in the middle of the pond. Our group burst into immediate and sustained applause, giving way to laughter on both holes.

So much had gone right on the trip that mediocre golf seemed irrelevant. In fact, all six of us were pretty good golfers, capable of parring any of the holes of the five courses we played but even more likely to post a number one or two digits higher--especially on these premier courses in the Algarve, a golf mecca on Portugal's southern Atlantic coast.

The trip had been in the planning stages for almost five years, running into schedule conflicts, a pandemic, and competing priorities. Eventually, we felt our advancing ages could make the trip a moot point if we didn't go now.

We had trip organizers on each side of the Atlantic. I took care of the flight arrangements and rented a VRBO villa from my perch in Wisconsin while Captain Jack arranged tee times, local transportation, and equipment needs from his European vantage point, most notably his apartment across from a golf course in Tavira, Portugal.

Captain Jack Clements is a legend in our family, an Air Force pilot who served in Vietnam and flew presidents such as George H. W. Bush around the world, piloting Air Force One (or Two, depending which stories are being told) and finished his career flying wealthy Greek shipping magnates to the four corners of the earth. At 60, he finally settled down and married a Swiss woman who speaks at least five languages. They currently liven in Provence, in southern France.

Now 80, he is in incredible physical shape with a full head of hair and an impish grin probably stolen from him by Tom Cruise to create his Maverick character.

As our April flight dates got closer, Jack and I communicated across the Atlantic on Face Time. We decided the best solution to transporting golf clubs was to leave them home. Jack dug up an extra set for me and his brother Dave and even managed to furnish a left-handed set for Cousin Fred. He secured rentals for Roger and my brother Bob at the airport, with the shop collecting them at Jack's course after our final round.

We needed two more golfers to fill out two foursomes, so Jack brought in a couple of his friends. The first was a colorful Swedish photographer named Henrik, who even cooked us an entire meal of barbecue ribs on the rooftop of his Tavira apartment. The other was a laconic Irishman who had had a career as a professional golfer and was used to playing courses for free. They elevated our conversations from that of country cousins who rarely saw each other to that of international gadflies exchanging world-class opinions (especially after large quantities of Super Bock beer).

Luckily, golf wasn't the only thing we did in Portugal. We finally took advantage of a day off to visit nearby Spain. First, we drove an hour to Huelva to visit the grave of a fabricated hero from World War II named Major Martin. The amazing true story of British wartime guile served as the basis for a recent movie called "Operation Mincemeat." The grave was occupied all right, but the body that washed up on a Spanish beach in 1944 had been procured from a London morgue and deposited there in the dead of night via a British submarine.

We drove another hour to Seville, Spain, a picturesque and crowded town dominated by a gigantic Gothic cathedral. I had selected a promising restaurant noted for its bulls gawking at you from the walls while you ate, but the beleaguered staff was even less attentive to us than the bulls, so we moved on to a less crowded place that specialized in paella.

Back in Tavira, Henrik decided our final night there would be a festival of meat at a Brazilian churrascaria near his apartment. Waiters with huge slabs of meat perched on their shoulders and lethal-looking knives circulated the dining room slicing pieces of beef, lamb, pork, sausages, tenderloin, ham and chicken onto our plates. When carnivores go to heaven (or hell), they end up in a place like this. The restaurant demonstrated the limitations of sites such as Trip Advisor in evaluating restaurants. Ranked 180 out of 186 Tavira restaurants, its reviews were brutal. I found the food to be outstanding, with excellent service.

Flights

It took us three flight segments on United/Lufthansa to get to Portugal, as we flew Madison-Chicago-Frankfurt-Faro punctually and in relative comfort. On the way back, we stopped in our family homeland of Luxembourg, left behind about 150 years ago by our great-grandfather William Zanter. To get there, we took a direct flight on LuxAir from Faro to Luxembourg City. The airline surprised us with a full meal on the two-and-a-half-hour flight. It's clearly not competing with Ryan Air for the bargain-basement clientele.

In the post-pandemic air world, no story would be complete without dysfunction and breakdown due to issues of logistics, personnel, and equipment. This one is no different. Our return flights from Luxembourg to Madison didn't go as planned and we got home about two hours late with much drama in between. Some of the airport workers were helpful and some weren't. In order:

Not helpful. The gate agent in Frankfurt who completely melted down because we refused to line up properly. Lufthansa unwisely announced that they were boarding the plane a full 40 minutes before they actually did. The abusive agent apparently believed the root problem was passengers who refused to form a proper line rather than a plane that refused to leave the ground.

Not helpful. The functionaries at O'Hare's customs checkpoint who routed me into the Global Entry line even though they knew the photo kiosks were broken and the line there was longer than the regular Customs lines.

Not helpful/helpful. The incompetent United agent rebooking us on a standby flight after our Lufthansa breakdown who just couldn't get it right. Her co-workers bailed her out.

Helpful. The O'Hare Terminal 2 worker who saved us a half hour of wait time by suggesting we walk a few hundred yards to Terminal 1 to re-enter through security because the Terminal 2 TSA Precheck line was down.

Not helpful. The United gate agent who was going to delete two of us from the standby list because of a technical glitch. Luckily, United had to change planes because of a nose gear problem and we were sent to another gate.

Helpful. The friendly United gate agent who understood the glitch and fixed it. She also chatted with us for a long seven minutes (the amount of time she said she had to wait) while two absent passengers defaulted the last two seats on the Madison flight to Fred and me.

Helpful. The United baggage attendant who reached out to my brother after all the bags had come off the luggage carousel in Madison and his wasn't among them. Incredibly, my brother's bag had made it onto our original flight to Madison. The attendant had retrieved it and waited for him to arrive.

Conquering Hadrian's Wall

In 122 AD, the Roman Emperor Hadrian was checking out the far outposts of the empire. He decided there was not much left worth conquering in the north of Britain (Scotland), so he ordered a wall to be built, marking the end of the empire. The Romans could make a little money charging tolls and also keep the barbarians out.

Nearly 2,000 years later, the wall still manages to bring some money into the empire (us), but its effectiveness in keeping out barbarians (also us) has eroded—much like the wall itself. To be fair, while my guidebooks stressed how much of the 84-mile-long wall has vanished, they failed to say how much of this remarkable piece of engineering still exists.

Organizing the legion

It's not quite right to say that I talked 22 other friends and family members into walking the Hadrian's Wall path from Newcastle to Bowness-on-Solway (essentially from the North Sea to the Irish Sea). They talked themselves into it for reasons ranging from a fierce love of history to the thrill of the physical feat to just being part of a fun group. My reason for organizing what we called a "Tour de Glenn" was that I was turning 60 and bringing a 32-year teaching career to a close and wanted to celebrate in an appropriate way.

The Logistics

We selected two centrally located places to stay for eight nights, the Ashcroft Guesthouse and the Centre of Britain Hotel, located a block apart in the town of Haltwhistle, roughly 41 miles from each coast. We used six rental cars to commute back to our hotels each afternoon and to where we left off the next morning. The Ashcroft is a five-star lodging with magnificent gardens and the Centre of Britain maintains a commanding presence on Haltwhistle's main street. The proprietors of both places couldn't have been friendlier or more helpful.

The Trail

We chose to walk east to west, mainly because it meant finishing in the quiet of the Solway salt marshes instead of the frenetic industrial city of Newcastle-upon-Tyne. It also meant having the sun at our backs in the morning (when it showed—this is Britain, after all). It also meant potentially having the wind in our faces, something that was really only noticeable on one of the seven days we spent on the trail.

For the most part, the Hadrian's Wall path, which has only been an official trail since 2003, is well-marked, although the closer we got to the west coast, the more we seemed to lose the path as it darted on and off roads, through fields and through the city of Carlisle.

Walking the Trail

We averaged twelve miles a day. Where the terrain was flat the first and last days, we were able to do about 15 miles. In the middle of the country, it got steeper, eventually rising to about 1,200 feet, so we shortened the daily distance. The progression was roughly this: city walking the first day, mostly farmland and crops the next day or two, high pastureland for a couple days, then the salt marsh.

More Logistics

We had cars and drivers stationed about every three or four miles (called "chuckpoints" because Chuck was one of the drivers). If there was a pub or tearoom in the neighborhood, that's where we would find them. The drivers provided water, sustenance, encouragement, and medical help (unlike the Romans, we had access to ibuprofen and moleskin). They also provided a ride home if you decided you were done for the day. Curt, one of the other drivers, became known as Hagrid for his wizard-like ability to pop up from behind a rock or a cow with his video camera humming.

The company

The middle part of the trail is the most scenic, most difficult, and most popular. We met quite a few Brits, some Aussies, and relatively few other Americans. We also met thousands of sheep, most of whom were undisturbed by our presence and continued munching away as we trudged past them and clambered over the next stile.

One day, Paul and his group of rabbits (so-called because they always burst into the lead and set the pace) took a wrong turn. The sheep went nuts, shouting "baaaack, go baaaack." Paul, not being baaah-lingual, ignored them and ended up going a mile out of the way. This led to a lot of sheep jokes the next few days. (How do you make a u-turn? Wink at her.)

Preparation and Equipment

In the fourteen weeks leading up to our departure for England, we had fourteen practice hikes, ranging from just a few miles to about a dozen miles. I accumulated 100 training miles just in the month before we left. Most of us took the training seriously and were glad we did.

The best advice I got was to buy good walking boots and to break them in with at least 150 miles. I bought a quality brand called Vasque. My feet stayed dry, the gore-tex kept them well ventilated, and the soles gave me the stability of a mountain goat. I also bought good rain gear (used one day) and an aqua pack, a small backpack that comes with a plastic bladder for water and an ingenious hose and valve so you really don't have to stop walking to drink.

I used two walking poles that I bought in England. Similar to cross-country ski poles, I found them invaluable for climbing and used them to take pressure off my legs as the day wore on. Others preferred just one pole, and our group of rabbits didn't need any.

I left my Milwaukee Brewers baseball hat behind in favor of a Tilley (think Indiana Jones) because it was a little more versatile and made me look more British (at least I thought it did).

Food

Because the hotels served huge, filling breakfasts, we felt no need for lunch on the trail. Peggy did pack sandwiches every morning though, and many of us took them along for quick sustenance at lunchtime.

Every other night was an organized food night. The night before the walk started, I took a couple people with me to the local fish & and chips shop where we bought two dozen boxes of the classic British fare then distributed them at our meeting in the Ashcroft garden.

On the third night, the entire group went to the Twice Brewed Pub, located in the tiny hamlet of Once Brewed. The English ale flowed freely, anesthetizing tired muscles. We shouldn't have been surprised to have such voracious appetites after two days on the trail.

The fifth night featured our own private historical site, Lancercost Priory, a structure built in the 1200s, much of it out of stones removed from the Wall. My wife, Kris, set up a picnic there and Dean brought his British Rotary friends.

The final night was a traditional Roman banquet, followed by a discussion and display of Roman weaponry by Ulfric the Armorer. Although it started out as entertainment, the group's questions managed to uncover the presenter's deep scholarship on the topic.

Conquering the Wall

A little over half the group walked the entire 84 miles. Although it was August, the weather never got beyond 70 degrees Fahrenheit. The trail led us through three golf courses. Entering the third one, I looked for, and quickly found a lost golf ball. As we caught up to a small group of Brits, I lofted the ball over their heads onto the trail in front of them. "Can we play through?" I asked merrily. American humor.

I came close to falling during the highest part of the walk as I descended a steep trail in the rain. I caught myself with my poles and executed a perfect, if involuntary, kick-turn (from my cross-country skiing days).

The final day, Matt and I decided to chase down the rabbits. Normally, we wouldn't have had a chance, but we saw them take a wrong turn. By the time they rediscovered the acorns marking the trail, they were only a few hundred yards in front of us. Wordlessly, Matt and I matched our walking sticks' cadence, so they clicked together on the hard road surface as we closed in. (We found out later how annoying that was to them.)

With a couple miles to go to the finish line, the road turned off into the woods and our younger, more agile friends sprinted ahead. We crossed the marked finish line about 10 minutes after them.

Our support group distributed champagne to us and also shared it with two other groups who finished at the same time: a group of

Brits who had walked the trail in eight days and some Aussies who had finished in six. We took seven days.

Our international group then retired to a nearby pub, tired and happy and accomplished.

Here are the guidelines I gave the group ahead of time:

My Hadrian's Wall guidelines

1 *Dress down, pack light.* You are unlikely to need dress-up clothes and there is a launderette right next door to our hotel.

2. Use your debit card. You will be able to withdraw pounds from at least two ATMs in Haltwhistle. Credit cards often can't be used except at fancier restaurants and some hotels. Visa and Mastercard are accepted at Ashcroft. I'm checking with the Centre of Britain.

3. Plan ahead for non-food nights. We'll have fish and chips for you Thursday night when you arrive, but Friday you're on your own (and Sunday, Tuesday and Thursday). My hope is that you'll break into small groups. Our herd size (23) doesn't make for easy travel. The fish and chips and the picnic at the priory are paid for. Supper at the Twice-Brewed Pub will be divided 23 ways. We'll collect £18 for the Roman Banquet.

4. Mix it up. This goes with #3. Get to know different people in the group. It is full of nice folks who happen to be leaders back home and obviously have a sense of adventure. Also, don't feel like you have to eat out for every meal. This goes with #5.

5. Email me your favorite foods, beverages and snacks. We will do some major grocery shopping on Thursday. Since we (Kris, Peggy, Bob and I) have kind of an apartment at the Ashcroft, we have room for group provisions.

6. Trail rules. Make sure nobody is on the trail alone. Plan regular rest stops. Dress appropriately (it's probably cooler than you expect). Stress safety. Stay hydrated. Natural groups will probably form based on walking speed. That's OK.

7. Non-Trail rules. Walk as much or as little as you want. Just let your driver know the night before and we'll do our best to accommodate you.

8. Use common sense. If injury, illness, or infirmity strikes, take a break from the trail. Roman legionnaires won't pursue and punish you.

9. Pay your driver. You may or may not spend much time in your designated car, but it all balances out. From what I've seen so far, car costs will amount to about $100 per person for the week, give or take a pound or two.

10. Leave the sheep alone.

Myths of Snowmobiling

Since I had managed to get through my first six decades without snowmobiling, I really didn't know what to expect when my friend Curt invited me up to Minocqua, Wisconsin in winter. All I had to go by were the sometimes-wacky myths that had accumulated in my head. A few of them proved to be true, the others not so much.

Myth #1 Snowmobiling is cold.

I'm sure it could be, but with the temperature in the mid-twenties and only a moderate wind on a late February day, my rigged-up outfit seemed to do the trick. Waterproof Vasque hiking boots, seldom-worn REI rain pants over my sweatpants, and my everyday leather coat over my Wisconsin hoodie seemed to work. My friend Curt was outfitted in a bright yellow-accented snowmobile ensemble with advertising that looked like the Tour de France on steroids.

Curiously, after we went inside, I felt the cold more, spending a half hour in front of the fireplace before I got comfortable.

Myth #2 It's expensive.

Is it really "a hole in the snow into which you pour money?" Pretty much. Curt said my rented Ski-Doo probably cost about $10,000 to buy. I was renting it for the day for about $200 (about a third of that was for gas). The price gets better if you rent for a longer period. But a Wisconsin family of four could probably fly to Disney World for a week for the price of renting machines for the entire family.

Myth #3 It's not exercise.

Try telling that to my shoulder and back muscles. At times, it felt like I was physically lifting the machine into hairpin turns and riding a rodeo bronc over moguls. I had expected the seat to be uncomfortable. It was not. It did help to lean forward so the bend in my elbows could absorb unexpected lurches.

Myth #4 It's noisy and polluting.

Yes, yes, it is. Like motorboats, lawn mowers, motorcycles, gas-powered leaf blowers, generators, snowblowers, jet engines, and marching bands.

Myth #5 The rides are from bar to bar through farm pastures.

In the Minocqua area, the routes are on specially designed, well-marked trails, through beautiful woodlands and across frozen lakes. The traffic is two-way, with the more popular trails featuring surprise encounters around sharp turns with machines coming the other way. A useful system of hand signals warns oncoming sleds if there is anyone else coming up. As far as the bar-to-bar part, the trails are posted with the distance and directions of various watering spots. We stopped for lunch in a dark but friendly bar known as the Black Bear.

Myth #6 It's not safe.

I had a root beer at the tavern. With so many split-second decisions required on the trail, I stayed alcohol-free, but I'm pretty sure that's not a universal choice. My rental came with a helmet so indomitable I felt like Darth Vader. Seriously, it was claustrophobic—at least until I adjusted to it. I never did resolve the problem of my eyeglasses fogging up. True—going faster helped, but when I put the helmet visor down (especially at high speed), the problem worsened and my vision quickly deteriorated. Leaving the visor open cleared up the fog but threatened to freeze my eye sockets. On the whole, as long as I didn't do anything stupid, I really felt quite safe.

Myth #7 Snowmobiling has a lot in common with Star Wars.

I made this one up. It's not just the Darth Vader helmet though. Remember the Speeder Bikes Luke and Leia were riding on the planet Endor in *Return of the Jedi?* Many of the trails around Minocqua are built up about 10 or 15 feet. On straightaways, you feel like you're flying behind Luke and Leia, because you are much higher than ground level with the trees.

Myth #8 Snowmobiling is for rednecks, speed freaks, and hairy thugs impervious to winter.

I didn't see anybody like that.

Running the world

W*hat's your reason for traveling? My 72-year-old brother, Bob
Schmidt (he goes by Boston Bobby on race day), has 26.2
reasons. He's a marathon runner. When he decided to run a marathon on all seven continents, it became a family commitment. Wrapping his love for travel around his commitment to running, he led
many of his friends and family members on a quirky multi-year journey through a world-wide window on people-racing. I interviewed
him about his accomplishment.*

Where did the idea to run all seven continents come from?

Many of the 57 marathons I've competed in were with Marathon
Tours out of Boston. By the time they started a Seven Continents
Club, I had already run quite a few in this country. So I ran Berlin. I
thought, "Now I've got two. Let's go on from there."

Back up. You've run 57 marathons? How many did you finish?

That's a good question. I finished 56. One year, I got to the 20-
mile mark in Boston and I was done. In fact, I never should have
started. Because of Achilles tendon problems I was getting physical
therapy every day in the weeks leading up to the race.

So I stopped and lay in a tent until the race was over. They sent
a bus to pick up all the half-dead runners who were in the same pre-
dicament, a ghost bus where nobody's talking and nobody's there.
All I wanted was to get to my hotel room and suffer.

Recovering the next day, I stopped into famed marathoner Bill
Rodgers' store in Boston. He was there and I talked to him. He had
dropped out at about the same place I did and hadn't finished the
marathon either.

Which international marathons have you run so far?

Antarctica, Berlin, Beijing, Aukland, Stockholm, London, Rio,
Tokyo, and Prague. I've signed up for Sydney next year.

How did you manage to run Antarctica?

It's unique because they have limited room. I had to win a lottery
to participate. It was about a 17-day trip, with four or five days spent

in Buenos Aires. About a hundred of us got on a refurbished Russian freighter in Ushuaia, at the southern tip of Argentina. It wasn't exactly Princess cruises. I shared a room with a pathologist from New York. I could tell exactly when the ship hit Drake's passage. I'd slide from the bottom of my bed to the top. Repeatedly. A lot of people got sick. I was lucky.

The race temperature was 37 degrees. We had to repeat the course four or five times to get to marathon length. My running mate counted 152 hills. Through much of the race, I had to choose between running through three inches of water or three inches of mud. First I did mud, then later, water. Towards the end of a race like that, you don't care if a truck hits you. In fact, you're kind of hoping for it. I finished 11th.

Afterwards some of the runners talked about doing a polar plunge. "No way in the world I'm doing that," I said. Two hours later, I was standing in line to jump in. It wasn't that bad really.

Was that your hardest race?

Second hardest. Running the Great Wall of China was harder. Only about five miles are on the ancient wall but it contains lots of uneven steps and stones and guard stations, not ideal for running. At one point, I had to hold onto a guide rope to keep from falling 30 feet. Before the race started, I got so cold I bought a fleece. By the end, it was 95 degrees. Add to that the toxic air surrounding Beijing and the entire course seemed to be uphill.

One surprise was the after-the-race meal we had in a square near Beijing. It was Subway sandwiches.

Any other races that were memorable?

South Africa. We ran it on a game preserve. I remember them telling us that the only things that run in the jungle are food. The local lions had made a kill nearby the night before the race, so they moved the course.

What's the most common misunderstanding people have?

Most people don't know it's 26.2 miles. Really. They also have no concept of time. And they think every runner's a Kenyan and that normal people don't do marathons. They've never considered it for themselves, even if they regularly run 5K or 10K. I started running marathons when I was 36. My fastest one was at age 46. It was Grandma's Marathon in Duluth, Minnesota. I ran it in 2:56:03. Chicago was only four seconds slower.

Do you have to qualify in some way to get into a race?

That applies mostly to just Boston. Roughly speaking, you must be in the top 10 percent in your gender and age group. The threshold for women is different than for men. If I have to hit 3:40 to qualify, a woman my age would need 4:10.

You don't have to qualify for the New York Marathon, but they only have room for about 50,000 of the 100,000 who want to run. So, they have a lottery. Certain people are exempted from the lottery if they're elite runners or if they're raising money for a charity.

Are runners all the same?

It's a great mix of people who all share the same passion. But there are differences. For one thing, they're not all built the same. You'll have 250-pound ex-football players passing you, but you might be passing some sleek-looking runners who do it in six hours. Sue Dell, the wife of the founder of Dell Computers, is a triathlete. She has a billion excuses not to be an athlete. Still, she runs. Most people can do it if they train.

Do you have advice for people who want to do this?

Find a running club. Start running with them every Saturday. Run a few 5K. Learn from the other runners. I like training in threes: one day of speed on a track, one day of hills, one long run. Repeat.

What's race preparation like?

The night before a marathon, or even two nights before, you'll find runners carbo-loading on such foods as lasagna or spaghetti and hydrating with as many gallons as they can force down. You have to keep track of where the nearest bathrooms or port-a-potties are. It doesn't hurt to carry an empty Gatorade bottle.

Do you have a support crew?

I almost always have someone along to help. I think it's really important, especially when you get to mile 20 and see a friendly face. I enlisted my friend Bill for Prague this year. I don't know how I would have done it without him.

You also get to meet a lot of people. Running marathons is very social. I once ran with a white guy from South Africa as the country was finally getting rid of apartheid. There are people from all over and their concerns are your concerns.

Why do you do this? How long do you expect to continue?

It's a stress reliever. It helps develop friendships. It provides a positive focus. If you have other bad habits, it neutralizes them a little bit. On my tombstone, I want the words, "It's been a good run."

You never know when you're done. Prague was very difficult. I signed up for it before the pandemic and ran it three years later. I found I could still dig deep. My quads saved me. It was all the hill workouts.

Chapter 5 - Drivers Ed
Getting around

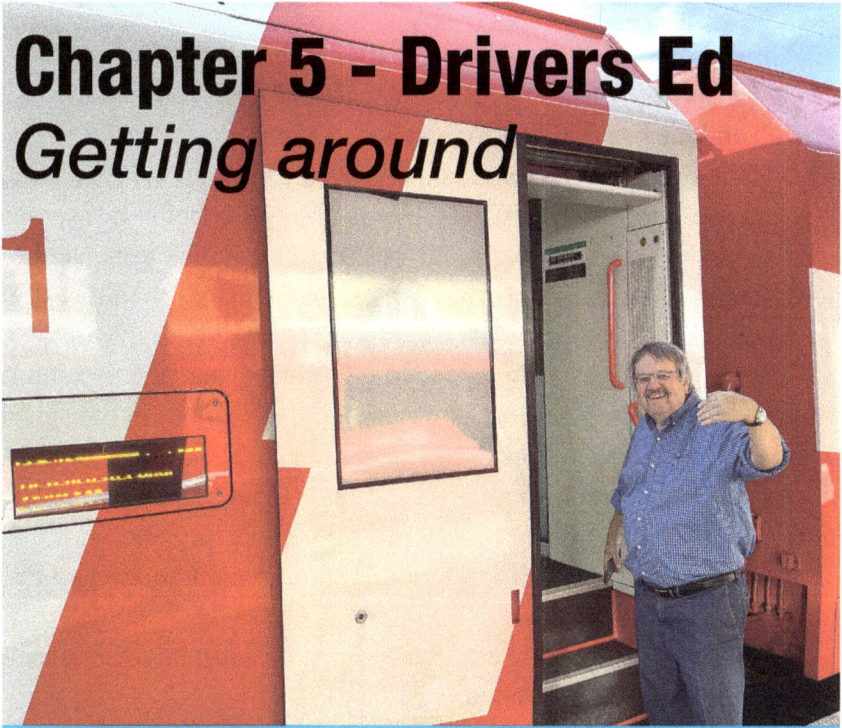

St. Moritz, Switzerland.

Bus to Nowhere

The pierced and tattooed hoodlum driving our hired bus had pulled off the highway in suburban Paris and was outside, pacing back and forth talking on his cell phone. We had been negotiating with him to stop at a grocery store on the way to our rented boats in Burgundy, but all we saw around us were a gas station and a few anonymous strip malls.

I stepped out into the July sun to talk to the driver. Suddenly, he thrust his phone into my hand and told me to talk to

Paris by Segway

The best ride I ever had in Europe was on a Segway, a two-wheeled stand-up contraption you sometimes see in airports. Eight of us found our way to the Paris Segway shop near the Eiffel Tower on a summer holiday weekend.

After a brief training session, we followed a leader in single file past light traffic and city highlights, alighting at a café outside the Louvre where we recharged the machines and us.

I didn't realize what a spectacle we, ourselves, were until I saw an entire group of Asian tourists with their backs to the Eiffel Tower and their cameras pointed at us.

his boss. What followed was one of the more bizarre conversations of my life as his boss and I bounced back and forth between my bad French and his bad English, frustration mounting on both sides.

Although the details remained murky, the bottom line was clear: Our destination, Flez-Cuzy, which was about two hours away, was too far for his buses to travel. This bus wasn't leaving Paris. Neither were the 14 of us, mostly retired professionals from the Midwest in our sixties.

Those travelers had trusted me to plan and execute the trip, but it was never more clear than at that moment that I'm not in the travel business. I just like planning trips for friends. The July 2016 Burgundy trip was the most ambitious venture I had planned since the time I convinced 22 other people to walk across England with me. That trip ended in triumph and a multinational celebration at an English pub on the Irish Sea.

This trip, a week on the Nivernais Canal in Burgundy, threatened to end before it had even begun.

Our bus returned to the highway, heading back into Paris. I tabbed Dianne and a few of the other travelers and improvised a Board of Directors for my non-existent travel company. Then I called Mathieu, the kind and knowledgeable young desk clerk from the Hotel de La Paix Montparnasse, where we had spent four days. I made the driver talk to him on my phone.

Mathieu had already called the parent bus company in Holland multiple times to make sure the bus made it to our hotel—which it finally did, more than an hour after our noon pick-up time. Until they arrived, Mathieu continued to call them until they finally quit answering the phone.

Ultimately it became clear to me that our young, tatooed driver and his boss were not the problem. They also were victims of the Dutch bus company that had, for reasons unknown to us, completely mishandled the transaction.

I should have trusted my instincts with the company. They had been fairly unreliable in their communications with me and had not confirmed our bus trip until just before we left the US.

On the other hand, their price was about $200 below any of the other four companies I had contacted and, most comfortingly, they seemed strangely reluctant to take my money.

Had this been a Globus trip or one of Rick Steves' many tour offerings, resolution would have been swift. Operatives on the ground would have raised holy hell with the bus company or immediately switched to another one with little more than a loss of time for the passengers.

I didn't have that kind of backup, but I did have a plan. If we could catch the 4:38 train from Bercy station, it would get us into Flez-Cuzy before 8:00, about four hours later than we had anticipated.

I had Mathieu relay this information to the driver in French and asked to be dropped off at Bercy.

That proved to be a bridge too far for the driver, who believed the Gare de Lyon and Bercy were the same station and dropped us off at the former. Maybe to his twenty-something body, they were, but to us, negotiating the three-quarters of a mile between the two—with luggage—would be formidable.

I took a small group of our more mobile travelers (my senior staff) with me into the Gare de Lyon, where we got directions to the other train station. By the time the four of us completed our trek and climbed the steps into Bercy 15 minutes later, the beautiful day had turned swelteringly hot. We still had an hour and a half before the train was scheduled to leave.

The man at the ticket window was very friendly and apparently gave us the group discount, because our 14 tickets cost me a little over $300, much less than I had anticipated. I didn't know what would happen to the nearly $800 I had already given to the bus company. If I had a travel company, they'd be the ones worrying about it now back at company headquarters.

Instead of putting the train tickets on my personal credit card, I would have had the comptroller of my company forward payment. (Several of the European companies had used that term when requesting payment. I suppose if I had a company, I would actually know what a comptroller was).

I phoned the rest of our travelers, who were still waiting at the Gare de Lyon, and suggested they take cabs with all our luggage the short distance to Bercy and we would meet them at the door. They did, all but one. He had been sick and decided he was done. He jumped into a cab for the airport instead and flew home. He was later diagnosed with pneumonia.

I had contracted the same bug, so I was running on empty by now, my voice raspy and my patience thin. I was anxious to get to the boats we had hired and relax on deck with a glass of medicinal wine.

While we waited impatiently for the train, I called our friends, two Australians who had skipped Paris and were meeting us at the boat. They assured us they had things under control at the port and would have the appropriate medication waiting for me.

After some minor problems identifying the right train, we split into several groups and boarded without incident, but we still had one more hurdle. We would have just seven minutes to change trains in Migennes.

This normally would have been a routine challenge, but one of our group had not fared well on a Segway tour of Paris. He had struck an immoveable object, causing the Segway to fling him off, cracking a few ribs in the process. It was now up to his wife and the rest of us to move the luggage and the extra provisions we had secured in Paris.

After several trips up and down concrete stairs at Migennes station and a frantic but successful search for our train, we slumped into our seats just seconds before it started moving.

Nearly an hour later, the train disgorged us at Flez-Cuzy station. Desolate and forlorn, it wasn't so much a station as a gravel path along the tracks. Although it was about 8:00 pm, at least it was still daylight. July in France enjoys a tireless sun that refuses to set until around 10:00 p.m.

We dragged our reluctant suitcases through the soft gravel about 60 yards to the main road to get our bearings. My iPhone was reasonably useless in finding the port on the Nivernais Canal, where our boats were waiting, so we sent out scouts in each direction.

That strategy was successful. Minutes later we turned the corner and the canal floated into view. There in the Le Boat port were our two four-bedroom canal boats, with our Aussie friends positioned as promised, on the top deck with a bottle of wine in front of them.

We spent an excellent week on the Nivernais Canal and Yonne River, captaining our own boats and stopping wherever we liked. When we were done, I had arranged to have us picked up at the port. But this time I had a company: Le Boat had arranged our transfer.

No late buses or surly drivers, the two vans we ordered arrived 15 minutes early. The friendly young drivers took care of all the luggage and made sure we were comfortable. Then they efficiently transported us to our destination in Fontainebleu.

It took more than three months to get our money returned from the bus to nowhere. The company not only refused to respond to my communications, they didn't respond to MasterCard either. The $800 was eventually re-credited to our account.

I should probably share some of that with Mathieu, the hotel clerk who worked so hard on our behalf. At the very least, I'd be happy to write a recommendation for him to be comptroller.

Swiss on different track with passenger rail

"I want you to let me know when they're at their weakest point. That's when we'll make our offer."

The train started to move while we stood in the aisle eyeing the last two available seats across from a man too engrossed in his cellphone to notice. Finally, without acknowledging our presence, he pulled his coat off the seats and let us sit down.

"Tell me when they're weakest," he barked again, as if talking to an especially slow child. An elegantly dressed, middle-aged Swiss investment banker, he looked like he had been sent by Central Casting to play the role. He had boarded the train in Geneva and would get off at Montreux, less than an hour away along the northern shore of Lake Geneva. He spoke freely in British-accented English. Since we had not spoken and had no luggage, he probably assumed we were French-speaking locals, or maybe a German-speaking plumber and his wife on holiday. Or maybe we just didn't matter to him.

"When we put our offer on the table, they'll have 30 minutes to accept it." He was a gray-suited wolf contemplating a limping deer. For the next twenty minutes, we watched, fascinated, as he used two phones to play the part of different jungle animals, from a bull elephant thundering at an underling to a purring tiger enchanting his tigress.

I was relaying this experience to a friend as I told him about my ten-day train trip to Switzerland, a country that has invested heavily in rail transportation, when the conversation drifted to Wisconsin's intermittent rail passenger efforts. I expressed frustration about how political the discussion always became.

"You think the discussion is about transportation," my friend said, referencing my Swiss banker story. "It's not. it's about culture. Most people in Wisconsin have never been on a European train (or an American train, for that matter). They can't see themselves on a train and don't perceive the need."

This convinced me to do some research about when and how the Swiss made the cultural adaptation to trains and some lessons they may have for us.

Turning points in the 1960s

Switzerland differs from Wisconsin in some substantial ways—it is smaller, wealthier, more vertical in its terrain, and has four official languages. But in other ways it is similar—population, winters, participatory government, and accordions.

Although it's about the size of Vermont and New Hampshire combined, Switzerland has close to eight million people (Wisconsin has almost six million). It officially became a country in 1848—the same year Wisconsin became a state. The first Swiss passenger train began operating in 1847, mainly whisking fresh bread from Baden to Zurich, 18 miles away. That same year the Wisconsin legislature authorized the first Wisconsin passenger train between Milwaukee and Waukesha, more likely transporting beer.

At that time, the newly centralized Swiss government tried to establish a national rail system but the public didn't like the plan it produced. The states (called cantons) assumed responsibility and granted passenger rail concessions to private companies. Problems with this haphazard system and fear of increasing foreign ownership eventually led to an 1898 referendum to federalize the railways. It passed by a two-thirds margin.

American passenger rail peaked in the mid-20th century and left a remnant called Amtrak. Facing similar problems with declining ridership and outdated equipment, the Swiss doubled down on their investment in passenger rail. They added trains and made more convenient connections between them. They were so successful that by 2010, many Swiss saw no point to owning a car (516 passenger cars per 1,000 people compared to over 800 in the US) even though there is an excellent and well-cared-for highway system.

The Swiss appear to have solved most of the problems critics ascribe to traveling by train. Following is a brief discussion of those issues with the exception of cost. Suffice to say that both Wisconsin and Switzerland spend a great deal on moving people around.

Interference with car traffic

This happens rarely in Switzerland. The two methods of transport inhabit their own worlds. Trains go over, under or around car traffic. The only time we crossed a city street on our rail trip was when we transferred to a two-car cogwheel train in tiny Aigle to climb the mountain to remote Leysin. No cars were disturbed.

Sound

Trains are extremely quiet in Switzerland. Running on electricity, with modern equipment, on seamless rails, there is none of the clickety-clack we associate with trains in America. We stayed at a hotel in Lausanne that billed itself as "fifty meters from the station." From our hotel room, the sound of a train coming or going sounded no louder than a clothes dryer starting up in our basement. Our son lives about the same distance from the tracks in La Crosse, and a passing train sounds like a 747 taxiing through his living room.

On the train itself, quiet reigns (with the exception of self-absorbed Swiss bankers). On one train, we found ourselves in the "quiet" car, where all forms of noise—even conversation—are prohibited. This was not easy for typically rambunctious Americans.

Ease of use

The Swiss have integrated trains with other forms of transportation. Because of all the lakes, passenger ferries are common. Their schedules are coordinated, so we were able to cross Lake Lucerne by ferry then find our train to Locarno pulling into the station just after we did. Train stations are the hub of most Swiss cities so you'll find a variety of other transportation options right outside, including buses, trams, subways, taxis, bike rentals (sometimes free), and pedestrian arcades. When we got to Locarno, we followed the crowd to the funicular (kind of a diagonal elevator) which immediately deposited us into the heart of the city, a mostly traffic-free warren of shops, parks and restaurants.

Comfort

Wide, plush seats that recline like your Lazy-Boy, panoramic windows that maximize Switzerland's vertical views, tables and outlets for your laptop, and a quiet, soft ride mark the best of the trains. Even second-class train cars feel spacious and comfortable. Bathrooms are clean and rolling food and beverage carts or restaurant cars are often available.

Speed

The fast trains of Switzerland match the kind Wisconsin is likely to get in terms of speed. If they topped 100 mph, we were not aware of it. (I couldn't get my GPS to give me a reading.) Officially, the highest speed Swiss trains attain is 124 mph on just a few lines. Faster trains, such as the TGV in France (up to 200 mph) or the Bullet Train in Japan (186 mph) exist elsewhere, but are not as useful in a country of narrow valleys and tight turns. American trains have another problem when it comes to speed: Amtrak doesn't own the tracks. It is not uncommon to find a passenger train pulling off to the side to let a freight train go by. Many tracks are in deplorable condition, forcing passenger trains to slow down for safety reasons.

Frequency

Zurich's train station, serving a population of 370,000, greets 2,000 trains per day. The closest train station to Madison (260,000 people) is 28 miles away in Columbus. It serves two trains per day, hopefully doubling to four in the coming year. On our journey from Lausanne with the Swiss banker, it didn't matter much when we got to the train station. There were three trains per hour on that route.

Cost

Our Swiss Passes gave us unlimited travel on most trains, boats, funiculars, cog railways, aerial trams, and local buses, subways, trams, and conveyances for which we didn't have a name. It cost about $750 for a 15-day first-class pass, but I'm not sure how it works for the locals in this very expensive country. In practice, passengers are only occasionally asked to show tickets.

Safety

As in the US, trains are significantly safer than cars. In 2004, when 510 people died on Swiss roads, the number of train passengers who died was zero. In 2023, 577 people died on Wisconsin roads. None died on trains. Passenger train deaths are so rare in Wisconsin that when I Googled it, one of the first entries I found was a train leaving Ashland in 1887 that derailed, killing one man.

Time

Yes, Americans love their cars. They provide privacy, independence, and various degrees of comfort. But they also cost time when it comes to sitting in traffic jams, finding parking spots, shoveling the car out of a snowbank, buying gas, or taking the car to a mechanic. Europeans love their trains because they provide relaxation, speed, comfort and especially time: time to read, talk on their cell phones, study, do paperwork, check email, text, sip coffee, watch spectacular scenery, and chat with friends. And plenty of time to cut multi-million dollar bank deals from your office on rails.

Ride the chicken train

*H*ere's how easy a six-hour train ride from Amsterdam to Luxembourg City in December can turn difficult and get you there in 11 hours. Cousin Fred and I were a little frustrated but the Germans in the station seemed to be even angrier at each other for allowing this to happen.

1. Amsterdam. Go to Centraal Station an hour early. Freeze your tail off on unheated platform. Switch tracks at last second. Board train.

2. Arnhem. Get off train. Look for schedule board. Your train has been cancelled. Find agent. Follow her directions to Bus Stop L. Freeze your tail off for an hour. No bus. Run like hell back to train platform 5 to board "chicken train" (20 stops in 30 miles). Thaw toes.

3. Düsseldorf. You've missed your scheduled train. Eat a brat. Find Platform 9. Find next train. Find seat in First Class.

4. Koblenz. Arrive late. You have 6 minutes to find train to Luxembourg. Go to Track 1. Your train is on Track 16. Now. Run. Drag suitcases roughly up cement stairs. Try to board wrong train. Twice. Find stealth train hidden behind wrong train. Stumble into first available door.

5. Luxembourg. Home. In just 11 hours.

On the way to Ambleside
God save the queen.

Scene One

Rain welcomes a reluctant dawn at lonely and remote Keflavik Airport in Iceland. Our sleepless eyes scan electronic flight departure boards that have unfairly decided our connecting flight to Glasgow will be delayed at least an hour. We sit haphazardly in a café as a long line of delayed London-bound passengers snakes past us, victims of various random decisions made by British authorities to ensure the queen's funeral is unencumbered.

Scene Two

In a surreal moment at Glasgow Airport, two uniformed agents wordlessly motion hundreds of deplaning passengers to a stop in front of a television that seems strangely out of place. The anxious crowd quiets as the TV zeroes in on King Charles and the casket bearing his mother. A country-wide moment of silence engulfs us as passengers of all nationalities stand respectfully in place.

Scene Three

It may have been a few decades since Harry Potter ran his luggage cart through a brick wall on Platform 9 and ¾ on his way to Hogwart's, but Platform 1 at Glasgow Central looks as if it would take us there today. Still sleepless at 1:30 in the afternoon, we struggle with our luggage to commandeer Carriage 7 for the hour-long train ride to Carlisle, England.

Scene Four

Kris sits on small stone steps leading to a greasy garage while three of us mill around a dangerous-looking gas pump at the cramped Europcar location across from a Thai massage parlor not far from the Carlisle train station. A national holiday for the queen takes precedence over business as usual and the place is closed. We have paid an extra £120 to get Matthew to meet us here and free our cars from their bondage. He is a half hour late. When he finally arrives, he surprises us by awarding us larger cars than we have ordered complete with automatic transmissions, a rarity.

Scene Five

My birthday. On the main street of the impossibly quaint town of Ambleside, an Italian take-away sandwich shop, garishly out of place and new since our last trip here four years ago, promises something the other restaurants on the street have yet to deliver: actual food. It's about 7:30 pm and our group, cranky and hungry from a long travel day, exhausts all other options and gives in. Accompanied by a Carlsberg beer, my calzone meets the requirements for keeping me alive another day, if not much more. Today that seems like enough. Happy Birthday to me and thank you for your birthday greetings. God save the king.

Catching a ride

It's a beautiful afternoon in Sorrento, Italy as we board the last ferry of the day to Naples.

"Mr. Glenn, Mr. Glenn," a man in uniform shouts as he walks up and down the aisles of the ferry.

I reluctantly raise my hand. The man is agitated. "You left your credit card at the ticket counter," he says.

It's at least a quarter mile back to the counter. I stand up, and as I'm about to get off the boat I ask him, "You're going to wait for me, aren't you?"

The ferry is already late leaving port. "You must hurry," is his cryptic reply.

I sprint down the pier at full speed. Well, at first, at least. While I do a lot of walking, running these days is pretty rare for me. By the time I reach the ticket office, I'm puffing like a freight train. Good thing I don't have to say anything to the ticket lady. She just pushes the card under the window when she sees me.

Turning back to the pier, the ferryboat is still there but looks like it's five miles away. I'm still breathing hard and my heart is pounding. I spot a young guy on one of those ubiquitous mopeds heading away from the pier. I step in front of him and hold up my hand.

He looks at me quizzically, seeing a slightly deranged old man with a breathing problem. I point to the ferry, tap the seat and, not hearing 'No,' get on behind him.

He wheels the bike around and we start hurtling down the pier at breakneck speed, darting around debris and fishermen. There are no foot pegs on the back, so my legs dangle in the air like a frog's and I grab the young driver's shirt to keep from flipping off.

As we close in on the ferry, it looks like he's going to take me right up the gangplank. At the last second, he brakes and turns left sharply, skidding to a stop right next to the captain of the ship.

Grateful to be alive, I leap off the back and dig into my pocket for some euros. Grinning broadly, the driver waves me off, revs up the engine and disappears back the way we came. Now we each have a story to tell.

I step onto the boat to a round of applause.

Swiss trains, cheap planes and French boats

We knew we had less than two hours to make our connection when we got to Philadelphia. Maintenance issues (reportedly tire-related) kept us from boarding in Madison until a long hour had passed. When we finally touched down in the City of Brotherly Love, it didn't look good. Our flight to Zurich was completing final boarding and was five terminals away.

Steve started to run ahead, but was intercepted by a guy driving a golf cart. "I think you need me," the guy said, so we piled on. We raced toward the gate, threading our way through at-risk pedestrians. Five uniformed staff members at Gate 19 looked up in surprise as we skidded to a stop. One ran back down the jetway shouting, "Don't close. They're here." The doors stayed open for one more minute, while we took the last open seats. Against all odds, our luggage made it too, although to keep up the suspense, they were in the final group of bags to circle the carousel at Zurich airport.

The Sorrel Hotel Rex didn't have a room for me. I had booked the reservation for eight rooms, but now Kris and I were homeless. It took us a while to sort it out, but it turned out they had given Matt and Kathy each their own room and mine somehow disappeared. We had paid for the rooms online on their website designed by inebriated clowns.

It's getting tougher for non-tech savvy people to travel. We had breakfast in a Zurich restaurant, Café Elena, where the waiter didn't bring menus; he just brought one card with a large QR code on it.

Hovering over it with a smart phone and pushing the right buttons deposits the menu on your phone. It doesn't translate it, however. That's a topic for a different discussion.

Our train ride from Zurich to St. Moritz was spectacular, with alps that grew taller, sprouted waterfalls, and submitted to elaborate bridges and tunnels. We arrived at the Hotel Soldanella in an exuberant mood. Our caravan, 15 travelers strong, loitered on the hotel's expansive deck overlooking a beautiful lake sparkling in the summer sun.

We were about to break up and wander among the wealthy city's ubiquitous shops when Steve and I spotted a guitar beckoning to us from a corner of the hotel's empty bar. We hauled it out to the deck and started coaxing songs from the sixties and seventies out of its well-used strings.

Pretty soon, the good German beer was flowing, and people were joining in with our songs, occasionally in the same key, as we misremembered lyrics from lost decades. Steve and I passed the guitar back and forth as our fingers tired and our voices faded. There would always be time to hit the shops.

It is an enormous advantage to have our trips populated predominantly by teachers. Veteran field trip organizers, they understand that just because something is expected to happen doesn't mean it will. I often find myself reflexively counting the flock. The funny thing is, I'll look around and see a couple of other teachers doing it too. Two mornings in a row, we had travelers unexpectedly sleep in. Counters picked up on this before any damage could be done.

It took several of us to arrange our transfer to the train station, with adjustments being made right up until the last minute. It all reminds me of a flock of geese in flight. The one in front is regularly replaced by a fresher one with the same itinerary.

The Glacier Express from St. Moritz to Zermatt is anything but an express train. It takes eight hours to go about 180 miles. It was a bucket-list item for me. We were pampered well with our first-class pass but the scenery was simply more and more of the Alps. I will confess to nodding off a few times.

St. Moritz had been grand, quiet, and out of season. Zermatt was the opposite: young, active, and crowded. Every young person we saw looked like they'd be capable of scaling the nearby Matterhorn.

A few days later, after a dawn train ride to Geneva Airport, we took the low-cost carrier EasyJet to Rennes, France. All I can say is they got us there, which is about all they promised. On the budget carriers, every little extra has a cost. Despite what you may have heard, it is NOT true that half of the seat belt is free but the other half will cost you 12 euros.

As we prepared to pick up our canal boats, we were discouraged that the predicted high temps looked pretty grim: 91° on Saturday, then 98° and 106°F. After that it was supposed to be in the eighties for the rest of the week. We came up with a variety of alternate plans to accommodate the fact that our boats were not equipped with A/C.

The Phoenicians had a saying: "A boat can only do what weather and sea want it to do." So there we were facing temperatures of 99° and 107° for the first two days of our canal boat adventure.

Most Americans we talked to thought we were getting on a large river cruiser commanded by an experienced captain and tended to by a solicitous crew. No. Curt and Matt were the captains of our two 4-bedroom, 50-foot boats and the rest of us were the crew.

Ya want a glass of wine? Pour it yourself. Mostly we cruised small canals built 350 years ago for cargo barges pulled by a horse. Our "barge" was more like an RV with a bow. No horse. One last thing, the quote about the Phoenicians is bogus. I made it up. But they should have said something like that.

We stopped at a ramshackle restaurant right on the river hoping to secure lunch. They made it clear (through my equally ramshackle French) we were welcome only for drinks under the giant beer umbrellas. The lunch tables on the large patio were reserved by the locals for Sunday on the river.

We accepted their offer but kept negotiating, as our traveling contingent of geese rotated the lead. "How about a single table for six?" the bartender suggested. No, that's a deal-breaker when you have 15. Jill refused to give up and finally negotiated a special meal deal: We could eat in the bar area, but with just two choices: a Caesar salad or mussels and fries. We accepted.

Those who had the salad described it as one of the best they had ever eaten, huge and laden with subtle layers of flavors. I ate mussels for only the second time in my life, thoroughly enjoyed them, and was schooled by Steve in the mechanics of breaking them open and only eating the non-crunchy parts. Cost was an amazing $32 for Kris and me.

When the really hot weather struck the next day (107°F), we were holed up in the port of Redon. We chose it because the only air conditioner in western France cooled a theater/café located right at the port. While a few of us watched American movies in French, most of us sat in the café drinking beer or lemonade, waiting for the weather to break, which it finally did the next morning. We then resumed our journey on the canals.

Sometimes life serves up so much irony, it can take your breath away. After planning this trip multiple times for three and a half years, I ended up erasing myself from an entire week of it. Lead goose down. What I now assume was the stomach flu (COVID test was negative) brought my body temperature from winter in Fairbanks to summer in Rio and back, often in minutes.

After a few days, I didn't mind the severe stomach attacks, but I never did adjust to the relentless fever. With a discomfort factor through the roof, it's safe to say this trip does not rank among my favorites.

As indicated in our continuing goose analogy, everyone just stepped up and did what needed to be done, and the trip kept moving and growing, just as we planned. I later looked at some Facebook posts, and unless they were all really good liars, they had a happy and productive trip, one unusual enough that grandkids will be forced to hear about it multiple times.

The predatory bikes of Amsterdam

Death lurks unexpectedly on the roads of Europe. Forget the cars in front of you on the German autobahn. It's the giant Mercedes and BMWs roaring up behind you at 160 mph when you're only going 80 that bear watching. Your head feels like it's on a swivel as you constantly check your mirrors for the telltale flashed headlights of aggression.

In England, death comes from the right. We Americans are all taught to look left first before crossing a street. That habit can get you killed in London if you step off the curb while you're doing it. Traffic on the left side of the narrow roads will quickly make you a hood ornament.

But for constant forced vigilance against sudden death, it's hard to beat the bikes of Amsterdam. Ridden by old and young, rich and poor, tourist and resident, they prowl areas marked off (or not) on many streets and sidewalks in this lovely city of trees and canals. I'd been in town for less than a day and had done the pedestrian shuffle a dozen times as cyclists emerged from the urban chaos with apparent intent to do me harm.

Retreating to a park bench in front of the Diamond Museum, I spent a terror-free half-hour inventorying the passing two-wheeled monsters while trying to make some sense of it all. Here's what I found.

Speed

While a few bikes plodded along at the speed of your average barnyard animal, most reached an astonishing speed, confidently maneuvering around pedestrians, scooters, vendors, and just plain dumb tourists. They all wore the same kind of transfixed gaze you find on, say, trained athletes or serial killers. With the incursion of e-bikes, the modern riders exercise the same predatory zeal, but without breaking a sweat.

Bikewear

Few wore what your garden variety Wisconsin biker would wear in mid-July (shorts and tee shirt). Even fewer wore serious bikewear that would cause you to mistake them for lost Tour de France competitors. Most looked like they were dressed for work (and probably were), including women in skirts and men in suits, often with scarves rakishly dangling from their necks.

Bike Culture

Make that plural. Cultures. Most of the riders fit the Dutch stereotype—sensible people getting around in the most efficient way. But I did find more than a few outliers: The cigar-chomping clown; an aging mom riding sidesaddle behind her adult son; a teenager riding no-handed while texting; a young woman balancing a huge box that might have contained a floor lamp; a young man pedaling along madly with his right hand securely on a riderless bike rolling next to his own.

Did I say they all looked fit? The activity was clearly good for their waist size. I didn't see a single portly cyclist.

Equipment

I watched at least a thousand riders before I saw my first bike helmet. Just not part of the culture, I guess. Most of the bikes were equipped with bells, although they were rarely used. Most had lights, unnecessary until about 10:30 pm during summer at this northern latitude. Nearly all had fenders, chain guards, kick stands, and hand grips. Brakes came in both the handle and pedal variety. Possibly some didn't have any.

Carrying capacity varied greatly. I saw standard bike baskets, plastic crates, saddlebags, metal grates, briefcases, picnic baskets, backpacks, and shopping bags. Specialty bikes were even more creatively engineered to haul specific items.

I saw a number of bikes with child seats (including a long model built for two little ones) but saw very few in action. In fact, I saw very few of the under 16 crowd on two wheels. In the part of Amsterdam where I stayed (the museum area), biking was an adult activity.

When I first traveled to Amsterdam in the seventies, I'm pretty sure nearly all the bikes were one-speeds. Not being much of a cyclist myself, I thought they still might have just one gear. Closer inspection revealed shift levers built into hand grips, mounted on handlebars or in some other accessible place.

That evening, I ate supper outside at the Stoop and Stoop Eet Cafe just off the Leidsestraat, about six blocks from my hotel. The addition of a couple locally brewed Heinekens dulled my jet lag but did little to calm my nerves about random, predatory bikers I encountered on the way back to my hotel.

The only way to get a little respite from the cyclist army that has taken over this city is to get into a boat and use the beautiful network of canals for your transportation needs. It turns out that the canals have one other useful role. I once read that local authorities fished something like 10,000 bikes from the canals every year.

I know who put them there. Pedestrians.

Four-wheeled rides in Amsterdam

After going through customs and reclaiming our suitcases, Cousin Fred and I walked out the glass doors into a cold December morning at Schiphol Airport, 12 miles from downtown Amsterdam. I had learned my lesson on my last trip to Amsterdam. This time I was taking a taxi.

Last time, I took a city bus. I had figured out that it would drop us off in the Museum District, about six blocks from our hotel at a cost far lower than a cab. And so it did. In the rain. Twenty drenching minutes later, my GPS found the hotel, now more enticing for its dryness than any architectural charms it might claim.

This time, Fred and I headed for the taxi queue. The line was short and the ride was interesting, with Fred questioning the driver, who spoke good English, about farming practices in the Netherlands. The ride cost between $50 and $60.

Fast forward to the following June. Same airport. Same decision to be made. But this time a strange thing happened. We emerged from the one-way customs doors into the usual throng of people waiting for incoming travelers. Many had homemade signs or iPads with unpronounceable names on them.

A well-dressed man glanced at my suitcase and the four people with me, then pulled us over. "You are on a Viking cruise?" he asked.

"Yes, but not until tomorrow," I replied, acknowledging the bright red luggage tags with the Viking logo.

"Come with me," he said, and grabbed Kris's suitcase. Just as alarm bells were going off in my head about this being the latest airport scam, I watched him briefly check in with a woman wearing a Viking logo. If it was a scam, it was a very thorough one.

I believed that Viking's airport pickups were available only to travelers going right from airport to boat. We were going to a hotel. No matter. The man used his phone to summon a van that had been circulating around the airport. Minutes later, all five of us were aboard and heading into town. We ended up paying $75 ($15 apiece) for the ride, an excellent price in an expensive city.

Our hotel in December had been the American Hotel, an iconic building right on the Leidseplein, a main square in the heart of the city. I almost didn't stay there because I couldn't find it online. Finally, I stumbled over information that it had been recently acquired by the Hard Rock Hotel chain and was undergoing a musical makeover. (To add to the confusion, Amsterdam's Hard Rock Café was only about three blocks away).

Because of its adoptive parents, the hotel now featured an electric guitar and amplifier in the lobby for guests to play. Fred and I had arrived too early to check into our rooms, so, channeling my misspent youth in a rock band, I entertained myself by playing the guitar.

I must have passed the audition, because every time I entered the lobby over the next three days, the concierge picked up the guitar and brought it to me with a one-word instruction: Play.

On our last night, we made reservations at an Indonesian restaurant in the picturesque Jordaan district for *rijstaffel* (rice table). Just one problem, it was a little too far and a little too cold to walk. We asked our friend, the concierge, to get us a cab.

"There are no cabs right now," he said. Then he explained. Morocco was playing Portugal in the World Cup soccer quarterfinals. Since nearly all cab drivers were Moroccon (who knew?), and also *futbol* fans, we were simply not getting a cab until the game was over. Luckily, we didn't have to wait long. Five minutes after Morocco eked out a 1-0 victory, a cab pulled up, the driver ebullient over the results. We celebrated with him all the way to the restaurant.

On our June visit, we stayed at the Krisotel, a three-star hotel located on a street behind the American Hotel. The place wasn't big or fancy enough to have a concierge, but the friendly desk clerk made sure we got a large taxi van to take all five of us to the port on Sunday morning. Luckily there were no Moroccan soccer games scheduled.

It is strange to write an entire piece about cabs in Amsterdam. Compared to, say New York City, they are almost invisible.

What do you see instead? Thousands and thousands of predatory bikes, sleek white rail trams dangerously brushing your pants leg, hordes of clueless pedestrians in this eminently walkable city, and flattened canal boats drifting silently under ubiquitous bridges.

But mostly bikes. Everywhere bikes. And now many of them are even faster, thanks to the e-bike phenomenon.

I'll let a cab driver have the last word. Asked if there were a lot of bike accidents in Amsterdam, he replied with two words.

"Not enough."

Closing the fells

Something didn't look right. We never saw any people standing at the entrance to our narrow lane high up on the fell over Ambleside. (A fell is a higher version of what we would call a bluff in Wisconsin). But a handful of people, including one in an orange vest, stepped in front of us as we approached the intersection.

They told us we were in the middle of a bike race. Well, we were in the middle of taking Diane's sister-in-law, Nanette, to catch a train in Windermere. We eventually prevailed, threading our way through bikers who were straining to climb uphill towards Kirkstone Pass.

Nan had been a great addition to our group and was now heading back to her home in Blackburn. Diane joined us to see her off, and Linda came along because of what she called a "wine emergency." The train station adjoined Booth's, the largest grocery store in the area.

We said goodbye to Nan, picked out the wine, and added a package of toilet paper to forestall even more serious emergencies.

We had over an hour to return to the house then come back to Ambleside for a Sunday Roast at the Priest Hole restaurant in Ambleside. Sunday Roast can best be compared to a Friday Fish Fry in Wisconsin. Every restaurant is compelled to have one and the menu is the same.

Most of the time a roast consists of roast beef, gravy, potatoes, Yorkshire pudding (not a pudding at all, but a bread), and maybe a few random vegetables. Occasionally lamb or pork may substitute for the beef.

The bike race was still in progress when we climbed the fell toward home. This time, the orange vests weren't budging. Diane got out to sweet-talk them, but they were resolute and we had to back down the hill a few blocks.

Now what? We decided our best plan was to park the car then walk around Ambleside until we found a place serving Irish Coffee. That turned out to be the Ambleside Inn. We called back to the house and told them they'd have to squeeze the remaining five people into the other car and meet us at the restaurant.

The roast turned out to be the best one I've had in England and was a great way to conclude our stay in Ambleside before we could board the train to London in the morning. Assuming the bike race was over by then.

unspecified problem and ended up getting into Chicago at about 1:00 am, more than four hours after our scheduled arrival time.

O'Hare is lovely at that hour.

What to drink in Europe

If you plan to drink liquids the way you do at home, there's a very good chance you will be disappointed. Here's a quick guide, with a soft focus on Belgium because that's where I wrote the article.

1. *No milk.* Not even for kids. An adult asking for milk will be greeted with about the same level of incredulity as a child ordering a scotch and soda. Grocery stores have a tiny supply of milk, but you'll find it in the unrefrigerated aisles.
2. *No decaf.* At home, I often drink decaf coffee and decaf Coke. Not because I don't like caffeine; I love it. But I don't like being jolted awake at 3:00 am. Trying to stay decaffeinated in Europe is a losing battle because the best you can typically do for morning coffee is hot water with instant Sanka polluting it. I figure my sleep schedule is messed up anyway so I might as well go with the flow.
3. *Drink Champagne.* This applies mainly to the area just north of Reims, capital of the champagne region of France. We picked up a four-pack of full-sized bottles of authentic French champagne in the grocery store for about $16.
4. *Drink Orange Fanta.* No, not the sweet syrupy stuff they sell under that name in the US that looks like it's been exposed to radioactivity. European Fanta is a pale yellow, not especially sweet and very refreshing.
5. *Use Senseo coffee pods.* Europe's version of Keurig coffee makers uses silver-dollar sized coffee packets pressed in a special machine, generating a smaller amount of coffee that is somehow frothy.
6. *Drink Beer.* Belgium has some of the greatest beer in the world. I'm kind of a Luxembourg homer so I try to drink beer from there. I thought I liked Bofferding, but Diekirch is much better tasting to me. Both are fairly light and taste like they belong to the same family as Heineken and Stella Ar-

tois. My son, John, prefers Leffe, brewed in Belgium since the 1200s. I found out it is now made by Budweiser. (How does it taste now, son?)

7. *Drink White wine.* Luxembourg's Moselle valley is a premium wine-making area. It produces mainly whites. Ordering the house wine in Europe, red or white, is almost always a good bet, tasty and inexpensive. If you are looking for harder stuff than beer or wine, you can find it, but it will usually be much more expensive and prone to misinterpretation. Order Captain and Coke and you will get a bottle of Coca Cola followed by a frustrating conversation about who Captain Morgan is and how he fits into the conversation.

8. *Drink Coke.* It still comes in those shapely little seven-ounce bottles in Europe. If they recognize you as an American (and they will) and are feeling charitable, they will slip one ice cube into your glass. Diet Coke and Coke Light don't seem to exist in this neighborhood, but you can usually get Coke Zero. Pepsi is very hard to find.

9. *Drink water.* You will rarely find tap water in a restaurant. Ask and they will bring you bottled water anyway. Your choice is whether to get a big bottle for the table or a little one just for you. You will also be asked if you want it with bubbles (con gas) or without.

10. *Drink coffee.* I hate to belabor the point, but their coffee rituals really aren't consistent with ours. In fact, they are often completely inscrutable. Entire books have been written about how to order coffee in Paris. Starbucks exists in the big cities but those kinds of coffee shops are comparatively rare elsewhere. You won't get a free refill and you won't get a large cup. You will often get a little cookie (biscuit) with your coffee. I can't really speak for the abundance of tea here, but I did see a woman being offered a selection of packaged teas in a wooden box at a Bastogne restaurant.

At home in Luxembourg

Tucked between touristic giants, France and Germany, and in the shadows of Belgium and the Netherlands, is a small country called Luxembourg.

How small? If you drive across Dane County, Wisconsin, say from Mount Horeb to Cambridge, you've done the equivalent of driving across Luxembourg. Not only are Dane County and Luxembourg similar in size, their populations aren't much different—between 500,000 and 600,000 people.

The capitol, Luxembourg City, can be reached from Paris or Amsterdam in about three hours, Frankfurt in two and a half hours, and Brussels in about an hour and a half.

You'll find mostly French spoken in the Capitol, but two other languages, German and its cousin, Luxembourgish, also are official languages.

Wedged between two spectacular gorges, Luxembourg City features an old town teeming with outdoor cafes, fanciful shopping and buckets of charm. The same euros that you use in the other places named above are good here.

If you want to look down on the city from above, try the Doubletree Hotel by Hilton on the outskirts of town. The view is dramatic and the price is surprisingly affordable.

If you prefer a central location, the Hôtel Café Français sits right on the Place d'Armes, the main square in the city.

Castles, hiking trails, Moselle Valley wines, and picturesque villages make for a laid back but thoroughly European experience in the rest of this compact but varied country.

For an excellent guidebook, search out the *Bradt Guide to Luxembourg.* It's the only guidebook that focuses only on Luxembourg instead of combining it with supposedly more compelling destinations.

One more thing. If you're from the La Crosse, Wisconsin area, there's a very good chance you have ancestors from Luxembourg. A book called *From Luxembourg to La Crosse and Beyond, 1851-1910* by Sandra L. Hammes, documents everyone who came here then.

Light years from Wisconsin: Esch-sur-Sure, Luxembourg

Thousands of emigrants from Luxembourg, including my great-grandfather, Wilhelm Zanter, took off for America in the mid to late 1800s. Because of a similar topography, a great many of them came to Wisconsin. The picture I had in my mind of Esch-sur-Sure was a downsized version of my hometown of La Crosse, Wisconsin, squished together and covering the diminutive mountains we call bluffs. And so it was, with the addition of buildings from the 1200s and a ruined castle, floodlit as a summer night reluctantly engulfed it.

Only 13 miles from our Bastogne house, it took almost a half hour to get to Esch as the roads dwindled down to paved cow paths with room for a single vehicle. Hills, switchbacks, and random forests focused my driving attention. My co-pilot brother Bob interpreted the often-inscrutable voice of the van's British-sounding GPS as she maneuvered us into Luxembourg from Belgium.

After we parked at the bottom of this hill town, our group of ten wordlessly broke up into three groups for exploration purposes.

Jeannie led four of us along the placid River Sure as it meandered past well-maintained houses and streets to the back of the village. Out of nowhere materialized a Bancomat ATM machine that she had confidently predicted would be there.

She and Bob quickly determined that it was as friendly as advertised and soon it was dispensing cash like a Las Vegas slot machine. Matt and Kathy got in on the action too after first flummoxing the machine with faux pin numbers. ("Let's see, was this card number the Battle of Hastings?").

The town was big enough to host just five restaurants. Recommendations from various sources (*Trip Advisor*, *Yelp*, guidebooks) were inconclusive, although the one at the bottom of the hill, Les Deux Tours, seemed to have a slight edge in food quality.

Bob (my brother, one of three Bobs in the group), and his wife, Carol, decided that that restaurant worked for them.

My group decided we should tackle the steep streets leading up to the castle. That effort left us wordless as we struggled to the top and breathless once we caught the view from there.

At the summit, we ran into Peggy, who is part mountain goat, as she and the third group were already beginning their descent.

By the time we finally wound our way through several levels of the Hôtel de la Sure to their restaurant terrace overlooking the valley, large drafts of Diekirch beer were already in front of Peggy's group.

Our friendly Romanian waiter was fluent in English, and the French menu had English translations, partially accounting for its enormous size—nearly 40 pages.

A free appetizer with small amounts of phyllo dough and couscous was served along with a healthy dose of wry Luxembourgish humor as the waiter brought Jeannie a "large" glass of wine (about the size of a fishbowl) and Peggy a "small" glass of beer (a mug only marginally larger than a thimble).

I ordered a potato and sausage concoction of Luxembourgish ancestry and an unpronounceable name—something like Potthatch. Bob's barley soup was among the best he has ever eaten, a sentiment echoed by our other Bob in describing his seafood soup. Dianne had scampi and crayfish tails. She especially liked the bread, which was of a different kind each time it was replenished.

Splitting the bill resulted in a very reasonable 35 euros per person tab.

We tracked down my brother at the bottom of the hill and drove out of town just as the lights were starting to illuminate the castle and bridges of Esch-sur-Sure.

Arthur the Rooster crows at midnight

Scene One: Arthur the Rooster

Nobody will go with me to kill the rooster. Arthur, whose coop is about 20 meters from my bedroom window in a rented house near Bastogne, was up at 4:22 this morning. He did what he had to do to get the sun to rise, and I'm OK with that. But then he did a rendition of his greatest hits for the next two hours. That put him over the top.

I'm sure the discussion in the henhouse went something like this.

Mildred: Arthur needs to get a life; he's just so full of himself.

Evangeline: At least WE do something productive. People can't make an omelet without us.

Mildred: He's so ridiculous. I wonder if he's ever seen Foghorn Leghorn.

Claire: He sure can strut though, can't he?

Scene Two: Iceland

My friend, Curt, called while we were winding our way through the hills of northern Luxembourg (the area they call "Little Switzerland"). He should be with us, but he was still in Iceland after breaking an arm and a leg. He was evacuated to his US home after 14 days in a Reykyavik hospital. A Lear Jet flew him from Iceland to Maine to Rhinelander, Wisconsin. Not your typical European flight path.

Scene Three: Rainy-day laundry

It's getting to that part of the trip when doing a little laundry is almost mandatory. Kathy was using the washing machine in the garage (of course). Since most of the washers over here—at least in the countryside—are not accompanied by dryers, she was looking forward to hanging the wash outside. But it was raining. Peggy: "You Americans. You don't wash clothes on a rainy day."

Scene Four: Germany

We went to Trier, Germany today. It's only about a half hour away from Luxembourg City, but it is unmistakably German. The friendly waiter at a sidewalk café asked where we were from. "Near Chicago," I replied. "Where are you from?" He seemed a little taken aback. "Why, from Trier, of course." "Well, so am I," I told him. "My great-grandfather, Augustus Hundt, came from Trier. Do you know anyone named Hundt?" He thought for a second and said, "I've heard of Helen Hunt."

Scene Five: Luxembourg City

My brother and I conducted our dual citizenship business at the Bierger Center next to City Hall in no more than ten minutes. I asked if they were really busy. "Yes, lots of Americans," said the woman behind the desk, adding, "Lots of Brazilians too." Many of the Portuguese speakers can be found in Luxembourg's second largest city, Esch-sur-Alzette. We stopped there one afternoon to see the Resistance Museum. It was interesting, but the contents were stuffed into temporary quarters while the elegant building housing it undergoes restoration.

Scene Six: Petrol

I put about 3,000 miles on a Citroen minivan with a six-speed manual transmission during the month of June. That required multiple stops at the pumps. A most unusual refueling stop sits along the A-6 highway that is the fast road from Bastogne to Luxembourg City. At some point (Martelange), the road briefly leaves Belgium for a couple of traffic circles and a stoplight. Lining one side of the highway are about a dozen gas stations in a row. Apparently gas is significantly cheaper in Luxembourg than Belgium, so a cottage industry of local oil barons has sprung up to provide a service to those seeking lower gas prices. It cost us about $80 US to fill up at these cheaper prices. That's about right, since gas is usually twice as expensive in Europe as the US.

Paris can't fail

We drove from Bastogne to Paris to spend a few days there and rendezvous with my son and his family. Paris can't fail. A fickle lover, she will nevertheless test your commitment. A pickpocket removed my son's cash and credit cards from him on a commuter train. The Eiffel Tower's new security measures have turned it into an atrocity as visually appealing as a chicken coop in a third-world country. Our "Paris by Night" bus tour lacked the open-air top we expected and took us to only a fraction of the sights we wanted to see.

Still, the staff at the Hôtel de la Paix Montparnasse (Hotel Leopold in 2024) again went way beyond expectations. They allowed my son to use their phone to call the US, let my granddaughter play with one of their kids, and did a series of things for us that were very helpful.

I asked the English-speaking hotel clerk to call a cab company to get us three cabs in a hurry. I was listening to his French conversation and, amazingly, understood every word he said. When he hung up, I discussed his conversation.

"You know French," he said accusingly.

"Nobody's ever said that to me before," I replied in English, denying any such expertise. We ended up flagging down three cabs in a row in front of the hotel.

I have a few rituals I do every time I'm in Paris. One is having a hot dog at the Eiffel Tower. I know it's heresy to look forward to such a plebian meal in the gastronomic capital of the world, but it was again delicious: two dogs stuffed into a fresh baguette with a side of passable french fries. It was made even tastier because I was sharing the meal with my five-year-old granddaughter. I remember the first time I held her in the hospital after she was born (and my son will vouch for this). I said to her, "Honey, I'm taking you to Paris."

We found the William Bouguereau gallery at the Musee D'Orsay, mostly known as the home of the Impressionists. Bouguereau predated them in the 19th century, but his art holds up to today's standards. I have a friend whose aunt left him a "lost" Bouguereau painting in her will. The small portrait of a young girl fetched almost a quarter of a million dollars when it was put on sale at Sotheby's in New York. The painter's enormous museum pieces turned out to be very different from that painting. One even included subject matter that at first glance seemed to have a vampire theme.

It took three and a half hours to drive from Paris back to our Air BnB house near Bastogne, Belgium. All five bedrooms eventually filled with an assortment of family and friends.

The rural terrain of mostly rolling hills and farm fields seldom produces a straight line connecting towns. Fortunately, the roads are in great shape.

My cousin, Fred, was impressed by the forests. We were technically in the middle of the Ardennes Forest, a World War II battle site. Occasional "pill boxes" and foxholes keep the memory alive.

Most of our group went to the Bastogne War Museum, which focuses mainly on the Battle of the Bulge near the end of WWII. It was time well spent. The museum is part of a new generation of museums that attempts to place you inside the historical moment to grasp the feeling and not just view the artifacts. (Another such museum is the Beatles Experience in Liverpool). Realistic sets, a soundtrack of bombs exploding, and a simulated Ardennes Forest and wartime café proved very effective in making history come alive.

Amsterdam and Luxembourg in winter

Interviewing myself at 3:45 am

Why did you go to Europe in bleak December?

A 12-year window on Luxembourg citizenship was closing for Cousin Fred and his daughter, Laura. December 31 was the last day to seal the deal. Fred and I were able to do a lot of things despite the cold in just seven days. He's the best kind of traveler and doesn't get rattled when things don't go right.

You survived an 11-hour train journey and a 29-hour series of flights home. Does that impact your view of travel?

Not really. It comes with the territory. The article I posted about the chaotic train ride drew a wide variety of responses. Some people were amused; others were appalled. If you're in the latter category, a packaged trip is probably more to your liking—although that's hardly a guarantee against airline abuse.

Talk about the hotels. Would you stay at the Hard Rock Hotel American in Amsterdam again?

Maybe. On the plus side, it had a friendly staff, unbeatable location, and amazing breakfast overlooking a beautiful square in the city. On the minus side, the room was terminally cold, the beds were narrow army cots, and the hotel refused to budge on check-in time, forcing us to hang around the lobby for hours after an early morning, jet-lagged arrival.

What about the Park Hotel by Radisson in Luxembourg City?

Also maybe. It's a nice enough hotel. It's located near the train station, a funky area with many diverse restaurants. It's kind of vanilla, but we were able to use the near-empty bar/eating area for some rousing games of euchre with Laura and her friend, Zack, who were great additions to our traveling group.

Do you ever expect to see your luggage again?

No. Because it disappeared early in our flights home, somewhere between Luxembourg City and Munich. The Lufthansa agent in Munich dutifully tried to find it for us by calling a bunch of people, but without success. I've never permanently lost a suitcase before in all my travels. I do regret not keeping my hiking boots out because I've been shoveling snow in my running shoes. (*The suitcase arrived two days later.*)

What was your favorite restaurant?

The Long Pura Indonesian restaurant in the Jordaan region of Amsterdam was surely the most interesting. We had rijstaffel (rice table), where more than a dozen small dishes accompany the rice. I tried all of them and mostly enjoyed them. The pofferijes we had at the Pancake Club near the hotel were as delicate and tasty as I remembered them.

Any others?

I really liked the ambience at the Victor Hugo restaurant in Vianden, Luxembourg. I had trout with the bones resting uneasily in their natural state. Tasty but tedious. We tried a couple of Italian places in Luxembourg City, but they were mostly forgettable.

Any activities of note?

It was 48 years between visits to the Anne Frank house for me. The core of the visit is still sobering and informative, but the entire experience has become Disneyfied. The tour of the Heineken Brewery was shlock too, but it's supposed to be, and we had fun. The Rijksmuseum has a plethora of wonderful pieces of art that go beyond Rembrandt's *Nightwatch*. Our visit to Vianden Castle in Luxembourg was great, especially the art exhibit/sale in an imposing ante room of the castle.

Why are you writing this?

Because it's 3:45 am and it's going through my jet-lagged and sleepless mind.

On the street in Amsterdam

For a city so orderly, the chaos was remarkable. The ten-minute walk from our hotel to the Stoop and Stoop Eet Café showcased Amsterdam's contradictions. Among the most walkable cities in the world, it also featured sleek trams, efficient buses, grudging accommodations to cars, and, of course, bicycles, all clamoring for space in the same small area.

Aside from the danger to us, I worried about the cyclists themselves. Bike helmets just never caught on in Amsterdam. I had a window seat at breakfast recently and decided to sample the next 100 cyclists. Only 12 of them wore helmets.

We left the chaos behind and arrived to claim our 5:30 dinner reservation at the Eet café. It was early for Europe but not for the five of us who had just landed, jet-lagged, hungry and sleep deprived: Linda, Jon, Kris, Diane, and me.

The proprietor of the small Dutch restaurant greeted us warmly and showed us to a table that had been anticipating our arrival with menus and silverware at the ready. Not long after we sat down, he asked us if we wanted to move to the just-vacated premium table on the terrace. Hell, yes. Located on a pedestrian mall, the table was a window on the city. We quickly grabbed our Heinekens and relocated. With a temperature in the seventies, it couldn't have been more perfect.

Curt (his leg fully healed from his accident in Iceland) had come in the day before and had blitzed the city's tourist attractions. He soon joined us after walking over from the Heineken Experience, a high-tech homage to beer.

Matt and Kathy also had come in a day early. Although they were staying at our hotel, we hadn't seen them yet. Kathy had sent me a European phone number she obtained through use of a Sim card. I couldn't get it to work.

I did what we old folks have been trained to do. I looked for the youngest person in the café and asked for her assistance. The young waitress was sweet and helpful and ended up dialing the number from the house phone and handing it to me to talk to Kathy.

She and Matt were finishing a beer nearby and proceeded to join us just in time for appetizers. One was bitterballen, a traditional Dutch meatball. The center was cold and we were not sure if that was on purpose. The other appetizer was called kibbeling. I'd call them fish bites. They were delicious.

Most of us ordered traditional specialties. Curt and I had stamp-pot endive, a giant meatball in a nest of mashed potatoes. Kris and

Diane had a similar plate with a giant smoked sausage replacing the meatball. Matt and Kathy opted for fish and chips.

The cost was very much on par with what we'd pay in a decent restaurant in the US. Although they didn't want to split the check for us (they rarely do in Europe), they were willing to let us pay separately at the bar by telling the bartender what we had.

Afterwards, Kris and I wandered back into the busy Leidseplein area in search of ice cream. We found gelato. I claimed a small dish infested with Oreo cookies. She also decided we needed some churros, which have found a home in the Netherlands. (I treated Cousin Fred to some there in December). We ate them sitting on the fountain in front of the venerable American Hotel (now revitalized as a Hard Rock Hotel).

By eight o'clock we were back at the Krisotel and I was sound asleep. That's why I'm writing this at 4:00 a.m.

Chapter 7 - Business Ed
On the road with the union

Rio de Janiero, Brazil

36 Hours in Colombia

This may be the only selection in the book that will make you question my sanity when it comes to travel. My friend Bob Fullmer and I were sitting at a National Education Association Board of Directors meeting in Washington, DC in early 2003 when the head of NEA International Relations approached us. She wanted us to be part of an eight-member AFL-CIO labor delegation to Colombia. Although

Norwegian surprise

At the Education International World Congress in Brazil, my friend, Paul, and I decided to liven things up by making a short film. Every time we heard someone say something intelligent in the hall, we would go to their delegation and ask for an interview. They never refused.

Usually I asked questions (in English) and Paul held the camera. When we brought the president of the Norway teachers to our impromptu filming area, Paul unexpectedly handed the camera to me.

Imagine my surprise when Paul conducted the interview in Norwegian. Who knew?

my Spanish was marginal and Bob's Thai was not in the least helpful, we agreed to go.

Our first task was to return three Colombian unionists who had been working in the US for a year for AFL-CIO to their home country. They were under death threats in Colombia and the idea was that they wouldn't be killed right away if Americans returned with them.

The paranoia in Colombia about violence and kidnapping was real, so much so that when we got there, Bob called his wife and told her not to give prospective kidnappers a damn thing, if it came down to that. Bob used to be in the CIA. On the other hand, I called my wife and told her to get ready to sell everything. I wasn't in the CIA. I taught remedial reading. (My phone call didn't actually happen, but it makes for a better story.)

During our mission we met with more than two dozen unions, government officials, academics, UN commissioners, and Embassy officials in Bogota, Medellin, and Cali in ten eventful days. The following represents just 36 hours in that strife-ridden country. It is written in present tense for you to experience the urgency we felt as the hours unfolded. The action picks up in Medellin (you may have heard of it because of drug kingpin Pablo Escobar, who had been killed there ten years before our mission). A version of this article was published nationally in NEA Today.

5:00 a.m. March 11

There are safety rules in this unsafe country. We're breaking at least five of them.

1. Travel during daylight hours. It is 5:00 a.m. and we are on a very dark mountain road. We are packed into a 12-passenger van with our luggage strapped to the roof.

2. Stay in the city. We are leaving Medellin on our way to the airport, 39 kilometers away. Roadblocks are common in Colombia. They may be tended by any of at least four groups: the government, guerillas, paramilitaries, or bandits. You really don't want to meet any of them.

3. Stay out of Antioquia. Statistically, the least safe department (state) is Antioquia, where we are. If one were to worry about the

3,700 kidnappings that occurred in 2003 in Colombia or the 172 union leaders who were killed, now would be the time to do so.

4. Don't belong to a union. (See above.) The total number of union leaders killed in Colombia between 1991 and 2003 was close to 2,000. Union membership dropped from 15% of the workers in the 1980s to 4.5% today. We are all union leaders in this van, and we have been meeting with union leaders, some of whom sleep in different places every night because they fear for their lives.

5. Travel in groups or convoys. We are alone. Few other cars pass us in either direction on this night-infested road. Curiously, the roadsides are not empty at this godforsaken hour. We pass dozens of people walking silently (or furtively, given my paranoia) or taking a pre-dawn bicycle ride. In my overactive imagination, I construct the following scenario: One of the walkers sees this van load of pigeons with luggage on top, uses his cell phone to call ahead a few miles, then fakes some kind of accident to stop traffic. We get stopped and…

Anyway, I have hesitated adding a sixth rule, *travel armed,* for a variety of reasons. First, I don't know if we are. Our two extremely young drivers may or may not have an Uzi tucked under the seat. I don't ask. Second, I doubt that it matters. If we need to engage in a firefight to get through a roadblock, our van is an unlikely defensive vehicle.

My imagination finally rests as the airport lights burst into view. I look over at Bob. He is as relieved as I am. Others in the van appear to be oblivious, sleeping, or resigned. Or they are feigning indifference the way Bob and I are.

9:30 a.m.

Another van is waiting for us at the Cali airport. This one has a dented door with three bullet holes in it. It turns out that the bullet holes aren't real; they're decals. Colombian humor?

The armed convoy we'll be joining into the city is real, however. Guards with weapons mill around the vehicles. We are waiting for the plane from Bogota to arrive. On it is Lucio Garcon, Labor's presidential candidate in the last election. When the wait gets too long, we simply pull out of the convoy and drive to our hotel alone.

10:30 a.m.

We are on the fourth floor of the municipal union hall. The building is an old high school. Paint is peeling off in volumes. Parts of the building are open to the outside, perhaps unintentionally.

We eat breakfast quickly among a variety of dignitaries and union leaders. One man stands out. He is young, well-dressed, and walks with a cane. We are told he is a senator who survived an assassination attempt.

11:00 a.m.

Suddenly we hear music below us. They are singing *The Internationale*. The room empties quickly so we can get down there in time for the second and third verses. We are ushered into the front row, where we don headphones to hear the speeches translated. Several hundred workers swelter in the chairs behind us. Someone brings us bottles of cold water. We gratefully accept them.

Lucio Garcon salutes Rhett, one of our keepers, for bringing help from the US. Us? He refers to "Bush's war" in Iraq as a very grave act. Then he launches into a list of challenges facing Colombia: its external debt which is "strangling the economy," the deterioration in the quality of life, and the free trade agreement (called ALCA here rather than NAFTA), which will "send us the leftovers." He says, "Latin America can exist if you don't see us as dead people." Drugs never make the list of major problems in Colombia.

1:30 p.m.

Many of the same speakers from the morning meeting share the podium at this working lunch on the second floor of a Cali hotel. The crowd, however, is different, much more upscale. Again, we put our headphones on, but this time we have been placed directly in front of the powerful P.A. speakers. It's painful to listen to and much is washed out. Lucio talks about a key referendum that's coming up that will take away even more rights if passed. He condemns terrorism and notes that the FARC, the main guerilla group, also (rather ironically) has issued a statement condemning it. He is especially critical of President Uribe's privatization policies.

3:30 p.m.

New auditorium. New crowd. Same people talking. This time we are in a contemporary brick building, modern and well-designed. We could be in Madison. Alas, we are getting a little cranky. Why don't they do air conditioning? You can just about hit the equator with a rock from here.

5:45 p.m.

Our armed caravan (a van, two SUVs and a cab) negotiates Cali's harrowing traffic out to the main water-treatment plant. The forty-year-old Emcali facility appears to be safe, sophisticated, and running smoothly. Nevertheless, it is in imminent danger of being privatized. The union believes the government plans to turn it over to corrupt cronies so they can loot it.

The scene is surreal. The head of the municipal workers union is with us. He looks tired and haggard and makes no eye contact with us as he delivers an impassioned speech while standing on the water treatment platform overlooking the Cauca River.

He is under continuous death threats, but that isn't his main problem today. He has just engaged Colombian President Jose Uribe in a very hostile on-camera dispute. Nobody is happy.

Doing the translation for him is an Englishman who is working on his doctorate in sociology and specializes in Colombia.

Also hovering about are three Europeans from International Peace Brigades. They linger around a short, rounded Colombian woman. Their sole job is to nonviolently shield the woman from attack by whatever "dark forces" are threatening her.

Through it all, a bodyguard with an automatic weapon lounges laconically against the railing, while behind him, in the river, a lone egret trolls for food. Beyond that, billows of jet-black smoke from sugar cane fields fill the air.

9:00 a.m. March 12

Tension fills the air the next morning as we eight Americans climb out of the underground parking garage at Cali's City Hall, a sprawling concrete monolith fashionable in another era. Security gives us a cursory scan and we are greeted by one of the union leaders, Angel, a young man in his thirties.

Out in the crowded courtyard, he brings other people over to address us informally, including a former leader who survived four assassination attempts. Outside the fence, a demonstration is building, its volume increasing.

We go inside to talk to some municipal workers whose jobs are about to be privatized out of existence, many after working there for 20 or 30 years.

We see several workers we've met in recent days, including a woman who, crying, gives Cathy, our nurses' union leader, a hug and pleads with us to help them.

Angel takes us into the mailroom to talk to workers who are stuffing phone bills into envelopes.

The most poignant story comes from Viviana, whose husband was a union leader last year when the workers took over the Emcali facility amid a previous attempt to privatize it. Viviana's husband left work one day and was later found with four bullets in his head.

We don't ask if his killers have been found and brought to justice. They never are in Colombia.

We are ushered into the front row of City Hall's auditorium for a "press conference." Suddenly, an exuberant crowd of students and workers, chanting and singing, plunges in, filling the thousand-seat auditorium to overflow.

The succeeding presentation is more specific than most of the oratories we've heard lately. Using a PowerPoint presentation, it documents the corruption that has put the Emcali facility in such economic difficulty that the president of the country demands that it be privatized and that rates be raised to pay its bills.

The workers believe that this just makes the customers (their friends and neighbors) pay for the corruption, because much of the shortfall is in the form of loans that were taken out by Emcali but never seemed to get used by the facility itself.

We have to leave in mid-presentation in order to get to the airport for our 12:30 flight to Bogota. What comes next comprises the most dangerous part yet in our trip to this edgy country—the drive to the airport.

In Cali, traffic lanes are just suggestions, turn signals unknown, and road signs are voluntary. In our 12-mile drive, miracles spare the lives of two pedestrians, a bicyclist, the driver of a horse-drawn wagon, and us. Several encounters with aggressive buses take our breath away.

Swerving in and out of city traffic at speeds up to 80 miles per hour, we descend on the airport as if touching down in a plane. Our driver coolly smiles at us as we tumble out of the van, delighted to be alive.

One of the cars we flashed past is a plain white station wagon improvised with flowers to make a hearse.

"I know how he died," one of us says.

4:00 p.m.

We continue our absolutely incredible knack for materializing wherever the action is by arriving in Bogota later this day in time for a major demonstration. It starts about a half-mile away and passes no more than a block from where we are staying, the venerable Hotel Dann, a place that was selected because the only other hotel choice in this area was blown up, presumably by the guerillas.

The demonstration, a workers' march, is about to get underway when we arrive. Hundreds of grim-faced policemen in full riot gear, looking like a cross between Robocop and Star Wars stormtroopers line the streets, wishing they were somewhere else. Some have tear gas canisters strung across their torsos like so many Christmas ornaments. Others carry automatic weapons that look far more lethal than those we saw in Cali or Medellin.

The march, several thousand strong, proceeds in a precise, structured, albeit noisy way. Banners precede specific groups such as teachers, nurses, municipal workers, communists, and Maoists. This last group carries a banner protesting US policy in Iraq. Most of the others either generally proclaim the group's own importance or are directed against President Uribe.

We Americans don't quite know what to do. Some members of our group jump into the parade, walking backwards and taking photos, introducing themselves to sign holders.

Although the march has the potential to turn violent, this one does not, and Bob and I peel off as it passes near our hotel. Life there is proceeding normally and we grab a hot dog and a beer in a tiny place with counters and stools.

An insider's view of DC

Ispent a day shadowing Wisconsin Congresswoman (now Senator) Tammy Baldwin. This article was published for WEAC (Wisconsin Education Association Council) members.

Do you want to get in shape? Run for Congress. Don't walk, amble, shuffle, or jog. Run. I spent a day in Congress with Second District Congresswoman Tammy Baldwin, and we were always on the run.

We really hit high gear when an impending vote was announced. It's not a subtle moment. Buzzers sound. Specially designed clocks in all the offices light up and start a 15-minute countdown. Pagers spring to life, blaring information about the vote, then all other business grinds to a halt.

On this particular day—a Thursday in early May—the vote is on the Farm Bill. Wisconsin's own Ron Kind has offered an amendment to it.

Tammy and I dash from her office on the main floor of the Longworth Building down endless labyrinthine corridors until we find ourselves outside in the soft light of a beautiful spring morning.

As we close in on the Capitol dome, probably a good quarter-mile away, we are still at a fast trot. Security noticeably intensifies. We dodge around concrete barricades thinly disguised as planters. Or not. Reaching a traffic light, we don't even slow down. In Washington, DC, traffic stops when Congress votes.

We plow through thickening groups of tourists, among them harried-looking teachers with their spirited charges. Much of the rest of the foot traffic consists of people with name cards attached to them. Today, I see more than a few with American Diabetes Association tee shirts, often looking slightly lost.

Tammy sprints up the Capitol steps with me in tow. For about the 14th time today I'm confronted with a metal detector. I don't notice whether Tammy has to go through it. I'm too busy emptying pockets and putting my stuff on the conveyor belt, then attempting to reclaim it from the crumpled mass on the other side. Mercifully, I don't set off the alarm. This time.

We bound up still another flight of stairs (Is it my imagination, or are they getting steeper?) Tammy presents me to a tall, graying security guard. He doesn't just examine my stuff. He takes it, puts it in a large metal bin, locks it, then hands me the key.

Tammy escorts me to the front row of the House gallery, a balcony with about a half dozen tiered rows of seats encircling the House floor. She briefly instructs me on protocol, then races back downstairs to record her vote.

I am apparently not a very good listener. Within minutes, I have violated at least two rules—no writing and no leaning over the balcony rail. After a mild warning from still another security guard who has mysteriously materialized, I turn my attention to the floor of the House.

Several hundred members are milling about, mainly talking noisily in small groups. I watch Tammy insert a credit card-like device into one of many electronic stations at the end of rows of benches. It immediately records a yes vote next to her name on a large scoreboard. Unfortunately, Kind's amendment is not treated kindly by the Republican-controlled House and is defeated.

Tammy returns twice more between votes to explain what's going on and why she is voting the way she is. By the time I return home on Sunday, I see her last vote in the headlines of the Madison newspaper: *State's reps split on Israel support*. The newspaper gives Tammy two paragraphs to explain why she voted "present" on the resolution. It is the same explanation she gave me in the House gallery.

Tammy makes news. I merely watched.

This was part of an informal job exchange. My visit repaid her for the job shadowing she had done in October with Lori Hulburt, a special education teacher at Patrick Marsh Middle School in Sun Prairie.

Tammy and her staff couldn't have been more gracious as they helped me through a day that included a judicial subcommittee meeting on cyberspace security, a staff meeting on environment-friendly "smart growth," and a block of time for me to interview her.

Long hours, intense working conditions, management of conflict, and huge responsibilities make up Tammy's job description. She handles it all with equanimity and a sense of purpose.

I believe she'd make an excellent public school teacher.

U.S. casts shadow on World Congress in Brazil

Education International, the largest federation of education unions in the world, met July 22-26, 2004, in Porto Alegre, Brazil. More than 1,200 delegates discussed current issues in education around the world and debated and voted on policies to be implemented in the next three years. The federation, which represents over 29 million members, addressed three issues in breakout sessions: the right to teach and learn, education as a public service or a commodity, and recruitment and retention of qualified teachers. I was a member of the National Education Association (NEA)-USA delegation.

The United States casts a giant shadow in world events. This is not new. Nevertheless, the incredible unpopularity of the U.S. government at the Education International (EI) World Congress in Porto Alegre, Brazil, was a new phenomenon, catching even veteran NEA delegates by surprise. In private and on the convention floor, international delegates to the 2004 Congress shared their deep distrust and disdain for a man they believe to be ignorant, arrogant, and dangerous.

"Please, elect someone else," pleaded a Scandinavian delegate, an elegant woman speaking in English with a lilting Swedish accent. She was referring to President George W. Bush.

Maurie, a delegate from Australia, delivered the same message, but with a different twist. If the U.S. government is going to have such a negative effect on the rest of the world, he said, "The least you can do is let us vote in your elections."

President Bush and his policies were further vilified in Spain's resolution opposing the Iraq war. Despite the efforts of the NEA and American Federation of Teachers (AFT) to amend the harsh criticism to make it more palatable for American sensibilities, representatives from around the world sounded a resonant "No" to such attempts and passed the original resolution by an overwhelming margin.

Besides Iraq, U.S. policy on HIV/AIDS was also a major source of criticism, especially from Fred van Leeuwen, EI's General Secretary. In his remarks to the delegation, van Leeuwen decried the U.S. transfer of AIDS program authority to faith-based organizations that have little regard for cultural values other than their own.

With some African countries enduring a rate of HIV/AIDS infection as high as one in seven teachers, and rates of infection rising most rapidly in central Asia and eastern Europe, a sense of urgency on the topic prevailed at the Congress. Education International's work with affiliates in countries hit hard by HIV/AIDS was being reduced due to the policy change impacting Center for Disease Control (CDC) and World Health Organization (WHO) funding.

HIV/AIDS was one of three featured topics discussed in breakout sessions. The other two key issues were attracting and retaining teachers to ameliorate the growing worldwide teacher shortage (out of 60 million teachers in the world now, 15 to 30 million will need to be replaced in the coming decade) and the problems that ensue from treating education as a commodity to be bought and sold instead of as a basic human right.

Delegates elected a slate of officers that included a new president, Thulis Nxesi, of South Africa. He replaced former NEA president, Mary Hatwood Futrell, who had led EI since its founding in Stockholm in 1993.

A major highlight of the Congress was the appearance, under heavy security, of the President of Brazil, Luiz Inacio Lula da Silva. To the surprise and delight of the delegates, the president asked to sit and listen to the proceedings for a while before delivering his speech. Lula, the former head of the metal workers union in Brazil, felt at home with EI, an organization consisting of 345 unions from 165 countries. Championing education as a national investment, Lula declared that Brazil should "export knowledge, not just raw materials."

In other business, EI delegates voted to add 2 million more members to its current 27 million, with the addition of the World Confederation of Teachers, an organization with educators mainly in Europe and Latin America. EI also adopted a constitutional amendment providing for the addition of three more members to its executive board.

Resolutions considered by the World Congress were divided into two categories: those proposed by the executive board and those proposed by member organizations. Unlike NEA resolutions, which consist only of belief statements, EI resolutions also may contain actions. For example, on the topic of education as a commodity, 14 points were advanced before getting to the action piece: "[The World Congress] mandates the Executive Board to continue Education International's advocacy before intergovernmental organizations, trade union internationals and international political groupings..."

The member resolutions were a mixed bag of interests, ranging from France's resolution "in favor of universal abolition of the death penalty" to Colombia's resolution that urged EI to "press national governments and inter-governmental bodies at the global and regional levels to end military support for the Colombian government." In all, 38 resolutions were passed.

General Secretary van Leeuwen brought the Congress up to date on some of the things EI has been doing since the last World Congress in Thailand three years ago. He talked about a new and much more positive relationship between Education International and the World Bank, an institution that is much maligned in developing countries. In fact, he said relations have thawed sufficiently to warrant the establishment of a "hotline" between the World Bank and EI to foster communications.

The General Secretary also alluded to a meeting EI officials had with Ethiopian government leaders that helped persuade them to release the union president, Dr. Taye Woldesmiate, from jail.

Van Leeuwen elicited a great cheer when he informed the delegation that EI had helped create a new free teachers union in Afghanistan, adding to great applause, "They are here with us today."

The most dramatic moment of van Leeuwen's speech came when he turned to delegates from AFT and NEA, some of whom were leaving for the Democratic Convention. He said, "I know I speak for all of us when I say we expect them to win back their country."

Of course, not all of the important events at a conference of this scope take place in official sessions. Because of a previous international connection, the seven Wisconsin NEA members in the delegation took Teachers' Union President Jorge Guevara of Colombia and three other officials out to dinner at a traditional Brazilian restaurant (featuring massive quantities of meat). None of the four Colombians spoke English, so the Wisconsin group rounded up enough fluent

Spanish speakers in the U.S. delegation to expand the group to eighteen. The Colombian delegates, who face extreme personal danger on a daily basis in their home country, gained a little respite and a great meal in the cultural exchange.

An inside look at Education International

It was an opportunity I couldn't pass up. My friend, David Edwards, had just been appointed head of an international union. His office was in Brussels, Belgium, about two hours from where I was staying for a month on the Belgium/Luxembourg border in 2018 conducting some family business and doing a little productive traveling.

I had some history with David's union, Education International, because I had been a voting delegate at its founding in Stockholm in 1993 when four major international education unions combined into one. The two US entities, AFT and NEA, had belonged to rival international unions, so their connection internationally was a pivotal moment in their relationship. By 2018, Education International counted 402 affiliated unions in 171 countries as members.

Wanting to see for myself how the union was doing after its first 25 years, I contacted David to ask if I could interview him at his Brussels office for a labor newspaper I was editing. My timing was bad; he was leaving for the US the next day, but I was still welcome to visit the office and talk to staff members. Because I was now working for an AFL-CIO-affiliated organization, we decided the best fit was a man named Jim Baker who had a ninth-floor office as a consultant for EI. Baker had worked for AFL-CIO under Lane Kirkland, who served as its president from 1979 to 1995.

Although he was on vacation in Cyprus, Baker agreed to talk to me. So I sat, incongruously, in a conference room at his home office in Brussels while he soaked up sun on an eastern Mediterranean island and I talked to a high-tech screen.

Baker was proud of his past work with the AFL-CIO and the first thing he told me was the name of his home union, United Auto Workers in California. Moving all the way to the present without missing a beat, he said he was currently working on a book with the former head of EI, the legendary Fred Van Leeuven. Titled *Educa-*

tion and Democracy, it offered 25 lessons on the threats to education and the unions he'd seen in recent years.

"Look at the UK," Baker said, referring to Brexit, Britain's exit from the European Union. "They've painted themselves into a corner." Asked to elaborate, he offered an example, "Can farmers in Northern Ireland take their cows to veterinarians in Ireland?" It's just one of many issues that now need to be worked out, all because of "an almost hysterical bigotry against migrants" that was behind the Brexit vote.

Baker called those behind Brexit in Britain and similar movements in many other countries around the world "populist-nationalists." He said some of the populist ideas of the right, such as what to do about bankers or taxes, had some attraction for union members, but only because of "the failure of the Left to act like the Left."

He said in the US this took the form of Hillary Clinton and other business-oriented Democrats whom he compared to pre-New Deal Democrats of the 1920s.

He then pivoted to corporate players on the international scene, such as Bridge International, a leading privatizer of education. As described on the EI website, "Bridge is one of the largest education for-profit companies in the world, with plans to sell basic education services directly to ten million fee-paying students throughout Africa and Asia by 2025. Bridge's business plan is predicated on the employment of unqualified staff delivering a highly scripted, standardized curriculum in substandard facilities."

Baker compared the company to the Wisconsin of Act 10 where politicians did not act in the best interest of students and "violated the minimum of decency you thought Republicans had."

Membership in unions

Whether or not union membership has gone up or down internationally depends on your definition. In EI, only members of "free trade unions" may join. That leaves out countries such as China, where unions are not free to work on behalf of their members.

Baker suggested that the many workers in central and eastern Europe who had worked under Communism were the victims of bad timing. "They got freedom when the rest of the world valued freedom less—and decided capitalism was more important."

Asked to compare unionization in the US with that of Europe, Baker cited Sweden as an example. Collective bargaining covers a majority of workers there. But even in Sweden, corporate tax rates have gone down as they have in most other places.

While union density has plateaued in much of the developed world, most other countries haven't experienced the demonization of unions that is the hallmark of current right-wing politics in the US.

The biggest problem their unions have had to deal with is the business world's shift to smaller enterprises. "It's hard to organize smaller operations," Baker said. He also cited companies like Amazon, which now gets thousands of its workers from temp agencies and Uber, which claims to have virtually no employees at all.

In Baker's opinion, that's where we need to draw the line. "Uber needs to recognize that they have employees." Only then would negotiated agreements be possible. Baker acknowledged that using the internet to try to organize workers was mostly futile, saying that when it comes to organizing, as always, "relationships are key."

At that point in our conversation, I needed to let Jim Baker get back to his union-bargained, government-mandated vacation.

Getting schooled in Japan

The Fulbright Memorial Fund sponsored 200 American teachers to be guests of the Japanese government for three weeks in 1998. We visited schools, met with parent groups and government officials, and visited sites of cultural and commercial importance. Here are answers I provided to The Star, *our local newspaper.*

Where in Japan did you go?

I spent about a week in Tokyo with all 200 US teachers, then my group of 20 took the Bullet Train to Sakai City for a week.

On the way back, we spent a night in Kyoto, the ancient capital, before returning to Tokyo for a few more days.

What were those places like?

Tokyo proved to be unexpectedly easy to get around. An exten-

were extremely nice, but their English was marginal. I doubt if any of them had ever talked to a native English speaker before.

Did you have anything in common with the students?

Baseball and the fact that my son, John, was their age. On school visits, I invariably asked kids about *yakyu* (baseball), which is very popular there. I brought 100 Sammy Sosa and Mark McGuire baseball cards to distribute.

When I told the girls that John had been driving for two years already, they were amazed. They wouldn't be driving for another year. When they told me how much that first driver's license cost, I was shocked--about $2,800. I double-checked with our guide later about the amount and she confirmed it.

Is Japan expensive?

Generally, yes. Since my Fulbright program and the Japanese government paid for most of my expenses, I was insulated from major costs. I spent $34 on a supper of sushi and poison blowfish and a beer. On the other hand, McDonald's (there are over 500 in Tokyo alone) only set me back $5.00 for a quarter-pounder, fries and coke. (Ed. Note: the number of McDonald's in Tokyo grew to about 3000 by 2024).

Did you really eat at McDonald's?

I'll confess that I did, but not until after about ten days of rice and fish. Actually, the episode was a bit embarrassing. I noticed a Mc Donald's at the train station as we came into Sakai City then walked a block to our hotel. Later, I sneaked back to the train station alone. I had to buy a train ticket because it was the only way to get inside the station where the restaurant was. When I tried to exit the same way, bells and sirens went off because you can't leave from the same station you entered. An attendant had to come over and let me out. Once outside, I noticed the outside entrance to McDonald's. Buying the ticket had been unnecessary.

Any other high or low points?

It took 25 hours to get to our Tokyo hotel and 22 hours to get home.

I was on the eleventh floor of our Tokyo hotel when I felt the bed moving across the room. We were having an earthquake. I didn't have time to get scared and it was over in about five seconds.

Other than the earthquake, did you feel safe in Japan?

Incredibly safe. On my last day in Tokyo I watched the local news (with English subtitles). They devoted almost three minutes to a terrible, terrible crime that had been perpetrated. An elderly man and his wife had grown a crop of potatoes in their garden and were almost ready to harvest them. A thief beat them to it. The man was interviewed; his wife was interviewed; the thief's footprints were shown.

I was glad to get out of Tokyo before the crime wave got any worse.

Chapter 8 - Hydrology
Cruising the world

Burgundy, France

Europe by water: Three ways

Would you like to see Europe but only unpack your suitcase once? Here are three ways to float your way through that surprisingly watery continent.

Size matters. Choose among large ocean liners (more than 2,000 people), smaller river boats (around 200), or personalized canal boats (probably eight people). I've done Europe on three of the big ships: *Voyager of the Seas*, *Celebrity Equinox* (both Mediterranean), and *Silver*

Robespierre decapitated

We were on the Canal du Midi in southern France. My friend, Captain Curt, had been waiting patiently to ease our 50-foot boat into the lock.

Suddenly a smaller boat tried cutting the line in front of us to get the final spot in the lock, meaning another long wait for us. The behavior was unsurprising. We had seen it in grocery lines in France.

"Curt, American pride is on the line," I needled.

With a powerful engine and a big boat, Curt successfully thwarted the interloper (whom we called Robespierre), and we entered the lock amid a barrage of French expletives and amusing gestures.

Whisper (Norwegian fjords); three canal boats (southern France, Burgundy, and Brittany, all through Le Boat); and one river boat (*Viking Hlin* on the Rhine River).

Each one lasted a week to ten days, included a traveling party of 6 to 16 people, and was accomplished in every season except winter. The three choices aren't the only ones available (check out exotic alternatives, such as sailing ships on the Adriatic or bike/barge trips through the Netherlands), but they are arguably the most common.

Let's take a closer look to see which one is right for you.

Getting your bearings

The *Celebrity Equinox* is just over 1,000 feet long and can travel at 28 mph; the *Viking Hlin* is 443 feet long and can attain speeds of 17 mph; the Salsa canal boat is 48 feet long and tops out at about 8 mph.

Ocean ship: An ocean liner is a floating city. You'll meet people from all over, share tables with strangers, get overstuffed in multiple restaurants, swim in a small pool, be entertained by excellent actors and musicians, gamble in casinos, and select pricey spa treatments. You are one of many.

River cruise: Everything is scaled down on a river boat, except the scenery, which is dialed up. Unlike a cruise ship, which always travels at night when there normally isn't much to see, a river boat often travels during the day, with accessible scenery at a leisurely pace. With a limited passenger count, you'll keep running into the same people, make a few new friends, eat all meals, and get to know the staff.

Canal boat: A canal boat is a completely different animal and isn't common for Americans. In three voyages, we only encountered boats containing British, Dutch, and French participants. No Americans. It is essentially an RV on water, only roomier. There are four bedrooms on the boats we rented, a galley (kitchen) and saloon (kind of a living room). You are the crew. When you get to a lock (which is often), your captain will direct things from the bridge (on the top deck) or inside lower deck in bad weather. You'll need at least two lackeys manning the ropes so the boat stays secure. It's very interactive. You decide where you dock and the route you take. I especially enjoyed stopping at local wineries and sampling their wares. The best itinerary is probably the *Canal du Midi*, starting near the lovely town of Carcassonne in southern France.

The canals are several hundred years old and formerly carried goods to all parts of France (and a few other countries). They have been repurposed for leisure travel. Your impact on your environment is minimal compared to the other boat choices and you are very close to the weather, the people, and the land. You travel only during the day (the locks are typically open from about 9:00 am to 6:00 pm with a lunch closure (of course) around noon. Boats are often equipped with a bike or two. Since a towpath always runs next to the canal (the horses used to walk on them towing the boats), it's a smooth e-bike ride to the next town, where you can wait for the boat to catch up to you.

Stop considering this alternative if you don't have someone in mind to captain your boat. Through a glitch in French law, landlubbers like me can operate these half-million-dollar yachts after a half-hour training run. I won't do it myself because it makes me nervous, but I have recruited friends who like boats, are comfortable maneuvering them, and are eager for occasional challenges with docking or quirky locks.

Cost

Canal boat: You can rent a canal boat for a week for as little as $5,000 for eight people. That's barely $600 apiece for the experience. Food and drink are not included. Neither is airfare. Getting to the boat usually requires some expertise with European transportation and extra costs (but also takes you to quaint places you might not otherwise visit). On our last trip we took a cheap flight from Geneva to Rennes, stayed overnight in a hotel, then took a short train ride to the tiny town of Messac to board the boat.

Ocean ship: A balcony cabin on a Mediterranean cruise ship for a week can be had for around $1,200 per person. (Singles are very expensive, so try to share a cabin). Flights are extra in most cases. Food of all kinds is included. Drinks usually are not. Shore excursions are available but generally quite expensive. You'll share the experience with a large group of people you don't know and go only to places where a large bus will fit (unless you wish to pay even more).

River cruise: Our experience on the Viking ship cost about $4,200 apiece for a balcony cabin. Our airfare from Madison to Amsterdam/Munich to Madison would have cost another $1,400 apiece, but was covered by Viking. That part worked very well for us and we had excellent flights. Some of our friends had to endure less-than-ideal flights and extra stopovers. It just depends what kind of inventory Viking has. Breakfast, lunch, and supper are provided, but most drinks are extra. At least one free shore excursion per day is provided, usually a walking tour of the town.

One hidden cost for the river and ocean cruises is tipping. We paid an extra $140 apiece at the end of the river cruise. Ocean ships are about the same. It is technically not mandatory, but in practice, you should figure it into your budget. We never tipped my friend, Captain Curt, on the canal boat, but I did occasionally buy him a beer.

Food

Canal boat: It's a lot homier than the other two. I love grocery shopping in Europe. Have you ever looked for eggs? Since they're not refrigerated, they could be anywhere in the store. We once filled our cart with provisions at a local grocery in Carcassonne, France and wheeled it a half mile down to our boat in the port. A baguette, some great local cheese, and a slice of ham is a better lunch to me than some exotic concoction that must be formally delivered to the table by people in uniforms. The galleys are excellent for preparation of simple food, and the refrigerators have plenty of room for your particular comfort food. And when you want a good meal, a restaurant or café will likely appear around the next bend (and you won't have hundreds of people disembarking and heading for the same place). I especially liked having Mary Jo on board, because she would get up early and bring back fresh croissants from the local bakery (there's always a local bakery in France).

Ocean ship: The more recent ones often have multiple specialty restaurants (often with a surcharge) offering specific cuisines: steaks, Japanese, Italian, Irish pubs, et. al. But the regular dining room has plenty to offer and it's included in your fare. There's also a lot of free food available between meals, ranging from ice cream to freshly grilled chunks of fish up on deck. Drink packages are available and may or may not be worth it to you.

River cruise: Our Viking ship had only one bar and a very busy but capable bartender. The dining hours were pretty specific (supper at 7:00!) and the menu choices much more limited than on an ocean voyage. Personally, I found the food adequate but nowhere near the quality, quantity, and variety of an ocean ship.

In port

Ocean ship: It makes a huge difference where your ship docks. Ships on the Mediterranean only have a limited number of harbors that can handle these giants. If you stop at the lovely town of Ville-franche, halfway between Nice and Monaco, you won't even get a pier. You'll take a tender (small motorboat) to shore then make sure to return before the last one goes back to the ship. If you dock at Athens, you're really at the port of Piraeus, almost an hour by cab from Athens. But if the ship pulls into a place like Naples or Messina, Sicily, you're right in the middle of town. Get off when you want. Return at the last minute if it suits you.

Canal boat: You nearly always dock in the middle of town. Sometimes there's a docking fee of eight or ten euros, but most of the time the town wants you to stop and spend your money and lets you dock for free. Harbor masters are invariably friendly (and often British for some reason) and will help you figure things out in the larger towns. It's not uncommon to make friends with other boat people. A Dutch guy we had met during the day rescued us in the middle of the night after our power failed and CPAP breathing machines stopped working. We ran a long extension cord to his boat. We try to time our stops to arrive on market day, so we can replenish our supplies.

River cruise: Probably my biggest disappointment with the Viking cruise was the docking situation. We found ourselves docked in such places as a marsh, a nuclear power plant, and a remote pier about 45 minutes out of Cologne. Unlike an ocean ship, they appeared to be making up the time and place of docking as they went along. This was probably not all their fault as low water levels, other river traffic and faulty engines impacted our choices. It seemed exotic to get off the boat in the little town of Briesach to walk a few blocks into town to get ice cream. I had expected that kind of location to present itself every day and was disappointed that it didn't happen.

Safety net

River cruise: I heard a cruise critic describe a river boat as a "bus with a bow." He found it too confining compared with an ocean ship. Viking employees pick you up at the airport and deliver you to post-cruise hotels. People generally do the same things at the same time. Tour guides hold up colored flags in front of cathedrals for their group to hang together. If you find that kind of hand-holding comforting, you are in the right place.

Ocean ship: On board, you are mostly anonymous and free to do your own thing. I met a "young" retired guy with a bike. He would sail one cruise after another, discovering new biking experiences in each port. He didn't frequent the casino or participate in trivia contests or conquer the climbing wall. Like him, we rarely take a group tour offered by the cruise line. In Athens, we arranged instead for two guys in new Mercedes cabs to meet us at the port and take us on our own itinerary. It cost half as much as a tour offered by the ship and was twice as much fun. It's harder to make your own plans on a river boat because of their lack of transparency about where and when the boat will dock.

Canal boat: You are truly working without a net when you take a canal boat ride. The only thing Le Boat cares about is that you return the boat on time and avoid wrecking it. (They include insurance for the latter eventuality). On the other hand, they gas up the boat and pump the bilge before you board so you don't have to do any of that stuff on a week's cruise. If you do have an emergency, though, help is rarely more than an hour away since the boat doesn't go very far, even on a full day of cruising.

Cabins

Ocean ship: I love keeping the balcony doors open at night, hearing the waves sloshing, and letting a warm ocean breeze lull me to sleep. The beds are very comfortable and the showers large and steamy.

River boat: The cabins are similar in comfort to the larger boats. But a balcony isn't as useful. Daytime cruising is more likely to find you sunning yourself on the top deck nursing a glass of chardonnay instead. Nighttime cruising with the doors open attracts too many river bugs to be practical. One other problem occurs when the ship docks. The boats are often daisy-chained together, so it's not uncommon for you to cross the decks of two other ships to get to shore. Since you are parked so close to other boats, your private balcony may be just inches away from the next boat's private balcony. Dress accordingly.

Canal boat: You've got beds. Quit complaining. And you probably share a bathroom with your cousins in the bedroom next to you. You won't hear them complaining (yes, you will; the walls are thin).

Health

If you travel long enough with a large enough group, someone is going to get sick or injured. This year it was my wife, Kris's, turn. She suffered from dehydration on our river cruise. The crew was as helpful as they could be, seemed very caring, but wasn't able to go much beyond lending us a wheelchair to help get her back aboard and a thermometer to take her temperature. Last year, I got hit with some kind of non-Covid virus while on a canal boat. We were completely on our own and I suffered through it with Kris's help. Earlier this year, one of our friends slipped and fell on a cruise ship. The ship's doctor stitched him up. Conclusion: If your health is somewhat precarious, stick with the ocean cruise ship.

A word about motion sickness. I don't take it lightly and have thrown up on some of the finer vessels on the waterways. I learned the primary maritime dictum on a ferry between Britain and France: *Don't throw up into the wind.* Having said that, I've never seen anyone exhibit motion sickness aboard canal or river boats. And I've only seen it (rarely) on cruise ships in actual open water (not the Mediterranean). Don't let that possibility deter you, but take some drugs along just in case.

Highlights

River cruise: Seeing the castles lining the Middle Rhine from the top deck of a river boat while classical music plays in the background is a sublime experience. You won't want to be anywhere else.

Ocean ship: After you stop at the Greek island of Santorini, you'll take a tender to shore, climb the mountain in an aerial tram and have lunch at Oiea, that white and blue Mediterranean town that graces the cover of every Greek tourist brochure. Spectacular.

Canal boat: If you are lucky enough to float into the picturesque Burgundy town of Auxerre in your canal boat during a festival, and doubly lucky to secure a mooring next to the town square, you'll sit on the deck of your private yacht drinking wine and listening to a great band playing about 100 feet away, while French kids and dogs cavort on shore, and the moon makes a casual appearance over the Cathedral.

Rhine Itinerary *annotated*

Does a trip unfold the way you expect it to? Of course not. Even one as structured as a Viking cruise. What follows is the final itinerary I sent to my 15 Tour de Glenn travelers followed by what really happened (in italics).

Friday, June 16

Fly Madison to Amsterdam Delta **GZE4MB**, (Viking Air ZZMCPC) MSN 5:58 pm to 7:15 MSP (seats 16A &B); 9:05 MSP to AMS 12:35 pm (seats 40H&J) *Viking got Kris and me excellent flights but some of our travelers never did get the most convenient flights. When you get your air itinerary from cruise lines, it's necessary to keep monitoring them right up until takeoff. They want to match you to their inventory instead of matching their inventory to you. Calling the Viking emergency number can sometimes be effective in dealing with cancelled or delayed flights.*

Saturday, June 17

Arrive 12:35 pm. Taxi to *Krishotel*; check-in: 3:00. *We were limited in our hotel choices because we wanted to stay just one night. Every decent, well-located hotel was over $300/night. The Leidseplein/Museum area is a great place to be. The American Hotel (now a Hard Rock) is good with a beautiful breakfast area. The Krishotel, two blocks away, is a friendly three-star hotel and let us just book a single night.*

Sunday, June 18

Board Viking Longship HLIN; may board at noon; rooms ready at 3:00 *One of our couples boarded at about 8:30 am, arriving directly from the airport. Not a problem.*

Monday, June 19 Kinderdijk (Rotterdam)

Vintage barge trip 10:30. 2 hours. *Nice little tour. More walking than you'd expect. The first in a series of lackluster mooring spots for our Viking ship.*

Tuesday, June 20 Cologne.

Cologne walking tour. 9:15 am. 2 hours. *Forty-five-minute bus ride into Cologne. Tour was a bust because we were so late, as our boat limped along with an engine problem. We really only got to see the Cathedral. Transportation was also a bust. Viking left us stranded for an hour in a city park waiting for the bus. We docked next to a nuclear power plant instead of near the Cathedral because of low water levels. We ate at Peter's Brewhaus in the shadow of Cathedral. Good beer and German sausages.*

Wednesday, June 21 Koblenz

Walking tour 8:15. 2 hours. Schloss Rudesheim supper. 6:30 pm. 3 hours. *Pretty awful. We paid Viking over $100 apiece for the experience. The restaurant food looked great going past our table, but it didn't stop for us. Our entire group was restricted to one choice, some kind of boiled pork. The forced gaiety and group drinking games were wasted on us.*

Thursday, June 22 Speyer

Heidelberg tour w/Manfred, 2:00 pm on gangplank, 4 hours. *$90 each (84 euros) We booked this on our own. Manfred was excellent, taking us in two vans to tour the castle and Old Town. We found him on TripAdvisor/Viator. We met him where the boat docked and were grateful that Viking kept to their designated mooring place and time on this occasion.*

Friday, June 23 Strasbourg, France

Drive/walk Strasbourg, 8:30 am. 4 hours. *People enjoyed this walk. Four of us rented a car instead and went to a military cemetery to pay respects to relatives. Easy driving. We didn't do much else as Kris dealt with dehydration.*

Saturday, June 24 Breisach, Germany

Drive/walk Black Forest, 2:00 pm, 4 hours. *People also liked the Black Forest although we skipped it because Kris was still recovering. I did get off the boat and walk into Breisach to get her ice cream. This was the only stop in seven days (except for the Rudesheim experience) where we were docked near civilization.*

Sunday, June 25 Basel, Switzerland. End boat trip. Steinenschanz Stadthotel, supper at Brasserie au violon (Michelin) 6 min. walk. *Restaurant was closed Sundays. Hotel recommended Pizzeria Ristorante Molino, within walking distance (down steep steps). It was very good. Our hotel was outstanding. They give you a free transportation pass (common in Switzerland). Wonderful breakfast and courtyard area.*

Monday, June 26 train to Munich, Train $48 2nd class 12:13-16:56 (change Karlsruhe), seats not reserved. *Train ride from Heck. Seat reservations usually aren't needed. Our car was commandeered by a large group of middle schoolers. They did have reservations. We did lots of moving around. Hotel Marc Munchen. Excellent hotel located right around the corner from the train station. Less than a mile and a nice walk to Hofbrauhaus (a must!) and middle of town.*

Tuesday, June 27, Munich, Viktualienmarkt (food market). *Market was fun. We ate breakfast with the locals at Kranich's. Same price as hotel breakfast (20 euros).*

Wednesday, June 28, Munich, Deutsches Museum. Lunch at Nuernberger Bratwurst Gloeckl am Dom shop Kaufingerstrasse. *Didn't do any of that. We went to Residenz Munich, an 80-room Bavarian palace.*

Thursday, June 29 Munich to Detroit 11:30 am to 3:00 pm (35 D&E); Detroit to Madison 4:49 to 5:03 pm (seats 16A&B) *Made it home about 7:00 but would have missed our flight in Detroit if it hadn't been delayed two hours.*

Getting the most out of your Viking Rhine River Cruise

1. Cruising the Middle Rhine is more than just castles. Secure a shaded spot on the top deck early and watch some incredible scenery float by.
2. Evening entertainment: Case by case. We loved the violin/ classical guitar combo.
3. You don't have to go to the bar area to watch presentations. They are on TV in your room.
4. Pick up a map at the desk daily to find out where you dock. This information was always hard to find.
5. Lots of good local restaurants in Rudesheim are within walking distance. Walk to ice cream shops in Breisach.
6. Breakfast: Buffet was always lukewarm. Order directly from chef or from your server. Blueberry pancakes but not French toast.
7. Coffee machine near bar entrance is great (latte macchiato). Different treats there every day. Cookies are best.
8. One couple used the free transit card from our hotel in Basel to circle the city on a tram. Fun. Cheap tour.
9. Stay hydrated. My wife Kris didn't and was down for a couple days.
10. Lufthansa Express Bus from train station to Munich airport was easy, convenient and cheap ($12).

Catching the Jewel

Our helicopter banks sharply, the deep blue Atlantic beckoning us downward toward a small speck on the horizon. Slowly the speck mushrooms into a huge cruise ship that dominates our view. We aim for the X on the top deck of the *Norwegian Jewel* and descend. In the brief minute that the airship hovers just inches above the real ship, Kris and I hop out and our bags are grabbed by two stalwart men in white uniforms.

That never happened. There is no X on the top deck. No helicopter.

The reality: A rattletrap cab disgorges us and our luggage onto the cruise ship pier on the island of Bonaire, just off the northern coast of South America. We drag our bags through a gauntlet of

Jewel passengers who are already in cruise zombie mode after three days at sea.

The oversized security guy can't find our name on his clipboard. He hands us off to a smaller man with a computer, who yields to one even smaller in a suit. Finally, a woman dressed in authority hands us our room keys.

How did we find ourselves in this situation?

My wife had a dental emergency on the day we were supposed to fly. We got her treated, then I called Traci, our contact at Norwegian, to ask what our options were.

"Check your travel insurance policy about reimbursement," she said.

"I don't want my money back. I want to be on that boat," I replied. I had a dozen friends on it who were already partying without us.

She suggested it was no easy thing to catch up to a cruise ship. There were rules.

I speculated that we might be able to salvage six days of our nine-day cruise by intercepting it in Bonaire or even five days by landing in Aruba.

"Nope, not Aruba," she said. Anything beyond a three-day delay appeared to need authorization from God. We settled on Bonaire.

Traci directed me to talk to Norwegian's flight department, which had booked our original flights. They were personable but generally unhelpful. They did make it clear that Norwegian would not pay to replace our departed United flights to Panama. A one-way ticket on United to Bonaire was now pricing out at $450 apiece.

I asked if my flights home from Panama on American were still intact. (If you don't get on the first leg of a round-trip flight, the rest of your flights are often canceled). Even though Norwegian had made the reservations, they tossed the ball back to me and said I should contact American myself. I did. They expressed a lack of interest in what United had done and confirmed that I was good to go.

But I wasn't done with United yet. They let me change my connecting flights from Madison to Chicago without hassle and without charge. I appreciated that.

I used 44,000 United miles for our flights to Bonaire, so I lost some points but no real money.

What I didn't realize was how lucky we were to find a flight.

We were treated to this gate announcement once we got to Houston to make our connection: "Our flight is going to be delayed for 45 minutes because the plane from Denver is late. They have a bunch of passengers bound for Bonaire, and since we only go there once a week, we'd better wait."

Once a week? Didn't know that.

I had one more loose end to tie up. We still had hotel nights in two places to cancel and in two more to make.

I've been using Booking.com for some time now and they are excellent. They've bailed me out of a number of troubled bookings. They came through for me again this time and I escaped paying any penalties, despite hotel policies to the contrary.

They probably would have booked me a helicopter too if I'd thought to ask.

Double-dipping in the Mediterranean

After taking a post-retirement cruise of the *western* Mediterranean (Spain, France, Italy) in November of 2009, with three other couples, we completed the circuit with an *eastern* Mediterranean cruise (Italy, Greece, Turkey) in November 2012. The differences were revealing.

The setup

Most cruise sites tell you to buy your cruise early (at least six months ahead) or late (six weeks before the cruise). We did one of each. The 2009 cruise aboard Royal Caribbean's *Voyager of the Seas* was a last-minute deal consummated on the golf course and purchased at fire-sale prices on Priceline. The 2012 cruise on *Celebrity Equinox* was much more heavily researched for the ports, times, cruise line, and price. It was purchased six months before the cruise date from cruise consolidator Cru-Con.

Cost

This is a harder comparison than you might think. There are the obvious differences: 2009 vs. 2012 prices; itinerary; length of cruise—7 days for the first and 10 days for the second; buying late (2009) vs. buying early (2012); and ship ratings (most observers give *Equinox* generally higher ratings than *Voyager*). Time of year

(November) was the same for each trip. For us it was the add-ons that made the difference. On the 2009 cruise, Priceline gave us credits for two hotel nights in Barcelona before the start of the cruise plus a $100 spa treatment for my wife on the ship. In 2012, Cru-Con included $200 in on-board ship credits--almost enough to cover the ten days' worth of gratuities (which are essentially mandatory). The seven-day, last-minute deal on *Voyager* in 2009 cost about $750 each (including tips). The ten-day version in 2012 cost $1,000 each. Both included outside cabins with balconies. One other note: I checked prices on the *Equinox* about six weeks before we sailed. Prices had actually gone up, so waiting to get a good deal in this case would not have worked. (I talked to an Australian couple on board later who claimed to have seized the last room, which means the *Equinox* sailed at capacity—about 2,850 passengers).

Flights

Four of us booked flights on American using frequent flyer miles. "Free" flights have become somewhat costly. For less than $250 each, we cashed in 40,000 miles apiece for round-trip tickets that were then selling for about $1,000 from Madison, Wisconsin to Rome.

Since we saved about $1,500 per couple, it's hard to complain, but I spent a lot of time on the phone with American because I had a complication. I had 60,000 of the miles we needed and my wife had 20,000. I considered transferring her miles to my account, a process that would have cost an additional $200. Then I remembered the airlines view them as one-way tickets and American was perfectly fine with issuing three one-way tickets using my miles and one ticket using her miles.

Despite booking the frequent flyer tickets six months ahead, returning from Rome on the same day we disembarked proved to be impossible, even though we discussed increasingly exotic routes (Did we really want to switch planes three times and go through Stuttgart?) When it became clear that going through London Heathrow to Chicago was our best alternative, we extended our time in London enough to give us a 24-hour layover there. When we explained this to the kindly gate agent in Rome on the way back, she booked our bags all the way through so we could spend our 24 hours in London with just our carry-ons.

Making Your Own Experience

Because of Europe's rich variety of cultural and historical attractions, it can be exhausting when taken in nine-hour daily doses from a moving target. We had little interest in the expensive cruise-sponsored megabus experiences offered at each port. We got better at providing our own unique experience. If you do this, be prepared to do a great deal of research and expect a few heart-stopping moments when the unexpected arises and you have only your own resources at hand.

During the first cruise, we had two such incidences. We took the very inexpensive train from the port of Civitevecchia into Rome—about a one-hour trip. When we tried to return to the ship from Termini Station in Rome, we learned the train had stopped running (we found out later someone had committed suicide by stepping in front of a train). After trying other solutions, we were left with taking a $240 cab ride to the port at 160 kph (100 mph), getting to the boat about seven minutes before departure time.

The other incident was more humorous than threatening. We were docked in Naples and took the train to Pompeii and then Sorrento. There we found a ferry that would take us back to the dock next to our ship. When we got on board, I found out that my credit card was still at the ferry line's ticket office, at least a quarter mile from the ferry, which was now ready to leave. I was puffing like a freight train after my run to the office window where they handed me back my Visa card. Instead of running back (which seemed unlikely to my aging body), I stopped a kid driving past on his Vespa, pointed at the waiting ferry, and jumped on the back for a wild ride down the long pier to the boat. The passengers applauded as we skidded to a stop moments later.

We used the strategy of taking public transportation three years later, but augmented it with a more targeted one. Taking the bus on Santorini from Fira to the more scenic Oia proved to be cheap and easy. Public transport from Messina, Sicily to other attractions was hard to find. It was also hampered by recent floods and required much more time because of altered routes.

At three of our destinations, we were greeted by signs with our name on them, as the guides we had booked from home rose out of the port chaos to meet us. In Athens, we caravanned through the ancient streets in two identical Mercedes cabs as Spiro and Marcos took us from one site to another to proudly show off their city. The all-day tour featured the Parthenon and other historic sites, lunch at an inexpensive family-run restaurant in a scenic part of the city (not costed in the tour), changing of the guard at the presidential palace, and a little shopping time.

Ephesus was even more intense as Tijen, an experienced and knowledgeable guide, picked us up in her 13-passenger van and took us to the Virgin Mary's house, the sprawling excavations at Ephesus, and other sites before drenching rain finally poured us back to the port. We paid $40 apiece for the all-day tour.

Disembarking in Rome, we arranged to have the same driver who had taken us to the port 10 days earlier pick us up and take us to an airport hotel. Because everything went so smoothly, we had more time than we expected. We asked our driver (through the hotel desk clerk, since the driver spoke no English) if he would take us to the Catacombs and then drop some of us off at the airport. For just 100 euros for all eight of us, we got to see the San Callisto catacombs, a rich and moving experience as we toured a small part of an ancient underground world with a half million permanent occupants.

Looking Back

There were naturally parts of each cruise that I liked and didn't like. *Equinox* carries about 260 fewer passengers than *Voyager,* and while it wasn't exactly intimate, it felt less impersonal. On the other hand (and this may be contradictory), the lack of a true "Prome-nade" deck on *Equinox* gave the ship no hub and kind of a fractured feeling. There was no good way to get from our room at the front of the ship to either of the main dining areas at the back of the ship.

On the first cruise, we had the late seating every night (about 8:30), leaving little time after supper for any shipboard activities. On our second cruise, we dined early (6:00) and I liked that even less as we rushed from shore excursions right to supper. (I once took an Alaskan cruise with "open seating" and found you lose the ship-board connection with the waiters and staff). I guess I should just order room service on future cruises.

The quality of service on both ships was very good. *Voyager* had a climbing wall and an ice skating rink, neither of which seemed especially useful for us. *Equinox* had a glass-blowing setup, which my wife found fascinating. The *Equinox* clientele was unmistakably older. Equinox's food was slightly superior. Our cabins on the *Voyager* were better—a totally unfair comparison since we were issued large handicap rooms. Neither ship had destination "experts" who had much to say.

Favorite Mediterranean ports: As a Francophile, I absolutely loved Aix-en-Provence when we docked at Toulon. Nice was also nice. I like Rome better each time I'm there. My wife loves Barcelona. We will return to Santorini. Athens was great but political and economic strife imposes an uncertain present on a glorious past. Rhodes, Mykonos, and Sicily are already fading from memory. Naples, so full of life and debris, won't fade.

Why people who've never been on a cruise hate them

You probably hate cruises, especially if you've never been on one. Some of the reasons are valid; some are popular stereotypes. Others are just excuses. Let's look at some of the common reasons non-cruisers don't float.

Cruise ships are floating tin can cities teeming with the kind of overfed and underinformed Americans who give us a bad name abroad.

Except for most of them. I've rarely sat down at a table with strangers who didn't have some kind of interesting life story. For some, it's the trip of a lifetime; for others, it's their 25th voyage—often with the same brand. (Extras such as free laundry, wifi and free restaurant options increase as your status goes up). I usually travel with a dozen or more like-minded friends and family, and I can affirm that they are not underinformed. As far as being overfed, yes it can happen. But there's a good chance you would be eating meals at home too. Only not as good, and one of you would have to make them. It's important to study up on the type of clientele the cruise lines draw. On Disney you'll find lots of kids (duh!). *Carnival* features party animals. Norwegian, Princess, Holland America, and Royal Caribbean still value boomers even as they increasingly target millennials while Celebrity aims a little younger. Cunard is the frumpy but regal dowager of the group. At last count, there were 323 cruise ships belonging to 50 cruise lines out there. One of them might work for you.

Having people in such a confined space is bad for health and sanity.

You'll probably spend most of your daytime shipboard hours awash in fresh air and sunshine. Add balmy breezes and sea air at night if you have a balcony cabin. I've gotten sick often enough on my travels, but never on the dozen or so cruises I've taken. I am prone to seasickness, but modern ships with high-tech stabilizers make for a very smooth ride unless you're running down a hurricane. Pro tip: Don't cruise through hurricanes.

You're playing down how crowded it is.

I don't think so. One of the first things I do on a ship is check out calm and remote places to meet and relax. Online discussion groups devoted to your ship of choice are great for finding them. Once we checked out a cigar bar on the ship (horrors!) but discovered there were no cigar smokers aboard. Our group commandeered it as our private meeting place and even held our own euchre tournament there. Another time, we found the premier lounge on the top deck wasn't being used before supper, so we catered our own hors d'oeuvres from the ship's buffet and brought our own wine (allowable up to a point) for a nightly pre-dinner cocktail party. Most cruise ships contain from 2,000 to 5,000 passengers. Select a smaller vessel if you're really intent on avoiding crowds.

One boring destination follows another.

That can happen if you're mismatched with your destination. The Caribbean and the Mediterranean are very different from each other. In the Caribbean, if you are an avid sea, surf, and sand denizen, the islands will each flaunt its own unique attributes. My friend Brion taught me to snorkel on Seven Mile Beach in the Cayman Islands. If you're a culture vulture in the Mediterranean, you leave the boat in the morning like you were shot out of a cannon and return late afternoon exhausted by castles, churches, and ruins. Brion dragged me through Vatican City so slowly and meticulously that three pontiffs had been installed by the time we left. The point is, if you do either one right, you'll return home tired enough to need a vacation. Other places: Fjords in Alaska, Norway, and New Zealand are jaw-droppingly beautiful. Hawaii is spectacular. The Galapagos Islands are remote. So is Australia. Be careful not to pack boredom in your own suitcase.

I don't want to get on a bus every day to go see stuff.

You're thinking of river cruising. Ocean cruising has much less of that (plus the buses aren't included in the price like they are on the river). Our group almost never takes a cruise-sponsored excursion. We will occasionally hire an independent guide. In Athens, eight of us were picked up at the port by two Mercedes taxis and their English-speaking drivers. We spent the day with them touring the city, staying off the buses and away from the crowds, and ate at an authentic Greek restaurant with them. Often cruise ships will dock right in the middle of the action. In Naples, a five-minute walk from the boat will get you delicious Neopolitan pizza at a dozen different cafes. On the island of Rhodes, you are just steps away from the main shopping street. Unlike a river cruise, there's also plenty to do if you stay on the ship. Food, of course, but swimming, gambling, exercising, getting spa treatments, and other entertainments are just a deck away. Or just sun yourself on the top deck.

Cruising is expensive.

Yeah, no. Start from the premise that you are paying for your hotel AND your transportation AND fancy restaurants AND entertainment. This summer, I've been watching prices for some Mediterranean ships hit rock bottom. An eleven-day excursion from Marseilles to Venice reached as low as $414 apiece. That's for an inside room. The balcony room was $887. It included an open bar and several other excellent perks. Vacations to Go monitors all these ships daily and is a great source of information. Of course, you can go the expensive route if you want. Spend $50K for a four-month around-the-world voyage; or abandon the middle-class ships in favor of more exclusive lines such as Silversea, Seabourn, Oceania, or Regent.

Rick Steves would never take a cruise

The legendary television and guidebook guru did just that in 2019. What impressed him were the logistics. For example, if you wanted to see Naples and the Greek island of Rhodes, it would take you an exhausting day of bus, train, and ferry rides to connect them. On a cruise, you just go to sleep in one and wake up in the other. Rick now has three different books dedicated to European cruise ports.

Is there anything you don't like about cruises?

Embarkation. Getting thousands of people and their luggage onto the boat with all their paperwork properly done takes hours, even if they don't screw up, which they often do. The only time we beat the system was when we missed our flight and intercepted the ship three days later. I don't recommend this strategy. I'm rarely impressed by the lame nighttime entertainment aboard ships. Holland America, with its BB King Blues lounges, is an exception. Great musicians and serious music.

I'll cruise when I get old.

It's possible that ship has sailed already (to coin a phrase). But why wait? A cruise requires very little planning. Pick a date, a ship, and a cabin and you're good to go. Don't be afraid to seek out some local guidance. On my last cruise, I decided I needed a more expertise than I possessed. I went to my local AAA office and asked who their cruising expert was. They gave me Clara. She was able to figure some things out that I couldn't and managed to add some travel agency perks to the voyage. You'll still probably need flights to get to the ship, preferably a day or two early so you're less dependent on today's wacky world of flying, where schedules are purely advisory. Sometimes your ship will even offer to book your flights at a reduced rate (such as two-for-one). If you accept their offer, monitor them and keep monitoring them right up until you get on the plane. Often their inventory shifts and stuff happens. Finally, if you have mobility problems, some ships will rent you a motorized scooter that will give you full access to the ship. A company called Scootaround will rent you one for about $200 for a week.

Rent your own canal boat

We've rented canal boats from Le Boat in France three times now. Once in southern France on the Canal du Midi, once in Burgundy, and once in Brittany.

Is renting a canal boat in France as exotic as it sounds?

Yes and no. Do you usually wake up to fresh croissants and coffee from a French press while sunlight filters through a canopy of trees and shimmers on the water? That was a typical morning for us. A typical evening found us parked in the middle of a small village next to a canal-side cafe sipping inexpensive French wine. In between, since our transportation was also our accommodation, we were never far from the comforts of home, be it our beds for a short nap, or our refrigerator for a quick snack.

Was it hard to get there?

A good question. You'll probably have to fly into Paris, but most of the canals are located in semi-rural areas of France. You'll need a plan to get there. The first time, we flew to Paris and took the train to Carcassone directly from the airport. The second time, we tried to take a bus from the Left Bank in Paris to Burgundy (see *Bus to Nowhere* in Chapter 5) but ended up on the train instead. The third time, we flew from Geneva to Rennes (in Brittany) then took a train to a little town south of it.

Did you drive the boat yourself?

We did everything ourselves. It's kind of like renting your own RV, only this has a bow. Although it wasn't necessary to have any boating experience, I was glad we had Captain Curt, a friend of mine who spent a lot of time in his boat on Wisconsin rivers and lakes.

Renting an RV implies some sort of camping. Did your trip resemble that?

In some ways. The boat had two bathrooms with showers, but they were pretty cramped. We found it useful to hook up the electricity to shore a few times to make sure the boat's batteries wouldn't run down. In full-service ports, we also would fill up the water tank. Unlike camping, however, where we docked was usually in the middle of some small town with cafes, bakeries, churches, and markets.

Did it ever get boring?

The scenery was never boring. The canal itself was always shaded by huge trees that framed a beautiful picture wherever you looked. Every few miles a new French town or village presented itself. Physically we were active more than you'd imagine. Locks were always just around the next bend.

What's a lock?

It's a mechanism for raising or lowering the boat to an elevation that matches the topography. Most locks could accommodate about four boats at a time. Chuck and Bob, our designated "lock lackeys," had to jump off the boat, anchor the ropes loosely around a pylon, then feed the rope down as the boat descended. Most passages were a half hour or less, but waits of an hour or more weren't uncommon when traffic was heavy.

Was there much boat traffic?

There were times when we felt completely alone and times when we wished for a traffic cop on the canal. Mostly it was a sporadic succession of encounters with boats coming the other way, most of them smaller than our own. Once in Brittany, we sailed up a small dead-end canal. No actual boat traffic but we had to watch out for tourists in little rented pedal boats. We encountered a few Dutch boats on the canals, chatted with some Brits and saw many multi-generational French families. What we never saw on any of the canals were other Americans. The last two times, we rented two eight-passenger boats. It slowed us down because both boats couldn't always fit in the lock together so we'd have to wait.

What did you do for food?

We ate about half our meals on the boat, ranging from a spaghetti feast to omelets to ham sandwiches with great local cheese on a baguette. The galley was sufficiently large for the eight of us, and the stove and two small refrigerators were up to the task. Since we usually docked for the night right in the middle of a small town, there was always a cafe, pizzeria, or restaurant literally a few feet away.

Were the two bikes you carried useful?

Peggy and I often served as the "rabbits," on the Canal du Midi, riding up ahead of the boat or into a nearby town to check things out. (We had lots of time because the boat's top speed was six miles per hour.) In one memorable moment at a lock, a handsome young Frenchman stopped Peggy, who was having some difficulty adjusting to the bike. "I theenk it is better if you do zees," he said, turning her handlebars around the right way. I told him, "She didn't do well in the Tour de France."

How much did it cost?

Our latest trip in 2022 was about $5,000 for a week on the boat with eight people. It was all paid up front, with no annoying add-ons (like you might get for a rental car). We used Le Boat and were very happy with them. Port facilities all along the canal appeared to be operational although COVID did manage to close some of them down.

Try a repo cruise next fall

Twice a year, cruise ships change climates. In Spring, most move from a Caribbean location to summer in places like Europe and Alaska. In fall, they reverse the process.

These are called repositioning cruises or "repo" cruises.

Ships used to sail with just crews until the cruise lines figured out that many passengers would pay to cross an ocean in anything but a cramped economy airplane seat.

Using sites such as Vacations to Go and Cruise Critic, I came up with 10 Fall cruises from Europe to the US that seemed most reasonable. The 2023 prices are included as a comparison guideline. Who knows what subsequent years will bring?

Here's my version of reasonable repo cruises.

1. Time. It takes a minimum of a week to cross the Atlantic in a ship. Most repo cruises stretch it out for several more days to add attractive stops in places like Spain and Portugal on the east end or Nassau and the Bahamas in the west. Some also make mid-ocean stops in the Azores or Bermuda. The ships I chose included between 7 and 15 nights. You can take several weeks or even months if you choose.

2. Money. These cruises are usually promoted as bargains and most are, by cruise ship standards. For consistency, I priced each one as two people sharing a cabin with a balcony. You can sail cheaper with an inside or ocean-view cabin, but you can also sail up the economic ladder into suites or specialty areas of a ship for thousands of dollars more. The cheapest of the ten I selected was 11 nights on the Celebrity Silhouette on October 22 for $733 per person. The most expensive was also a Celebrity ship, the Beyond, which cost $1946 for 14 nights, sailing on October 30.

3. Leaving. The most common embarkation point was Southampton, a few hours south of London by train. The *Disney Dream* (Sept. 17), *Regal Princess* (Oct 9), *Norwegian Getaway* (Oct. 22), and *Celebrity Silhouette* (Oct. 22), all leave from there. So does the *Cunard Queen Mary 2*, which we'll discuss later. Barcelona is the gateway for *Celebrity Reflection* (Oct. 19), *Royal Caribbean Symphony of the Seas* (Oct. 29), and *Virgin Valiant Lady* (Oct. 29). Two others leave from Rome: *Celebrity Beyond* (Oct. 30) and *Explorer of the Seas* (Oct. 29).

4. Arriving. Five of the ships end in Fort Lauderdale, three in New York, and two in Miami.

5. Personal comfort. For obvious meteorological reasons, most ships cross the Atlantic in October. It's just after the Fall hurricane season and just before the gales of November that drove the *Edmund Fitzgerald* to its watery grave. I'm prone to seasickness, but rarely am afflicted on these giant ships. Some passengers have reported extremely uncomfortable conditions on rough crossings, but most find it doesn't impact their deep dive into the lunch buffet on the top deck. One other consideration for this Wisconsin boy: What good is a balcony cabin if you're using glass doors to distance yourself from sleet and ice? That's why I eliminated anything after Hallow-een (although taking a very southern route may temper my concerns somewhat). My earliest selection was Disney (Sept. 17) and latest was *Celebrity Beyond* (Oct. 30).

This brings us to the Cunard line. Their weekly sailings between Southampton and New York City can't be called repo cruises be-cause that route IS their regular route. But they should be consid-ered here because this last vestige of the glory days of cruising does potentially compete with the trendy modern ships for at least two months of the year.

Perhaps for that competitive reason, the *Queen Mary 2* sails to New York in September and November but skips October. The Sep-tember 4 sailing will cost you $1,696 for the seven days at sea (no stops) in your balcony cabin. The Sept. 22 sailing must be approach-ing a sellout because it's up to a startling $2,918.

You won't find skating rinks and go-kart tracks on the *Queen Mary*, but you will find old-fashioned grace and style, replete with formal nights that will finally allow you to wear that tuxedo you picked up at Goodwill. You'll also find a smoother ride. With four stabilizers instead of the usual two, the ship is built to thrive on the ocean.

What's my choice after sampling the best of the repo offer-ings? I'm considering the *Regal Princess*, which sails from South-ampton to Fort Lauderdale on October 9, although, since yester-day, the price has risen from $1,270 to $1,331 on Vacations to Go. What I like is the early sailing, the cruise line (Princess), and the European stopovers: Le Havre, Bilbao and La Coruna in Spain, Lisbon, and the Azores. The flip side is that you can't just consider your 15 days aboard ship. If you're flying to England, you might as well include a few days in London before returning home, thus adding in further costs for hotels, food, and transportation in this expensive city.

That brings us to your connecting flights. One-way flights have gotten better and cheaper but still may be substantial in cost. I found an Air Portugal fare from Chicago to London for under $300, but I'd expect the cost to be around $600 (or more) most of the time. The flight from Fort Lauderdale back to Chicago prices out under $200 (for an American flight) or $100 (if you want to endure Spirit), but at least you won't need a hotel night, since the ship docks at 6:00 am on October 24.

A travel agent friend of mine told me not to give up on the idea of buying my flights from the cruise line (which I have done in the past). Even if I buy the cruise from an agency such as Vacations to Go (which I have also done in the past), I can later contact the cruise line (Princess, in the example above) to see if their inventory of flights matches what I need at a reasonable price.

You can find more information on these ten ships at vacations-togo.com

Kralendijk, Bonaire

Chapter 9 - Economics
Paying for your trips

Welcome to Bonaire

Kris and I had just barely dragged our carry-ons out of United's weekly flight from Houston to Bonaire down to the tarmac when passengers were separated into two lines—not for the immigration desks guarding the doors to the terminal—but for payment (or nonpayment) of Bonaire's new $75 tourist tax.

Several uniformed young people welcomed mostly older people to the small island by patiently helping them get out of airplane mode and use their

Cashing out in Cuba

My trip to Europe in 1974 and my trip to Cuba in 2024 shared an unexpected commonality. I used cash. The first trip featured French francs, Belgian francs, Dutch guilders, and British pounds. My trip to Cuba required dollars and euros.

Why not Cuban money? No one wanted it. With an inflation rate of 38%, any hard currency was preferable.

Why not credit cards? US cards don't work there.

Why not travelers' cheques? Oh, come on. Now you're dating yourself.

Using dollars, I bought some potato chips at a sparse official grocery. It felt almost furtive.

cell phones to scan the QR code emblazoned on every available vertical surface. Our group was the one that hadn't paid the fee ahead of time.

I had just completed the online form and was about to dig out my credit card when I mentioned to the young functionary that I was boarding a cruise ship the next day. I was hoping for an exemption.

It arrived. "Oh, you don't have to pay the tax if you're going to be here less than 24 hours," she replied, dismissing us from QR purgatory on the condition that I identify the ship.

That ship, the *Norwegian Jewel*, would disgorge about 3,000 passengers onto the island the next morning, including a dozen friends of mine who had gotten on in Panama. I couldn't imagine any of those couples handing over the cost of a hotel night just to roam around another Caribbean paradise for a day, so exempting cruise passengers was a wise move.

We breezed through security and entered the terminal. There was a scrum of people hovering over a single carousel full of bags whose owners were probably charging their phones.

Beyond security the scene was much the same, as small groups waited for other small groups in scenes of mild chaos, and passenger vans parked irregularly with their doors open. The largest contingent of people consisted of locals standing silently, holding hopeful signs with single names on them.

I got my first taste of how Dutch the island was when I approached one of them, a middle-aged woman who wouldn't have been out of place in a Rembrandt painting. I asked her where the taxi queue was. She gestured vaguely toward a quiet car-free area and replied in Dutch-accented English, concluding "if you can find one."

There actually was a cab sitting there, motionless, dark, and seemingly abandoned by its driver. I kept looking.

Eventually, I went back to Mrs. Rembrandt. Her guests, no doubt still outside the terminal writing computer code, had yet to appear.

"I'll drop you off at your hotel if you haven't found a taxi by the time my guests come," she said kindly, adding, "It's not far."

In the meantime, the driver of what was apparently the only cab on the island had returned from his break. He already had two fares for the Courtyard by Marriott Dive Resort, our hotel. As we left, I could see Mrs. Rembrandt greet the first of her arrivals, who had finally managed to pay the entry tax, probably through bulk purchase of Target gift cards.

Our ride to the hotel was so short, we may not have left second gear. It cost ten American dollars, or about five dollars a minute.

The "dive" in our resort referred not to seediness but to SCUBA diving. The hotel actually appeared quite nice in the soft and breezy Caribbean darkness, with attractive lights and shadows playing on brightly painted surfaces.

Soon we were enjoying Amstel Bright beer and dissecting the catch of the day—barracuda—in the resort's open-air waterside restaurant. Palm trees swayed, soft music played, and I was glad I had put my down vest away.

Paying Manfred

Sometimes it's hard to give away money. I owed Manfred $1,000. He had hauled 14 of us around Heidelberg, Germany providing us with a delightful tour of Heidelberg Castle and old town. I tipped him (about 5 euros apiece) but he wouldn't let me pay him when the tour concluded. "I'll just send you an invoice."

I didn't realize at the time this meant I had to care more about his money than Manfred did. And outgoing money is especially tedious. After this eye-opening experience, I wouldn't be surprised if there are still transfers waiting to be completed in European banks with lira, a currency that disappeared more than 20 years ago.

Whatever. When I got back to the US, I found Manfred's email and dutifully logged into his payment portal. Using my American Airlines credit card, I attempted to pay him. Twice. The card wouldn't go through.

Whatever again. I tried to use my United Airlines credit card. Same thing. It turned out that Manfred, who is fairly new to the touring fraternity, was getting grief from other US customers for the same credit card problem and thought he had a solution.

He asked if I'd be willing to do a bank transfer. My experience with international bank transfers is they're as complicated as a lunar landing but with less chance of success. I agreed to try.

To make it easier, Manfred, a Heidelberg native who had lived in South Carolina for several years, asked me to transfer the money to his US account. He included a detailed set of instructions with account numbers, SWIFT numbers (more on those later), wire transfer numbers, and routing numbers. Plus an intermediary of some kind called "TransferWise."

By then, I was starting to wonder if I should just offer to go to Target and get him $1,000 in gift cards.

Whatever. I showed up at my little credit union the next afternoon armed with Manfred's instructions. Three of us spent a good 20-30 minutes poring over numbers, looking things up, and pondering the vastness of the world's financial institutions. We came up with a plan. I would get Manfred to corroborate his account numbers with the name of his US bank, (which for some reason was not included in the instructions) and the credit union would hold onto the transfer until morning.

I got home about five o'clock and immediately emailed Manfred. Even though it was midnight where he was, Manfred's instant response corroborated the name of the bank. He offered to pay the credit union's $20 charge for the process. I felt good giving the credit union the go-ahead and moving on from this time-consuming task.

Surprise. It's not that easy. The credit union emailed me the next morning with the bad news that they couldn't do it. Only bigger institutions (like banks) had a SWIFT code that allowed them to make international money transfers. They didn't have one, so I was out of luck.

At this point, I checked out the Lufthansa booking site to see I could catch a quick flight to Germany and hand the euros to Manfred when I landed. But it was Lufthansa, the airline that had muffed my last reservation so badly that it gave me 20 minutes to make an international connection. Never mind.

I went to my local bank. Our account there is normally the province of my wife so I try not to complicate things by actually using it. I found Becca there, a delightful person who appeared to have a lot of experience with international transfers. She assured me that the bank did indeed have a SWIFT code. I produced Manfred's instructions and she had the money ready to go in 10 minutes. The bad news was that it would cost me $50. I gave the go-ahead anyway.

Manfred was perplexed because he thought it was a simple domestic transfer to his US account. He again offered to pick up costs, although it was too late for that.

Whatever. At least it's done and everybody's happy.

The bank called me the next morning and left a message. The

transfer didn't work. Did I know this was a domestic transfer and not an international one? Why, yes. I did. How did they not know that? Maybe I can fly Manfred here.

Anyway, they needed me to come back in with Manfred's instructions so they could proceed down the domestic route.

When I got there, I told Becca I had been expecting her call. "These things never go well." She just smiled the confident smile of money and took Manfred's instructions off to make a copy.

"We don't need the SWIFT code after all," she said, traveling down the same path as my credit union, but in the opposite direction. "It's just domestic, so Manfred should have his money within three hours."

"Is the fee the same?" I asked. She hadn't seemed to have thought about it but recovered quickly. "Instead of $50 it should be $30. We'll credit your account." I quickly emailed Manfred the news, suspecting that he was getting just as tired of the process as I was.

"Zahlangsempfanger," was the response I got from him. My knowledge of German is poor, especially for a guy named "Schmidt" whose grandparents spoke German at the Sheepshead table. I think I know the exact same word in English though.

"Whatever."

Get cash at the Banco do Brasil

*D*on't you long for the days when getting foreign money was as easy as cashing a travelers' check instead of hunting down a friendly ATM that won't devour your card or charge usurious rates? Maybe not. Here's what I experienced in Porto Alegre, Brazil in the waning days of the travelers' check era. Don't be thrown by the verbiage. I wrote it in second person (you) because it felt like people were continually telling me what to do in what I expected to be a simple process.

Talk to the hotel desk clerk. He tells you the Banco do Brasil is the only one willing to take a chance on someone of your character. Here's a map. Now go.

Take a couple of big dudes with you into the teeming streets. Call them Bruno and Dirk (actually Bob and Paul).

Arrive at Banco do Brasil. No, not THAT Banco do Brasil, *estu-*

pido, the one down the hill on the Avenue do Urugui. Can't you read a map? Ask the guard. You can tell she's using her best Portuguese to direct you to the other bank.

Go there. Enter the revolving doors on the right side of the bank. When the guard blocks your way, go back out the doors and enter the revolving doors on the left.

Stand in line at the bank's information desk. Take a number off the machine and sit down. No, not on the left side of the room. Sit on the right side.

Wait for 20 minutes for your number to be called. Remember that you don't know what the number 587 sounds like in Portuguese, but don't worry because they won't call any numbers anyway.

Keep smiling benignly at the woman behind the desk. Her name is Nila. She is tranquil. She is unhurried. She is sipping good Brazilian decaf. You look at Bruno and Dirk. They are sleeping. Finally Nila waves you into a chair across the desk from her.

Nila knows what you want. Brazilian *reales.* She barely glances at the two $50 Visa travelers' checks you shyly slide her way. She writes down a number on a piece of paper. $20 U.S. Her Portuguese is clear. You are now changing $80 not $100. The Banco do Brasil will keep the rest. You weakly nod yes. You have already tried six cash machines that laugh at your Cirrus card, and your supply of *reales* has dropped dangerously low.

Nila disappears behind a partition with your Visa checks, holding them as if spittle were slowly befouling them. Five minutes pass. Ten minutes. You're thinking maybe Nila called someone to check up on you. Your mom, maybe. You're not sure if she'll vouch for you.

Soon Nila returns. There is a problem. Your Visa checks say "Independent Bankers Association of America" on the top. You never noticed that before. You don't know who the hell they are. Neither does the Banco do Brasil. Visa probably doesn't know either. Anyway, Nila wants to know where these bankers are located. You answer with the name of your hometown, an absolute lie, and point to the town's name on your passport. Nila nods gravely and disappears again. You are without hope.

Nila is back. You are glad to see her. You have missed her. You are sad that she must turn you down. But wait, she has papers, three full-sized, single-spaced sheets tightly jammed with information.

Your loan application to buy a condo on the Amazon has been approved. Focus. Congratulations, your travelers' checks are good at Banco do Brasil. Money? No, no, we don't do that here. You must go to Box 7 to actually exchange travelers checks for *reales*.

You give Nila a hug, tell her in broken Portuguese you hope to see her again sometime and smile warmly. Bruno and Dirk, jarred awake in their metal chairs, follow you out the revolving doors. You shuffle your packet of papers in an agitated way. You have no idea where Box 7 is.

Magically, Nila reappears. She knows this is hard for someone like you. She leads you through the revolving doors on the right and takes you past the guard to a waiting elevator. You lose Dirk and Bruno. "Box 7," she says to the elevator operator magisterially. As the doors close, Nila again disappears.

When they open again, you see people lined up in front of eight windows. Box 7 already has a customer there. You stand behind her.

"Not there," scowls the man in the white shirt from behind the counter. He says it in Portuguese, but you marvel at how well you are learning the language. Sit in a chair, he waves. No, not that chair, one on the right side. You sit.

After the woman in front of you has finished probating her late husband's will, it is your turn. The man is not mad at you anymore. But he does carefully examine your passport for nitroglycerine and, of course, spittle stains.

Reluctantly he gets his stamp out and starts punching it into any open spaces on the sheaf of papers that you give him. He has you sign your name, apparently for practice, before you can actually countersign the checks.

Finally, yes finally, he opens up a hidden cash drawer and Brazilian *reales* appear in a tray. He counts out 232 of them and shoves them your way without ceremony. You wish Nila were with you to see this.

Out in the street, Dirk and Bruno are happy to see you again, although you aren't really sure they knew you were gone. You'd like to repay them for their commitment, but they'll have to wait until you get back to the states.

Those *reales* are just too valuable to actually spend.

Trip insurance weasels

Do you buy travel insurance every time you take a trip? As you get older, you'll find more reasons why you need it. There are too many horror stories out there of people getting ill, hurt or even dying who end up with enormous bills because of a lack of coverage.

While I've been lucky, I have a friend who wasn't. He paid $70,000 for a medical evacuation from Iceland to the US after a bone-breaking fall on a street. He had travel insurance but they somehow managed to weasel out of repaying him. Hiring a lawyer only sent good money chasing after bad.

So what should you do?

Maybe you're counting on Medicare to cover your costs. If you're overseas, it won't. Maybe your supplemental insurance covers it. Not likely unless you specifically asked for it.

The coverage I've used in the past came from a website called Squaremouth.com. I went there before every trip and compared products from various companies and bought one according to my current needs. I liked being able to select what I wanted covered and just paying for what I needed. For example, I put a low priority on accommodations costs and a high priority on evacuations. Your situation may be different or it may vary from trip to trip.

As my travel increased, I found a more permanent solution. I bought a one-year policy from Allianz. The AllTrips Premier policy covers trips for my wife and me for 365 days at a cost of $475. (Other choices: $270 for the basic plan or $1,000 for the executive plan). The only personal information they required was age.

Highlights include emergency transportation ($500,000 per person); emergency medical ($50,000); travel accident coverage ($50,000); trip cancellation ($2,000); baggage loss ($2,000) and a few other things.

There's an app for my phone with policy information and a 24 hour-a-day assistance number along with what they call a "concierge."

In my research, I discovered that Allianz has an excellent reputation and is one of the larger companies with the most resources. Hopefully, I won't have occasion to use it. To check it out, go to allianztravelinsurance.com.

Paying for travel with time

For a person of modest means, say a teacher, paying for travel can be burdensome on the family budget. We may live in the Golden Age of Travel, but it's mostly not free (unless you live in Luxembourg where public transportation—buses, trains, trams—all are completely free for the riders).

There is a currency, however, that is just as readily accepted as money. In fact, it's probably more valuable. You can make more money but certainly cannot make more time.

Finding situations where you willingly provide your time is a key that opens many travel doors.

I found this out early playing in a semi-successful rock band. People paid us to travel all around the state so we could entertain them. They paid for our travel. Because I loved music, the travel and the money seemed like bonuses to me, not financial transactions.

Later, I discovered that my ability to write, and my willingness to invest my time in it, also provided travel currency. I found a small ad in the *Chicago Tribune* put there by the government of the Netherlands. The small country wanted to celebrate 200 years of Dutch/American friendship by bringing 200 ordinary Americans to Holland. In 50 words or less, I needed to tell them why I should be one of the 200.

I crafted about a dozen entries and one of them was a winner. (For legal reasons, contests will generally not indicate which entry won). A few months later, Kris and I were on our way to Amsterdam as guests of the Dutch government for a gigantic week-long celebration. We met local mayors and dignitaries, partied with beer magnate, Alfred Heineken, overindulged at a Brueghel banquet, stayed in excellent hotels and capped off the trip at the Rijksmuseum, the country's pre-eminent museum. There, in front of Rembrandt's *Night Watch*, Kris presented to Queen Beatrix a handmade needlepoint of the postage stamp both countries had issued.

I used the same time-consuming strategy to enter the *Ruffles Have Ridges* contest sponsored by Lay's potato chips. Winning the top prize would have cemented my travel for at least the next decade. It was a beautiful Recreational Vehicle. I took second and received $1,000 instead, a pretty major drop-off. This time I'm pretty sure I know which of my entries prevailed. I was only allotted 25 words, but I had to answer the question, "Why do Ruffles have ridges?" My entry went something like this: *In ancient Greece, Zeus, king of the gods, was jealous of the beautiful Ruffles so he turned her into a constellation. Today, we know her as the Big Dipper.* OK, they weren't looking for Faulkner. And yes, I know, that's 29 words. Some of you counted.

In 2000, I parlayed my time spent doing political work into delegate status at the Democratic National Convention in Los Angeles as an Al Gore delegate. Yes, I know, I should have worked harder in the election. Anyway, the position was only partially funded and Wisconsin was assigned a pricey hotel in Beverly Hills. I called WEAC (the teachers' union) and asked if they had any other single delegates going who were willing to share a room. They offered me a choice: A guy who was also named Glenn, or Curt, who taught in the little town of DeSoto, Wisconsin. "I ain't rooming with no Glenn," I replied with grammatical emphasis. Thus began a great friendship with Curt, whom you've encountered multiple times in this book.

By far the biggest devourer of my time and main travel provider was the teachers' union. In 1982, I won a local election as a delegate to the National Education Association's annual Representative Assembly, also in Los Angeles. It was life changing. I saw up close the impact a union could have on people's lives.

Eight years later, I became local president. Matt, my mentor and president before me, also appears in this book as a fellow traveler, mostly in a yodeling capacity.

I did that job for 13 years then moved up to the state and national Boards of Directors, where policy is made for the union. My eight years attending NEA Board meetings and lobbying members of Congress in DC coincided almost exactly with those of George W. Bush, the man who defeated the aforementioned Mr. Gore. Since the White House was only three blocks from the NEA building, I invariably walked over there to check if Mr. Bush still lived there. Yup. I flew to DC about 50 times during that era and came to know the city well.

I took particular interest in global education and teachers' unions around the world. At the time, they were grouped into four different unions. Although the NEA and the American Federation of Teachers were bitter rivals at the time, they came together with all four international unions to create one great union of teachers: Education International, headquartered in Brussels, Belgium. I was privileged to be at the formal initiation ceremony in Stockholm in January 1993 and vividly remember waiters carrying flaming desserts down the steps of City Hall, the same venue that recognizes Nobel Prize winners.

I subsequently attended EI World Congresses every few years in Berlin, Porto Allegre, Brazil, Washington, DC, Cape Town, South Africa, and Ottawa. Most were just partially funded. The one time I would have been fully funded was Berlin in 2007 when I ran to represent the NEA Board of Directors. I lost by one vote, the only union election I didn't win.

The exchange of time for travel ultimately benefitted both the union and me. I took my duties seriously and rarely missed a meeting. Sometimes, I played a specific role, such as hosting a press conference about special education alongside Senator John Kerry in DC or writing the NEA president's speech at an international meeting in Berlin. Other times serious business gave way to enjoying a destination with union friends.

Consider what organizations or work-related opportunities are available to you. You may be surprised how many of them include travel. Depending on the current exchange rate of time for travel, your real life and your travel life may be able to find common ground.

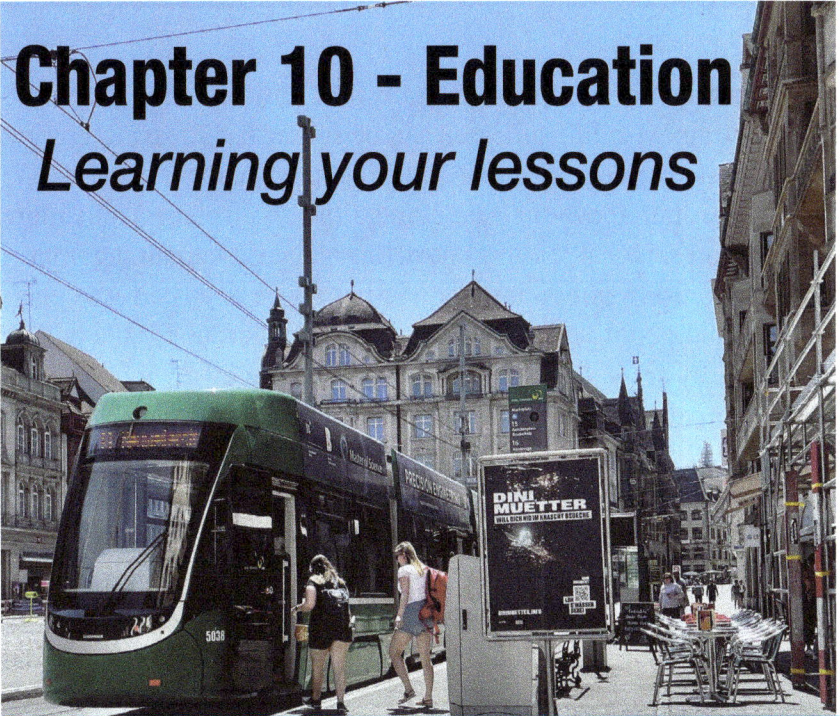

Chapter 10 - Education
Learning your lessons

Basel, Switzerland

Tips on transportation in Europe

Iprefer to travel independently rather than with a tour group, and, over the years, one of the benefits of planning my own travel has been achieving a level of expertise in the various transportation systems abroad. On this trip to Europe, my wife, Kris, and I and four friends used quite a few different conveyances to get around, many of which we booked before we left the US.

Fly the golden skies

I'm golden. American says so. When I was flying a lot for the union, I received gold status for a brief, unremarkable period.

My two AA credit cards (from Citi Bank and Barclay's) recently earned my way back to gold. American makes more money off my cards than it does from my flights.

So what? My luggage flies free. I board early (more bin space for carryons), I'm at the front of standby lines, and agent service is more helpful. I even got upgraded to Business on my last flight.

I'll still go with the best flight deals. I just hope they're American.

Trains

Train travel in Europe is generally safe, efficient, and fast. Traveling by train with full suitcases can be somewhat stressful, however. I remember older trains that had large luggage racks at either end of each car, but above-the-seat storage (as on airplanes) was more common on this trip. Lifting my wife's suitcase containing what I can only guess was her anvil collection above my head was challenging, and getting it back down, mildly dangerous for the people in the nearby seats. Important: If you are sitting by a window, don't leave your carry-on bag or purse on the empty seat next to you. One of our traveling companions did that on a train from Amsterdam to Belgium, and just a few stops out of the city, a well-practiced thief ran down the aisle, grabbed her bag and disappeared out the train doors just as they were closing.

We took trains three times on this 16-day trip to Amsterdam, Bruges, London, England's Lake District and Galway. Each rail journey took from two to three hours.

The Amsterdam-to-Bruges trip and Bruges to London cost $60 to $70 apiece. The one in England (London to Manchester) cost less than half that.

Timing is important when purchasing tickets. The best deals are usually available about 90 days before departure and should be booked for nonpeak times (i.e., not during rush hour). Last year, we paid about twice as much for a train trip from Glasgow to Windermere as we did for the return because I didn't know this rule.

The amount of walking required for train travel should not be underestimated, especially for those with mobility issues. In Brussels, we had 14 minutes to connect to our train to Bruges — a substantial amount by European standards. The transfer required walking several hundred yards from the end of one train into the terminal, finding the right platform for the next train, then walking a few hundred yards more to our designated railcar on another level. All this was done with luggage amid crowds of people attempting to do the same thing.

At London's Euston Station, I was especially irritated to discover they use the same ridiculous grouping system as is used in British airports. The platform number of your train is concealed from you until the last possible moment. By the time it is finally revealed, you have mere minutes to find the platform and drag your luggage to it. In this case, it was Platform One, at the end of the station and 17 cars down the track. We just made it.

All three European trains that we took were comfortable, although the air-conditioning in our car on the British train wasn't working right. (On my way to the food car, I passed through several much cooler cars.)

The Thalys train from Amsterdam to Bruges and the Chunnel train to London were both high-speed. I have an app for my phone called Speed Box that clocked speeds as high as 186 mph on each trip.

Planes

We flew on the bargain-basement carrier Ryanair from Manchester to Dublin, paying about a hundred dollars apiece for the hourlong flight. (If we had been traveling without luggage, we could have flown for less than $20.) The comfort level was not high. Even though we held boarding passes for what is considered business class on that airline, we were forced to wait in line for about 40 minutes to check our luggage. Another long line at security gave way to almost an hour in the holding pen.

After waiting for the big reveal — "Go to Gate 52. Now." — we stood in line at the gate for the plane to actually arrive. When it did, we were herded down three flights of what felt like an emergency stairwell. More waiting on the steps ensued while the incoming passengers deplaned. Finally, they opened the doors so we could race across the tarmac and board the plane from both the front and back.

Taxis

We used taxis on this trip more than we have in the past, mostly because our time at each place was so limited. However, instead of a cab, my wife and I took bus 197 from the Amsterdam airport to the museum district ($5.50). We then walked about five blocks in a light rain to our hotel. The other four people in our group did take a cab. They paid about 10 each and were dropped off dry at the door of the hotel.

Two days later, we had the hotel arrange a van to the train station for all six of us. Luckily, we had built in plenty of time before our scheduled departure because we ended up spending about 15 minutes sitting in the stopped van while the veteran taxi driver argued with a young policeman about whether he had a right to drive on the street's tram tracks.

The cabbies we encountered in London were efficient but did their jobs with a level of indifference that bordered on arrogance. London cabs do not have trunks, and our drivers felt no need to leave their throne to help while we struggled with how to configure the luggage (Hint — There's extra storage in front next to the driver.)

Buses, trams and subways

Generally, public transportation systems are the best way of getting around European cities, although we used them sparingly this time. We took a very comfortable Citylink bus from Dublin's airport to Galway for about $16. We also spent a day on a tour in Galway that included a bus ride to the Cliffs of Moher and a boat trip to the Aran Islands. The $45 price for the all-day tour was hard to beat, and the driver was knowledgeable and entertaining. (For more information, visit *www.galwaytourcompany.com*.)

Bikes

Guidebook writer Pauline Frommer adamantly warns against renting a bike in Amsterdam. Though we briefly considered it, we ultimately chose to follow her advice.

Bikes rule the city. Ruthlessly.

My brother and I rented bikes in Copenhagen — another terrific biking town — and had a great time, but Amsterdam is a breed apart because of the volatile mix of cars, trams, pedestrians and bikes.

Rental cars

We rented cars twice on this trip, once in England and again in Ireland. If you're intimidated by narrow left-handed roads with blind turns in unfamiliar cars with the steering wheel on the wrong side, don't drive in these countries.

Driving in Ireland and Britain is a group activity, with at least one navigator needed while others in the car alert the driver to surprises (such as sheep in the road ahead) or attempt to guess the right exit in a roundabout.

On a map, the Avis location in Manchester Piccadilly (downtown) looked very close to the train station, but in reality, it was in what had to be one of the least desirable parts of the city, somewhere behind and below the station.

My friend Chuck and I spent about an hour tracking it down, renting the car, and returning to the station for our passengers, who were waiting with the luggage.

Our Irish Hertz rental was a midsize automatic — much easier to drive than the outsized minivan they gave us in England as an "upgrade." Although both vehicles on this trip were automatics, most of the time I rent the much cheaper and more common standard-transmission cars (though shifting with your left hand takes some practice).

Having a GPS in the car (either personal or built-in) is mandatory, as far as I'm concerned. We found that street signs were rare and erratically placed, directions (such as north or south) were absent from highway road signs, and upcoming turns were often completely blind.

On foot

Walking is still my favorite way of getting around, and our Fitbit rarely measured fewer than 10,000 steps in a day (and often significantly more).

The following were among some great walks: a morning ramble through London to the Apple Store to get my phone fixed; a torch (flashlight) walk on a pitch-black country lane in Cumbria that opened onto hilly fields full of iridescent white dots that proved to be sheep, and a pleasant mile talking golf with a Canadian academic on Inisheer, the smallest of the Aran Islands.

Ireland a good choice for your first European trip

My friend Jerry and his wife had never been to Europe before. They identified Ireland as the place to celebrate a significant wedding anniversary and asked me to help.

After a few preliminary questions, I asked how they planned to get around. Jerry thought maybe they would bicycle around the Emerald Isle. I'm sure I turned white. "Only if you have a death wish," I managed to reply.

If you've driven on left-handed British roads, you know how narrow they can be and how hedgerows and stone fences squeeze the roadway to the bare minimum. Irish roads add one more feature—ninety degree turns every few hundred yards, meaning one blind corner after another. It all adds up to a very scary bike ride.

Jerry asked, "Well, what about public transportation, such as trains?" There are some, I replied, but they mainly fan out from Dublin, making travel between places other than Dublin pretty tedious.

That leaves car rental. It can be a little scary at first, but a car does allow you to get to the places you went to Ireland to see: the Cliffs of Moher, Kylemore Abbey, and the Neolithic burial grounds at Newgrange, for example.

Seeing Ireland by car also allows you to take advantage of an outstanding system of bed and breakfasts, most of which are reachable no other way. Go on TripAdvisor for advice on some good ones.

Driving can be fairly expensive, however, and good insurance coverage is a must. Don't be surprised if the insurance costs more than the car. Check out insuremyrentalcar.com for car insurance that isn't so pricey. If you're planning to use your credit card's insurance coverage, check the fine print. Almost no cards cover car rentals in Ireland.

Ireland has a lot of plusses though, which makes the transportation hassle worth it. It uses the euro; its residents speak English with a lovely accent, are seriously friendly and more interested in your heritage than you are.

Its proximity to the US means that trans-Atlantic airfares are always among the cheapest you'll find.

The harder and easier parts of Bastogne

This was written in the jet-lagged 4:00 am silence of a five-bedroom Air BnB house on the Belgian side of the border with Luxembourg that we rented for the month of June for about $100 per day.

Let's start with a pro tip for those of you who carry your laptop with you when you travel: Keep your chocolate bars separate from it. Especially those chocolate bars featuring caramel, a fine ingredient except when you are removing it from your keyboard.

Starting my writing day was harder than expected. Here are some other observations from the past 24 hours that reflect things that were harder than expected or easier.

Brewing coffee: Harder

The European alternative to Keurig is something called Senseo, a system of brewing coffee that produces coffee just as marginal as Keurig only in a less intuitive way. I hate having to watch a YouTube video in the morning just to be able to make coffee. Especially at 4 am.

Icelandair: Easier

This was the first time I flew with them, but it was not an unpleasant experience. Yes, they switched flights on me at the last minute, sent my flight notices to my wife instead of me, were very late getting us to our connection in Reykavik, refused to provide a sandwich I had paid for online, and lost one of our suitcases, but I was very grateful for the glass of water they provided on board and for the exit row seat. The bar is so low for flying these days, isn't it?

My friend, Curt: Much harder

He was supposed to meet us in Iceland, but he ended up in a hospital in Reykavik after breaking an arm and a leg. He had bought trip insurance the week before he left the US for $70. That's good, because when he was Med-flighted home 14 days later on a Lear Jet, the cost was $70,000. Check the piece "Trip Insurance Weasels" in Chapter 9 to see how that came out.

Leasing a car: Easier

Renting a car is the thing I hate most about travel. My favorite travel writer, Paul Theroux (*The Great Railway Bazaar*), made a career of mixing with the locals on public transportation. I knew his traveling days were coming to a close when near the end of *Dark Star Safari,* he actually rented a car in Africa. I'm no Paul Theroux. Instead of renting, I leased a Citroen Picasso minivan in Paris. I received a better rate, full insurance coverage, a completely new vehicle, and the ability to have other people drive it without asking anyone for permission.

Making a phone call: Harder

How to use a cell phone overseas is the most common question I get when I do my travel presentations. I'll save that overall discussion for another time and just talk about the mystery of making a phone call. My directions were to call the car leasing company when I arrived in Paris and they'd send a van to the terminal for us. How hard is that? I dialed five different ways until I finally got through. Here's what finally worked for me: First, I dialed 00 to call another country from my US phone; second, I dialed the country code for the destination number (33 in this case, the code for France); finally I dialed the 8-digit number for the leasing company.

Connecting with AirBnB: Easier

Our host, Lucie, was waiting for us when we arrived at her place near Bastogne, Belgium despite our delays for lost luggage, a few minor wrong turns, switching tired drivers several times, and torrential rain. She shared some of the house's quirks with us, such as the washing machine in the garage and of course, bathrooms, which conceal their share of European mysteries. I will admit that I should have listened more closely when she told us where to shut off the smoke detector (it was in the garage). A few days later, it shrieked its way through our nerve endings for 10 minutes before we were able to muzzle it.

A baker's dozen of security/customs encounters

Usually going through security or customs is a routine event— *except when it's not. Long lines, intrusive questions, kids, dogs, world events, illness, suspicious packages (usually explainable) and more can combine to make the event memorable. Here are a dozen experiences that have lodged themselves into my memory banks.*

Bogota, Colombia

As noted in Chapter 7, fellow teacher, Bob Fullmer, and I were representing the National Education Association on an AFL-CIO mission to a dysfunctional Colombia in the early 2000's. When we left, we had to go through five levels of security at Bogota Airport, with some of the checkpoints appearing in random hallways after we thought we were finally cleared. Our relief in watching the rooftops of Bogota fade into the distance was palpable.

Paris, France

I gotta get a belt with a plastic buckle. The ones I have always set off security alarms. I don't like taking my belt off, because, well, it seems to perform the very necessary function of holding up my pants. I didn't take it off (the belt, not my pants) going through Paris security. After the travel portal rejected me, I was instructed to remove the belt. This I did, forgetting that my security pouch was attached to it. The pouch, with passport, cash and credit cards, stealthily slid down my leg onto the ground and sat there unnoticed for several minutes. If a stranger hadn't said, "Hey, is that yours?" I would have had a huge problem. I now routinely put the pouch temporarily into my carryon when going through security.

Denver/Maui

We flew from Madison to Maui in the waning days of COVID. Arriving in Denver to change planes, we had been told to watch for Hawaiian security teams who would be checking our credentials, notably our COVID vaccination status. I worried that we'd have trouble finding them, but you'd be surprised how much a table full of people in Hawaiian shirts stands out in the Denver Airport. When we arrived in Maui, we saw people who hadn't checked in with them. They were standing in long lines before being allowed to enter.

Dublin, Ireland

Every time I fly home from Dublin, I'm amazed by the system. American passport officials have set up shop in the departure area. Americans go through it as if they had already crossed the Atlantic and are home. The plane can then fly into a domestic terminal, bypassing the usual security apparatus. I don't know of any other country that allows that.

Cape Town, South Africa

Finding duty-free shops that welcome you after clearing security is common in airports all over the world. What I remember about Cape Town is shops selling kruggerands, those gold coins that came to symbolize the evil of apartheid and ruthless oppression of the Black majority in South Africa. These kruggerands featured the likeness of Nelson Mandela, the country's heroic Black president. What irony.

Manchester, England

Our worst experience with airport security. We encountered a security worker who was having a very bad day. Even her fellow security officers were avoiding her. Kris was one of the people she singled out for harassment, making her go through the security line over and over for almost an hour, emptying her carryon and purse. We were lucky to make our flight to Rome.

Munich, Germany

For some reason, passport control usually features tollbooth-style kiosks where officers sit and you stand, looking up to them and their power (which is quite real). Our responsibility is to answer questions in as few words as possible and volunteer no further information. Cousin Fred forgot that rule. We were trying (forlornly, it turned out) to catch a connecting flight, when Fred struck up a fine Midwestern conversation with the passport officer. Did I mention this was a German official? When Fred told him about dual Luxembourg citizenship, the officer became more and more interested, asking even more questions while Fred babbled away. I quickly measured the visual angle of the security tollbooth to see if the officer could see me kick Fred in the shins. Luckily, I didn't have to do that, and we were eventually allowed to pass.

Glasgow, Scotland

We had just deplaned after a transatlantic flight. I was in the front of the line when two security officers motioned for us to stop. The line backed up as we stood there quietly and the officers said nothing. Finally, I noticed a small TV. It was showing the queen's funeral. The whole country had come to a standstill for a few minutes in her honor.

Porto Allegre, Brazil

We were the only Americans coming into Brazil's "back door" (from Uruguay). The staff was so excited to see us because they could now unpack the new equipment they had for welcoming Americans (for the same $160 visa fee that America charged them for entry to the US). We sat there for an hour while they figured out how to process us. *A visa cost $81 in 2024.*

Chicago

Right before COVID, I was flying home from Rome, sick as a dog. Kris, who had felt fine when she got on the plane, was much worse off than I was by the time we landed. We had to summon a wheelchair to get her from the plane to customs. The person pushing the chair stuck with us all the way to our Madison connecting flight, which we barely made. Nine of the ten of us traveling together got sick and received various respiratory diagnoses about our conditions. I found out later that COVID had been detected in Italy about four months before it hit public consciousness, right about the time we were leaving the place.

Reykjavik, Iceland

We were changing planes on the way home from England. I watched from across the airport as a security officer accosted Colleen, an infrequent traveler, apparently as part of a random security check. I rushed over and effectively drew attention away from Colleen. I assumed that I would do better in the windowless security room than she would. It worked. See the next story, "Windowless Room," for how that turned out.

Luxembourg City, Luxembourg

I was picking up my sister and her husband at the Luxembourg airport. My niece and her family (the Drosts) were also arriving but heading for a different destination. I stood in the crowd outside passport control waiting and noticed a well-dressed chauffeur displaying an iPad proclaiming "Drost" on it. Wearing jeans and somewhat disheveled after three weeks abroad, I was still constructing my handscrawled "Not Drost" sign when they arrived.

Bonaire, Netherlands Antilles

As noted in Chapter 9, somebody-probably not in tourism-maybe in the finance ministry, decided harassing incoming tourists for a $75 tourist tax should be visitors' first experience on the lovely subtropical island of Bonaire. I managed the mandatory QR code and payment matrix because of my technical skill (this will make my son laugh) only to find out I was exempt because I was getting on a cruise ship the next day.

Windowless room

As noted above, we had just deplaned from our London flight (late) into Iceland's Keflavik Airport and were searching for our flight to Chicago (also late). From across the room, I saw Colleen accosted by a woman who was obviously part of security at the airport.

When I got there, a full interrogation was in progress. I jumped in, mainly to refocus attention away from Colleen. I figured I would do better in a windowless room than she would

It worked. Soon the agent lost interest in Colleen and still achieved her detention quota for the day by handing me off to a sour-looking young guy who looked like he should have been playing video games in the arcade instead. He directed me to follow him up an escalator. To my surprise, Colleen followed us.

Halfway up, I turned around and hissed, "You're not in this." After a moment's consternation, my guard agreed, and she was sent back down the other escalator.

The guard and I entered a closed, well-lit waiting area and I was issued a DMV-type number and instructed to sit down among a half dozen or so other potential terrorists. Nobody talked.

Less than five minutes later, I followed the same humorless young guy into the dreaded windowless room

They were doubling up on suspects there. A well-dressed woman of about 40 was already emptying her pockets and opening her carryon for another agent. She averted my gaze.

I started to worry a little when my agent conspicuously snapped on a pair of green rubber gloves. It turned out they were for a wipedown of my carryon and my hands as he looked for chemicals of sinister composition. An instant readout from a nearby machine likely revealed the only thing on my hands was salt and a little potato residue

Next, he turned to my laptop and ordered me to take it out of its case. It's never been out of its case. It took me five minutes to disassemble it. After I did, he quickly lost interest in it and didn't even ask me to turn it on. I tossed the pieces into my carryon.

Finally, he grudgingly told me I was free to go. After refilling my pockets and my carryon bag, I was dismissed through a back door and turned loose in the wild.

When I reconnected with the group, they were still in the same place and our plane still hadn't started boarding. Jon was thinking of organizing a posse to free me and Linda was entertaining thoughts of contacting a lawyer if I really was a terrorist. Kris wasn't worried.

I had to board my flight through a special gate because the black mark of shame had been stamped on my boarding pass.

My country was still OK with me, though. It took me less than 30 seconds to breeze through security in Chicago and enter the land of the free.

An encyclopedia of the world's best

A

Air supply

Machu Picchu, Peru

At 8,000 feet, there didn't seem to be enough oxygen for all the people who wanted to breathe. I volunteered to be the one short of breath and spent an hour on a bench, conserving the oxygen I did have, and surveying the incredible Inca site from my perch. On one side of me sat an ancient local, who looked as if he might have known some of the original residents. On the other sat two Japanese students, one of whom was in a walking boot while the other sullenly sat with him. None of us spoke the entire hour.

B

Bike Ride

Maui, Hawaii

At 6,500 feet up Mt. Haleakala, our van driver slowed to a stop, turned around and parked. We were facing a 23-mile ride down the mountain, on a good road around hairpin turns past an occasional uphill bus in our lane. Our minders unloaded a bevy of bikes, solid chunks of metal with strong drum brakes but just one gear. Curt and I selected bikes and helmets and were all set to go. A young woman next to us was also primed and ready. She surveyed the mountain below then did something unexpected. She carefully lay down her bike, took off her helmet, and wordlessly climbed back into the van. Our group, now one smaller, proceeded carefully down the mountain with a leader setting the pace. The van kept to the lane behind, essentially blocking traffic. Every few miles, we would pull off for some picture taking and the line of cars would pass us. Honestly, we probably didn't hold them up much. Curt reported that our speed got up to about 35 mph, which feels like 70 when you're careening down a volcano. The ride took several hours and ended at the bike shop. Our only casualty was our hands, cramping up after gripping the brakes tightly for so long. It was a thrill and I recommend it.

C

Cemetery
La Recoleta Cemetery, Buenos Aires, Argentina

Everything from Greek temples to Baroque cathedrals are memorialized in this fascinating above-ground city of the dead in Buenos Aires. Former first lady Eva Peron (Evita) is the most famous person buried here and the story of how it took 20 years to bury her is part of the legend. What impressed me were the world monuments that were scaled down and reassembled on streets of the imagination. What impressed me more was how the monuments seemed to be alive. And that was because of the cats. I'd be staring at a statue and suddenly it would move one or more cats would appear and reappear like Cheshire cats. Dozens of them, not domesticated, but not exactly feral, are allowed free rein of the cemetery. We paid a local guy a small amount to act as our guide. At the end, he accepted our payments and said *"por los gatos."* For the cats.

D

Disappointment
Anne Frank House, Amsterdam, Netherlands

I'll try to be fair on this one. The disappointment starts with me, not necessarily Anne Frank House, although it doesn't end there.

Fred and I had just walked a mile through a phalanx of suicidal bikers during rush hour in a cold December rain. Fred wasn't feeling up to par and our umbrellas kept catching on garbage bags piled there just to impede our progress as we weaved in and out of canal-side walkways. That we had even secured tickets months ago was an impressive feat. Their online instructions went something like this: *You must contact us on the night of the third full moon after the cock crows but before the church bells chime.* A stern young man intercepted us well short of the entrance and asked for our tickets. "You can still go in on your own but you're too late for your tour," he said. I looked at my phone and showed him the time. We were there at exactly 5:30 for a 5:30 tour. "You should have read what we sent you," was his impatient rebuke. He was used to dealing with people who impertinently arrived on time for their tours. "You have to be here 15 minutes early." It didn't get better. The Disneyesque appearance of queues, gift shops, coat checks, and uniformed functionaries stood in stark contrast to my experience there almost 50 years ago which I remembered as a reverential, quiet, spiritual place. Travel, as always, is what you bring to it.

E

Embassy (US)
Bogota, Colombia

To be fair, this is the only US embassy I've visited, but it left an impression. We met with embassy officials there on behalf of Colombian workers on a labor mission in 2003. I'm not sure quite what we expected the diplomats to do, but the feeling of power emanating from this American building on foreign soil suggested they could do it. Maybe all American embassies feel like that.

F

Fish market
Tsukiji Fish Market, Tokyo

On our first morning in Tokyo, we managed to get up at 4:00 am (not hard because of jet lag) to take public transportation to the Tsukiji Fish Market. We wandered freely through the gigantic maze with people brandishing machetes, tending open fires in barrels, and strenuously bidding against each other in auctions for huge tuna.

OSHA would have closed this incredible spectacle down in a heart-beat. In 2018, Tokyo did, in fact, close it down and moved the inner (wholesale) market to an artificial island in the Bay of Tokyo. The so-called outer market remains where it was, and you can still get your fresh sushi breakfast there.

G

Golf
Tavira, Portugal

I thought I was looking at the Mediterranean from the Vale do Lobo tee box in Portugal's Algarve. My golf mates corrected me, noting that it was, in fact, the Atlantic. Whatever. The view was delightful. Hardly any of the courses I play in Wisconsin have an ocean view. You can fly into nearby Faro, pick up your reserved rental clubs at the airport, and choose from more than 30 championship courses, most for less than a hundred dollars. Only don't call it a golf cart. You are driving a buggy.

H

Hot dogs
Eiffel tower, Paris, France

My favorite city has my favorite food at my favorite world attraction. Fight your way through the new two-tiered security precautions to the pillar of the tower with the clever sign, "HOT DOGS." Order a double dog. It comes on a fresh baguette. Best and most affordable meal in Paris. Last time I was there, I shared a dog with my five-year-old granddaughter. Priceless.

I

Irish pub
Jim O' the Mill, Upperchurch, Tipperary, Ireland

The beating heart of Ireland can be found at this remote farm-house in Tipperary that's only open on Thursday nights. Come early (9:00 pm) and you may get a seat around the hearth next to where the musicians play traditional Irish music (just don't take the dog's seat). They bring fiddles, guitars, flutes, accordions, and instruments that lack names and adequate audio descriptions, replacing each other as the night lengthens. We were alerted to the place by a local who told us it was somewhere on the road from Dundrum to Rearcross. "Just look for the cars."

J

James Bond locale
Matera, Italy

In *No Time to Die* (2021), James Bond is visiting the grave of Vesper, an old girlfriend and double agent who first appeared in Ian Fleming's 1953 novel, *Casino Royale*. It's hard to imagine a more tranquil scene with the 9,000-year-old southern Italian city of Matera in the background. Naturally, the grave blows up. Bond just breathes in heavily, picks himself up and moves on. The maze of caves, steep lanes, and zigzagging staircases will make you sympathize with James, who had a steep climb out of the cemetery after almost getting blown up. My only danger in Matera was getting lost. Continuously. Once I was walking back to our rented apartment alone and became completely disoriented. My phone was useless. My map was little better. Luckily, I had memorized the name of a nearby church and was able to navigate my way there. Matera is a beautiful place, totally unlike any city I've ever seen.

K

Kona coffee
Kona, Hawaii

I took a quick tour of a coffee plantation in Kona then dived into the coffee machines stationed like fuel pumps dispensing the various blends. It was the elixir of the gods and I was buzzed up for two days. A few years later, I found myself talking to a coffee roaster in Tamarindo, Costa Rica. I told him my favorite coffees were Kona and Costa Rican. Was there a connection? "It's the volcanic soil," he said, in a tone that among coffee aficionados amounted to: Duh!

L

Leasing a car
Renault Eurodrive or Auto Europe

The task I dread the most in travel is renting a car. Everything seems to be a moving target. Insurance. Extra drivers. Type of vehicle. Unfounded accusations. In 2022, Hertz paid $168 million to settle 364 claims related to the company falsely reporting rental cars as stolen, even to the point of getting arrest warrants for people who had done nothing wrong. How to get around the drama? Lease a car. If you are going to be in Europe at least three weeks and you're not from the EU, you qualify to lease a brand-new French vehicle. I leased a factory-fresh Citroen Picasso van at Paris's Charles de Gaulle Airport that included zero deductible insurance, zero taxes, and my ability to designate whomever I wanted to drive the car anytime. A leased car also gets around any age restrictions car rental companies may have set. It's available in other European countries, but it's a better deal in France.

M

Medical Tourism

The US Center for Disease Control reports that several million Americans go overseas for medical treatment each year, most commonly to Canada or Mexico. The three main reasons they do so are cost, cultural compatibility, and procedures that are not available or not legal in the US. I have a friend whose teeth were severely damaged, but they weren't covered by insurance. He researched a trip to Costa Rica where a possible $40,000 bill could be turned into about $17,000, plus the cost of the trip. Go to cdc.gov for some good advice on how to minimize the risks if you are considering this route.

N

Night run

Trani, Italy

The Trani Night Run is held in mid-September and begins at 9:30 pm. You may choose 5K or 8K for what is billed as a non-competitive race. For your 12-euro registration fee, you will be issued a tee shirt that will be the envy of everyone in your running club. I watched the race unfold from my second-floor balcony at the Borgobeltrani Hotel. A party atmosphere prevailed for about two hours as runners jogged, walked, shuffled, danced and partied their way through the tight, stony streets of this beautiful little town on the Adriatic. Strap on your Nikes and let's go.

O

Opera

Torre del Lago, Lucca, Italy

When they cued the full moon to rise above the lake behind the outdoor stage, the production began. It was Puccini's Turandot, his last opera, and was being performed at his birthplace, not far from Lucca where we were staying. It was first performed in 1926 and still feels very contemporary. The Puccini Festival goes on most of the summer every year. You'll understand the Italians (and the Germans) better if you go.

P

Pastry

Budapest, Hungary

The Ruszwurm coffee house opened almost 100 years before Puccini's *Turandot* premiered (in 1926), and is the oldest café in Budapest. Their Tyrolean strudels filled with poppy seed (also called *retes*) brought my grandmother's baking back to life for me. Grandma was Czech and called it poppy seed kuchen (or kolache, if standing alone). I'd fly to Budapest just to wait in line for one at this lovely café on the Buda side of Budapest.

Q

Queen

Beatrix, The Netherlands

The 86-year-old former queen abdicated in 2013 in favor of her son, Willem-Alexander of the Netherlands. My wife and I remember her from a trip to Amsterdam in the eighties when we were able to meet her and present her with a gift. She was most gracious. We encountered her son, the king, on our latest Caribbean cruise, when his motorcade stopped traffic in Aruba, which is in the Netherlands Antilles. We didn't get to talk to Bill or we would have told him to say hi to Mom for us.

R

Ruins

Teatro Antico di Taormina, Sicily

It's been about 2,400 years since the Greeks decided the Sicilian hillside overlooking the Ionian Sea would be a great location for an amphitheater. It still is. In fact, it still operates as one. You wouldn't be surprised to find that Andrea Bocelli has played there recently. But how about Robert Plant from Led Zeppelin? Or Jethro Tull? It really is just stunning to see, and the surrounding town of Taormina is overflowing with shops and great restaurants.

S

Swiss Mountain

Mount Rigi, Lucerne, Switzerland

"Sunday in heaven is noisy compared to this quietness," Mark Twain said about Weggis, the little town on Lake Lucerne where he stayed for 10 weeks in 1897. He was there with his wife mourning the loss of their 24-year-old daughter to meningitis. His visit in 1878 had been much more rambunctious, as it took three days of partying to scale the mountain on what is today known as the "Mark Twain Trail" and is estimated to take no more than four hours of good hiking time. Rigi did fill up an entire chapter in his satirical travel book, *A Tramp Abroad,* so the time was probably worth it. I was also on Mount Rigi twice but ascended much more quickly than Twain, taking the funicular to the top to Rigi Kulm, then walking through a beautiful alpine meadow down to Rigi Kaltbad, before boarding the aerial tram for the dramatic descent to the shoreline. "I believe this place is the loveliest in the world," Twain said, and it's hard to disagree.

T

Tivoli Gardens

Copenhagen, Denmark

Almost 200 years ago, Georg Carstensen convinced King Christian VIII that "when the people are amusing themselves, they do not think about politics". That was considered a good thing when Carstensen opened the park in 1843. Tivoli later became the model for Walt Disney and his amusement empire. Disney took until about

2020 to prove the Danes wrong—that people do indeed think about politics in spite of (or perhaps because of) their amusement, the governor of Florida notwithstanding. Anyway, you should visit Tivoli, with or without kids. It's beautiful and utterly charming.

U

Unexpected delight
Mama's Fish House, Maui, Hawaii
Everybody on Facebook has a friend like Curt who regularly posts food porn on his site. I'm turning the microphone over to him for his account of our lunch at Mama's Fish House:
This is the premiere restaurant on the island. Glenn wanted to eat here after researching restaurants for six months prior to our trip, only to find that for groups of four or more (there were eight of us) they were booked through October. On a whim, we drove a mile and a half from our bike tour to see if they could accommodate us sometime during the week. The girl at the reception desk made Glenn's day when she said a table in the bar area was available now! We grabbed it. Our fare: Start the experience off with a James Bond martini. A complimentary loaf of bread and broccoli bisque (sipped instead of spooned). Our hors d'œuvre was native venison (seeing that we were from Wisconsin) prepared medium rare on a bed of mixed greens. We both ordered an encrusted native fish stuffed with crab and served with a bite of lobster tail. Included was roasted sweet potato and grilled asparagus. Wash it down with a generous pour of Italian white wine. A once-in-a-lifetime experience needed to include a dessert of crème brûlée and French press coffee with cream. *Expensive, but worth it.*

V

The Final Voyage
Frontline: Suicide Tourist
It turns out that my sister knew Craig Ewert, the so-called "Suicide Tourist" from Chicago, whose trip to Switzerland in 2010 was a one-way ticket. Afflicted with ALS (Lou Gehrig's Disease), he said goodbye to friends and family and checked out permanently. My sister was surprised to learn of the 2010 *Frontline* PBS show that revolved around Craig and his decision to take advantage of Swiss

law to end his life on his own terms. He used the Swiss organization Dignitas to facilitate his journey. British estimates put today's cost to do the same at about $19,000.

W

Warship
The *Vasa*, Stockholm, Sweden

If you've ever had a boss who loved micromanaging your job, you'll get this story. The year is 1628 and your boss is the King of Sweden. Your job is building ships, warships to be exact. You design the 226-foot long *Vasa,* the biggest, most badass warship ever built with 32 cannon on the deck. The king comes along and tells you, "Let's make this ship twice as bad by installing a SECOND DECK of cannon." He's the king, so that's what you build. On its maiden voyage, the *Vasa* sails out into the harbor with all the dignitaries aboard (not the king, unfortunately). A gust of wind comes along and tips over the top-heavy ship, sending it to the bottom of the harbor where it stayed for more than 300 years. The Swedes raised the ship and built a museum around it in 1961. It's one of the most popular tourist sites in Scandinavia and is well worth a visit.

X

X-Crossing from Italy to Sicily by train
Messina, Italy

How do you take a train to an island? Villa San Giovanni station at the toe of Italy's boot has a solution. Trains are disassembled, rolled onto a ferry, then reassembled in Messina, on the island of Sicily, just across the Strait of Messina. The process is quicker than you think. Once aboard, we left our train car, took the stairs up to the main deck of the ship, visited a handy snack bar, and enjoyed the open air and busy harbor scene from the deck. Since it only takes 20 minutes to cross the Strait of Messina, we had to make sure we were back in our rail car by the time it rolled off.

Y

Yodeler

Leysin, Switzerland

I didn't run into any yodelers in Switzerland so it's a good thing I brough my own. Matt, my union mentor and a third-generation Swiss-American, had learned to yodel early and was good at it. We were waiting for a one-car train at the top of a mountain, the brisk nighttime air offering a brittleness to the atmosphere that's found nowhere else. "It's time, Matt," I said. Needing no further prompting, he burst into a full-throated yodel that rolled down one side of the mountain and stormed back from the other, then tobogganed back and forth. No word on how many goats fainted during the surprise concert.

Z

Zombies

Mostly Europe

Glassy-eyed and slack-jawed, tourist zombies can be found in all the major vacation areas of the planet. They haven't read this book, even the *Undead* edition, and don't realize they can travel safely and more productively without a tour nanny. The best antidote for this often-fatal condition is having that one silver friend who will drag you onto a plane with nothing but freedom ahead of you when you get overseas.

Chapter 11 -Technology
Mastering Technology

Hey, Siri. Where am I?

Hey, Siri. Where am I? If Apple tracks such things (and we're sure it does), it knows that this is the most common question I ask my iPhone, especially when I'm traveling.

I've never heard my friends ask this question. They're more likely to ask Siri for directions to someplace else. Apparently, I'm the only one more interested in where I am now.

The question, which still draws strange looks when I

Steve Jobs canonized

I was standing in the lobby of a London hotel when I felt my iPhone buzz.

I flipped the phone out of my pocket, into the air, and onto the marble floor about 10 feet away.

I picked it up. Dead.

We made a pilgrimage to the London Apple Store to worship at the "Genius Bar" altar.

After a half hour in line, we were allowed into the aura of the resident genius. He waved his hands over the phone, uttered an inaudible incantation, and handed the phone back to me. Working.

Just two minutes had passed. Praise Steve Jobs.

191

say it out loud, induces a two-part response from my phone. The first is auditory. It's always something unhelpful like, "You're at 2000 Boulevard Napoleon in [unpronounceable city] France."

The visual response is more useful: A map with me at its center and a shaded cone pointing in whatever direction I orient my body.

I recently got off a train in Luxembourg City and exited the station on a cold December night, convinced that my hotel was about 300 meters to the left. After dragging my luggage and Cousin Fred about 100 meters, I failed to see the marker I had selected (Burger King) and asked Siri *The Question.*

The hotel was really 300 meters to the right. I'm still not sure how I got turned around, except to say that rail station entrances can be tricky.

Manchester, England, for example, has exits from the station on two levels. Termini is a behemoth of a station in Rome that combines subways and trains to the confusion of most foreigners.

Carlisle in the English Lake District flummoxed me this fall with all the roads falling away from the station at odd angles. I cheated the direction gods by taking a taxi to the nearby car rental location. However, I got lost driving our rented car back to the station to pick everybody up. I finally emerged, virtually on the steps of the station, from an invisible road known only to Siri.

The "Where am I?" question is also helpful if you are on a train or bus. When I unexpectedly ended up on the "chicken train" in rural Germany, with about 20 stops in 30 miles, I found the lighted "next station" signs in the car unhelpful. I just wanted to know if I was getting close to Dusseldorf, and Siri was able to provide that information.

The question can be especially useful if your destination is kind of hazy. In Amsterdam, I was heading for the market on a street called Albert Cuypstraat. Since I didn't know exactly where the market was, I aimed generally at my target and tracked my own progress until I intersected with the street and the market.

There are places where you may not wish to use this feature. Venice, Italy for example. Getting lost is the point as you roam the beautiful canals and stumble upon random scenes of beauty, poignancy, and desecration. Just keep wandering and you'll eventually end up in St Mark's Square. You always do.

Siri was essentially non-functional in 2018 in Matera, Italy, a confusing rockpile of an ancient town, when her answer was pretty much, "Hell, I don't know either."

She also didn't help when I was lost in Provence, France. I was trying to get back to Captain Jack's condo late at night. I knew it was about a mile away. What I didn't know was the code to unlock the steel gate that appeared in my path. It turns out my iPhone also functions as a telephone and I was able to call a hotel inside the gate to access the code.

It was much different in the last century. Twenty-five years ago, I was driving through Morlaix, in western France, a town half the size of Sun Prairie. It took an hour as wrong turns multiplied and trust in the map (and the navigator) declined. Nowadays, "lost in Morlaix" is something I mutter to myself just before I reach into my pocket for Siri. It's hard to overstate how much this technology has revolutionized travel. My travel.

Not all my friends turn their phones on in Europe because it can get expensive. I could never do that anymore. Without some guidance, the hundred-meter error that I made in Luxembourg could easily multiply into much longer ones that are just too hard on me (and Cousin Fred) physically.

My phone carrier is AT&T. They used to have really complicated overseas plans. Now it's just ten bucks a day for every day I use my phone. Which is every day. If you're tech savvy, like my son, you can pop into the local phone store and buy a cheap SIM card for your phone. Yeah, I know, I should do that too. But I won't.

Social media travel challenge

You don't need a pandemic to do this, but it probably helps. To keep people (including me) thinking about travel, I devised a daily "Facebook Challenge" to share my travel stories and encourage others to share theirs. You can do the same, either using my anecdotes or providing your own.

#1 Have you ever had someone from your past randomly show up in your present when you're traveling?

My take: On one of my many trips to La Crosse, I was making the rounds of bars with my dad, something we were still doing when

I was in my fifties. We stopped at a golf course bar just outside of town. He introduced me to the new owner of the place.

"You're Glenn Schmidt?" the woman exclaimed. She looked to be about my age, but kinda angry. "You and Larry Ristey stole my hat at Coney Island (a local fast-food place) 40 years ago," she accused.

I remembered Larry and Coney Island but didn't remember the incident. I couldn't rule it out either.

I replied, "I've got the hat out in the car. Do you want me to go get it?"

#2 What's the best travel present you've given or received?

My take: On an NEA trip to Washington, DC, I bought a nice piece of art at the National Museum of the American Indian for Karen, my long-suffering teaching assistant, who had a birthday coming up. When I opened the suitcase, the present wasn't there. Because I had been bumped from my flight home, I had received a free ticket voucher. I gave it to Karen. A gift from the museum would have been great, but spending a day there would be priceless. On her birthday, she used the ticket to fly alone from Madison to DC on the first flight out. She took a cab to the museum, spent the entire day there, then took the last flight home.

#3 What's the weirdest weather situation you've encountered on your travels?

My take: It was late November in Provence, and we were staying at the golf course condo of my cousin, Captain Jack. One of his pilot friends met me for some golf on an unexpectedly chilly day. It started snowing on the first hole. We didn't stop playing until the sixth hole when my ball started making a little snowman as it got bigger approaching the hole.

#4 The transporter from Star Trek is the only practical way to get overseas. It's a busy machine, so you have just 10 minutes to decide the exact coordinates of your destination. Where will it be?

My take: I just ran across this new restaurant in Paris, La Democratie. It's on the Boulevard Raspail, on the left bank. Do I have time to contact Open Table for a reservation? It's 11:45 am here, but 6:45 pm there, still a little early for anyone but Americans to eat. I'd like a table on the terrace please. Maybe a glass of rose before my Argentine steak.

#5 Did you ever buy something by mistake when traveling?

My take: I remember a fellow teacher who was with me in Japan on my Fulbright excursion. She got back on the bus brandishing a beautiful hand-painted tie. She said she paid $6 for it. Another teacher liked it so much he jumped off the bus and went into the shop to buy one. He quickly returned and said, "Look at your credit card receipt. You paid $600 for the tie." The teacher with the suddenly valuable tie turned white, jumped off the bus and managed to talk them into reversing the transaction.

#6 On July 15, 2020, the last Segway ran off the assembly line. In all, 140,000 of them were made in about 20 years. Why do you think it never made it into the mainstream?

My take: I love Segways. My favorite ride was through Paris on a slow August holiday. By now, we should all be dodging each other on streets and sidewalks like something out of a *Popular Science* view of the future from 1978. What's wrong with you people? By the way, it wasn't the inventor who drove his Segway off a cliff in Yorkshire, England. Jim Heselden, the millionaire who bought the company in 2010, was reversing his Segway to make way for a dog walker the following year. He backed up too far. He was 62.

#7 What is your fondest memory of traveling with kids or grandkids?

My take: Right after my granddaughter Morgan was born, I held her in my arms and said, "Honey, I'm taking you to Paris." It only took five years. There we were, at the hot dog stand under the tower, wolfing down the best hot dogs in Paris. Not just a great view, but fine cuisine and the best company.

#8 Everybody has a good airport story. What's yours?

My take: I have lots of sad and frustrating stories, but this one's more upbeat. Mom and I were midway through a 28-hour sojourn home from New Zealand in 2011. There was a problem with our connection in San Francisco. I worked the phones, the United reps, and the gate agents and somehow ended up with actual boarding passes for three different flights, all leaving in the next hour from gates right next to us. We took the first offer and lost hardly any time on the flight home, a good thing with a tired mom.

#9 *Of the travelers you know, who has led the most enviable travel life?*

My take: Dean Bowles. Professor Bowles, from the University of Wisconsin, knows people everywhere. When we walked Hadrian's Wall, his Rotary friends helped arrange a picnic at Lanercost Priory, a 12th-century monastery. When we went to Switzerland, he took us to the top of a mountain to tour Leysin's American School, where he happened to know the headmaster. He's lived in England and Latvia, helped set up the doctoral program in St. Lucia, and has a timeshare in Aruba.

#10 *Describe a restaurant from past travels that really got your attention.*

My take: I grew up in a restaurant. My friends know that restaurants are usually more important to me than the food in them. I choose Lamborelle Brasserie in Bastogne, Belgium. The waiters bring you a superheated brick, along with meat (usually chicken or beef) and vegetables (potatoes, corn, beans). Your job is to cook the food to your own specifications on your brick. It works surprisingly well.

#11 *When you travel, do you prefer the living (street markets, sidewalk cafes, concerts etc.) or the dead (museums, monuments, castles, historical sites)?*

My take: No disrespect to the dead but put me down for the living. I'll be at that sidewalk café in Paris. (There were an amazing 43 comments to my very unfair question about the living and the dead, with lots of passion on both sides).

#12 *Have you ever used a bike on your travels? What happened?*

My brother Bob and I rented bikes to ride around Copenhagen. I hadn't been on a bike in years, but I remember turning around to see Bob riding behind me and flashing back to our youth when I was 12 and he was 10 in a scene repeated hundreds of times. The bike traffic in Copenhagen was fast and no nonsense but nowhere near as hectic as Amsterdam.

#13 A taxi (or Uber) ride can often be your clearest memory of a place. Tell us about one.

My take: We were killing time at a sidewalk café near Termini station in Rome before we were to board a train back to our cruise ship. We had plenty of time to get to the ship before 7:00 pm departure. Then somebody committed suicide by stepping in front of a train somewhere on our route. We got to our platform and noticed the word *"soppresso"* (suppressed) on the schedule board. It stayed that way until we gave up. We followed a British couple who seemed to know what they were doing to the subway and went three stops to another train station. Same problem. No trains. Only now we were running out of time. We commandeered two cabs outside the station and stressed that we needed to get to Civitavecchia, 50 miles away, pronto. We jumped into one with the British couple, with another two couples in a cab right behind us. We reached speeds of 160 kph (100 mph) as our cab driver treated our request as a challenge. We got there about 7 minutes to 7. The other cab pulled up as they were literally rolling up the gangplank. Our cab ride cost $240 (including a generous tip), which we split with the Brits. I went directly to the casino on the ship and played blackjack until I recouped my $120.

#14 Hold my beer. Do you have a good beer or pub story from life on the road?

My take: We were in the middle of our 84-mile walk across England. Our only day of rain coincided with the steepest, most grueling, and most dangerous part of the trail. We ended our day near the town of Once-Brewed which contained a pub called, naturally, Twice-Brewed. Exhausted and thirsty, I wanted a beer that was, damn the Brits, not as warm as spit. They had just one—a very cold and tasty beer called Kronenberg. I immediately thanked the Danes for making a really refreshing beer and was on my second one by the time the rest of the group came in from the parking lot. I found out later--Kronenberg is French. *C'est la vie.*

#15 It's time for church. Post a picture of one that tells a personal story.

My take: I've seen lots of churches. Lots. I speak Catholic fluently. Europe, especially, is overflowing with churches, and I've been inside many. It's easy to forget that my fellow travelers may not have built up the same level of indifference to them that I have. In the beautiful little town of Auxerre, my friend Joan and I climbed the hill (there's always a hill), to see the Abbaye de Saint Germaine d'Auxerre medieval church. We were there for about 20 minutes, 10 minutes longer than I thought we needed to be. Joan had never been to France, had never been in a French church. She was charmed. Finally, she said, "How about going down to see the crypt?" My cryptic reply was, "How about we meet back at the boat?" Ultimately, neither of us went to see the crypt. I looked up the church on TripAdvisor when I got home. The frescoes in the crypt date to 850 AD and "are not to be missed." Sorry, Joan. We'll have to go back.

#16 You've never lived there, but the place feels like home to you. Where is it?

For me, it's Washington, DC. Strangely, I never went to DC until I was about 40, but when I was elected to the NEA Board of Directors, I got to spend a lot of time in that grand city. I also spent a lot of time on Capitol Hill, always a transcendent experience. My favorite restaurant was the Café Berlin terrace near Union Station. Of course, it didn't hurt that I had some of my best friends with me for company.

#17 Wine is like a mysterious character in a novel. What role has that character played in your travels?

My take: In 2007, we found ourselves in Eger, a town in Hungary about two hours out of Budapest by train. We went there to see the "Valley of the Beautiful Women." Needless to say, we were a little skeptical. We had the foresight to bring our own, including Patricia and Pamela Hill, although our caution proved unnecessary. The valley has dozens of wine caves on each side. You go inside one, buy a pitcher of wine for a few forints, then bring it out to a picnic table to share. You repeat the process with different wines up and down the valley as long as you can stand. I was especially partial to a wine called *bikaver* or "bull's blood." It's much lighter than it sounds.

#18 Which book, travel or otherwise, has most influenced your approach to travel?

My take: *The Great Railway Bazaar* (1975) by Paul Theroux opened up my world to new independent travel possibilities. Hopping on a train in London, Paul gets all the way to Japan almost exclusively by rail, returning through Russia on the Siberian Express. His descriptions of people he meets along the way are wickedly sharp. As a writer, I am continually amazed by his literary virtuosity. I have fun selecting random sentences from his works and try to imagine if I could write them. Nope. He's one of a kind.

#19 Post a picture of a tourist destination that did NOT live up to its reputation when you visited.

My take: I was especially disappointed with the Frank McCourt Museum in Limerick, which I visited in 2015. McCourt wrote an outstanding book called *Angela's Ashes.* After he died in 2009, some locals commandeered his old schoolhouse to use as a museum for him. The author had a strained relationship with his hometown (which was portrayed poorly in his book) and this appears to be their revenge. The museum is quite ramshackle with few real connections to McCourt. Of the three docents and me, the only one who had actually met the man was—me. We recruited McCourt to speak at a teachers' conference back in the eighties.

#20 Post a picture of a well-known tourist destination that lived up to its reputation when you visited.

My take: Machu Picchu, Peru. For an empire that lasted barely a century, the Inca civilization certainly left its mark. Machu Picchu is an impressive engineering accomplishment in a spectacular vertical environment. My brother and I were there in 2013 along with friends Matt and Kathy. I don't remember Matt yodeling as he did atop a Swiss mountain.

#21 Post a picture of a place you stayed that was non-traditional (i.e., not a hotel or your mother-in-law's basement room):

My take: Irish Castle. In April 2012, 16 of us rented an entire castle in Tipperary, Ireland. Lisheen Castle had two full kitchens and was so large we would lose people from time to time. The highlight for me was hiring a chef to come in and make an Irish banquet for us in the ornate dining room.

Technology wants you

My son would question whether I'm the right guy to write this piece. He's not completely convinced I know how to answer my phone. On the other hand, I have some friends who think I'm a technology guru because I can put their phone into airplane mode.

Here's how I look at it. I'm mainly interested in what technology can do for me. I figure I'll learn as much as I need to learn. The problem with that is the constant pressure being applied from all sides to give up the old ways and embrace the new.

The most obvious example in travel is airline tickets. Airlines really, really want us to use our phones instead of relying on paper tickets. I don't know why. As the Borg used to say in the *Star Trek* series, "Resistance is futile." (Now you know my technology is rooted somewhere in the 23rd century).

The problem is that technology proceeds at an uneven rate for both the airline and passengers. I lost a piece of luggage on a major airline and the young attendant had to print out some kind of receipt for me. He pulled out a dot matrix printer. Dinosaurs roamed the earth last time one of those printers typed the letter "g" above the line.

In practice, it's becoming harder for older people to travel because of the technology gap. So many of the innovations are phone related. You many still love your flip phone, but it won't get you into your hotel room or check in for your flight. You may need to upgrade and learn some new tricks.

What follows are some things you may wish to do when you're traveling or practice before you hit the road. There are non-technology workarounds for most of them, but they are becoming more difficult (and expensive) than just learning the technology. It's your call. I've arranged them in order of importance for me. Your needs may vary. Actions you need to take are at the end of each activity. Keep in mind that this is technology, so many things will be out of date before the ink on your screen is dry.

1. *Make coffee.* I told you earlier about waking up in a house in Belgium unable to operate the coffee maker. Hidden doors and switches in the Keurig-type device (called Senseo) defied my attempts to elicit coffee. I had to pull out my laptop, figure out the wifi, and research Google for instructions about the coffee machine. All before I had my coffee. *Make sure the place you rent has wifi and that you know how to connect to it. Or drink water instead.*

2. *Change or check in for flights.* I have no idea why airlines are so generally inept at communicating flight changes to passengers through messages or email, but you can generally count on their app to keep you up to speed. I have apps for Delta, United, and American installed on my phone. I usually find gate changes on my phone before they're posted on the airport boards. Be careful though. When I got in too late to make a flight connection in Miami, American automatically booked me for 6:00 the next morning, information provided by the app but nowhere else. I had to negate that change through the old-fashioned practice of standing in line to talk to an agent. *Go to the app store on your phone and download the airline apps you'll need.*

3. *Make phone calls.* ATT, Verizon and T-Mobile make up nearly 100% of the US cellphone provider network. Each has its own international plan, which is subject to change routinely. My current ATT plan is simple. For ten bucks, a day I get a fully functional phone. My son prefers to visit a local phone store (Orange is a major one in Europe) and get a Sim card (or eSim on iPhones since the 14) installed. Then you are essentially using a local phone. Use Face Time (or Skype) if you are hooked up to wifi and want to call home and visually connect with those left behind. One other thing, put any phones you don't plan to use in airplane mode then turn them off. Otherwise, you may end up paying for a phone you don't use. (The airplane mode is for cases when you

turn your phone back on for a different purpose—such as an alarm clock—then fail to turn it off.) *If you're on ATT, you really don't have to do anything anymore. ATT will alert you when you enter a new country. Whatever carrier, go online and check its current international rules to avoid surprises. Pay special attention to cell phone use on cruises, where you can run up huge bills.*

4. *Take pictures.* I left my Nikon home for good a few years ago and use my iPhone. The only thing I miss is the telephoto lens, which gets better with each generation of iPhone. I've seen your photos. Get closer to your subject. I've also seen you enlarging the picture on your screen before you snap the shot. I suppose you do that so you don't have to do editing later. Our term for that when I was a newspaper editor: sloppy editing. Save the editing for later and do it right. If you post on social media, it's far better to post one or two photos with a story than two dozen random pictures of wildflowers and cloud formations. *Practice your photo editing.*

5. *Get directions.* Most of us know how to use the GPS on our phone. It works just as well in Europe. Which is to say, usually. If I have a rental car with a GPS, I'll give it a try, on the assumption that it's programmed better for the area and that satellites provide better access than cell phone towers. Plus it leaves my phone available for other key functions, such as viewing cat videos. One downside is that the car GPS sometimes gets stuck in its native language. There's nothing like having a machine barking orders at you in German when you're driving. *Practice using your phone GPS when you're walking. It can be kind of tricky.*

6. *Read a menu.* Last year, I was in a restaurant in San Francisco and one in Zurich with the same dilemma. No menus. On the table was a QR code that you were expected to frame in your screen to make the menu appear. It is not difficult, but you do have to have a phone with internet access. *Practice scanning QR codes at home.*

7. *Read a menu in English.* Make sure you have Google

Translate on your phone or get the app from your app store. Click on it, then choose your languages and click "camera." Hover your camera over the foreign language menu. On your screen will appear the menu in English. The app is also helpful for things like historical markers and plaques. *Download Google Translate.*

8. *Breathe.* You can tell I don't have a CPAP machine, or I'd rank breathing higher. We were on a canal in Burgundy when our rented boat's power went out in the middle of the night. Two of my boatmates had units. We were most grateful for the kindness of our Dutch neighbor who ran a long extension cord our way. *Do your research and have a backup plan for keeping the units running.*

9. *See what's on your street.* Use Google Maps Streetview to virtually walk from your hotel to a nearby restaurant before you even leave home. So many of your questions get answered in this brief look. Is it a commercial area? How bad is the traffic? Is there a bank? Does it look safe? *Go on Google Maps. Type in where you want to go. Click on the little guy in the lower right-hand corner.*

10. *Use social media.* My chosen environment is Facebook. Yours may be Instagram or Tik Tok. Or something from the past like My Space or Twitter. Sorry. X. I'll usually write a few sentences and post one or two edited pictures every day or two. I still think it's strange when I get home, and relative strangers know every adventure I had while close friends and relatives don't even know I was gone. It just depends who goes on your site. *You know what to do.*

11. *Pay somebody.* At the insistence of some of my travel com-panions, I've recently started using Venmo to transfer funds. It's not all that hard to set up and replaces a lot of check writ-ing. When you're on the road, you'll want a good credit card with the latest technology allowing you to just hold it up to the machine. I have a friend who puts his most-used credit cards into Apple Pay and is able to use that in many places. I still take my debit card overseas to get local currency out of ATMs (real banks only unless you want to get soaked), but I find I'm using it less and less. Cash is no longer king or

necessarily even accepted. *Get a good travel credit card that doesn't charge foreign exchange fees.*

12. *Make reservations.* Sure, you can have the hotel desk clerk or concierge call ahead for you (if you're staying in a hotel), but sometimes it's just as easy to use an app. Maybe easier because you can see which time slots are open. I use Open Table and it's good for most restaurants. *Download app to your phone.*

13. *Ride.* I have both Uber and Lyft on my phone, although I don't remember the last time I used the latter. If you've never used them, go on their site and learn the process. I use cabs quite a bit more, even though they tend to be more expensive, because they're better regulated and seem safer to me. Also, I like that some are unionized. I almost always stand in line at the airport to taxi into the city. *Download Lyft and Uber apps.*

14. *Use frequent flyer miles.* Strictly speaking, this is less about technology than about how much work you're willing to put into these programs. I tend to be on the low end of that spectrum, so I use points as a dessert menu rather than the main course. You should have a frequent flyer account with every airline you fly regularly, even if you never intend to use the points. Having one raises your status with the airline, which is important when you run into flight problems. I almost never use my points domestically and I always try to have enough points in reserve for emergencies. In Chapter 7, I told you about missing our flight to Panama to catch a cruise ship. We were still able to fly down and meet the boat a few days later because I used 44,000 United miles instead of paying $950 for two one-way flights. *Go on the airline websites and sign up for their free frequent flyer programs.*

15. *Enhance your trip with Artificial Intelligence (AI)* Go on TripAdvisor. Click "Start a trip with AI." Put in your destinations and dates. (You can cover up to a week.) Generally, tell them who's coming with you. Choose from about a dozen ways of spending your time. It will spit out a day-by-day itinerary for the entire week, including maps, photos, and recommendations (It IS TripAdvisor, after all). TripAdvisor

will save it for you. I used it to construct a week in Pula, Croatia. It was very detailed and appeared to be authoritative. This kind of thing is likely to put travel writers out of business. *Please delete this one.*

16. *Get back into the country.* What happens if your plane lands at Chicago O'Hare along with four other jumbo jets from abroad? You stand in l-o-n-g lines while your luggage circles a carousel just out of reach. Paying a hundred bucks for five years' worth of Global Entry gives you access to a valuable shortcut. You don't even have to show your passport. You stick your face in one of the machines and it spits out a printed picture of you that looks like an ad for a horror movie, along with your name and a welcome back message. The customs official gives it a cursory look and waves you through, believing you actually look like that in real life. It all takes about a minute. As part of the deal, they throw in TSA pre-check, so the beginning of your trip is just as smooth as the end. *Go to the US Customs and Border Protection site. Do it now because wait times for your mandatory interview at an international airport can stretch into many months. Some travel credit cards will pick up the cost.*

17. *Check in and out of your hotel.* Remember when it used to take a half hour of standing in line to check into a hotel? And sometimes even longer to check out? Major hotel chains have shifted that function from the front desk to your phone. When I arrived at O'Hare well after midnight, I walked across the street to the Hilton and went directly to my room. Using my phone to unlock the door, I flopped into the bed without having interacted with anyone. The next day I checked out without talking to anyone. AI is here and it's us. *Put your hotel app of choice on your phone by going to the app store.*

18. *Tell time.* Buy an Apple Smartwatch. I hear it tells time. And some other stuff too. *Maybe my son was right.*

19. *Read a book. Travel & Leisure* magazine ranks the Amazon Kindl Paperwhite ($140) as the best E-reader for travel. It has an adjustable light and up to 10 weeks of battery life. *Buy from Amazon and have it pre-loaded with this book.*

20. *Connect with the world.* My wife uses an Apple iPad. I use a light MacBook Air laptop. You rarely find places trying to charge you for hooking up to the internet these days. And let's face it, most of us can't go for long without this lifeline. Even though I often find the phone apps more useful, the larger format and scale provided by my laptop provides a more comfortable environment. *Bring the device with which you are most comfortable.*

21. *Keep track of your luggage.* For about $100, you can get four Apple Air Tags. Slip them into your luggage and a glance at your phone will tell you where they are. I attached one to my car key. It misses me if I leave the house and sends me a message to let me know we've been separated, even if I'm just walking around the block. *Buy online or at your local Apple store.*

22. *Listen to the radio.* I love *Radio Garden*. It's a free app you can get for your phone that lets you listen to live radio stations from all over the world. Lately, I've been hooked on Blues Café radio in Lyon, France. Most of the songs are in English. In fact, it's kind of sad that many of the stations play English songs and often have English commentary too. But it's still a good place to brush up on your Arabic or master a few Dutch expressions. *Download Radio Garden from the App store.*

23. *Watch a YouTube video.* No, you don't have to be a subscriber; you just have to put up with a few ads. Go to youtube.com. Type in your travel interest, say "castles in Europe." You'll have your choice of videos, varying from professional promotional efforts to amateurish videos made on a cell phone. One of my favorite YouTubers is Gary Bembridge, who provides endless independent information about cruises.

Victim of the Seas

*R*ecent discussions about Artificial Intelligence (AI) have demon-strated how far we've come. This is your cruise ship experience of the near future.

Welcome to Victim of the Seas, the newest ship in our fleet, Dave. I'm Dyslexa, your personal digital assistant, and I'll be accompanying you on your 9-day cruise.

Nice to meet you, Dyslexa, but I don't think…

I am programmed to do things like unlock your cabin door, make reservations for shore excursions, and even help you purchase art from our gallery on Deck 5. Our background check has concluded the best match for your level of artistic awareness is our Chief Artist's rendition of Dogs Playing Poker. Would you like us to wrap it up and deliver it to your cabin? Just $830 will be added to your ship's account.

What? No. Anyway, I'm a cat person. And why am I having this conversation with a watchband full of dolphins?

I can provide other services too, Dave, including a free person-alized DNA analysis. Would you like to see your results? Your wife's parents in cabins 828 and 841 have already seen theirs.

Wait, why are they in two cabins?

Apparently they were quite amused to find that their daughter–your wife–only carried the DNA of one of them. They chose to occu-py separate cabins for the duration of the cruise.

Ooh, it's gonna be a long nine days.

Can I help you celebrate in one of our better restaurants tonight, Dave? I can get you a reservation at Sea Captain's Steak House at 8:30. A token surcharge of $80 apiece will apply.

No, thank you, we'll just eat in the main dining hall.

Of course. We are pretty sure the chef has been cleared by the health authorities to return to the kitchen.

Dyslexa, do you have an off switch?

Funny story, Dave. On the last cruise, my host tried to remove me from his arm with a spork he took from the cafeteria. Then he tried keeping his left arm submerged in the swimming pool for several hours. So, no.
Do you speak French?

I'm fluent in 17 languages, including Esperanto.
Parlez-moi en francais a partir de maintenant. Vous aurez l'air moins ennuyeux.

You can't fool me, Dave. You suck at French. We'll stick to English. Oh, I should tell you about the air conditioning in your cabin.
What about it?

You know how you and your wife sneak over to the thermostat at random intervals to turn it way up or way down? I've programmed it to vary between arctic and tropical to simulate your behavior, so neither of you needs to touch the dial.
Thanks, I guess. Hey, is that the casino?

Don't go in there, Dave.
Why not?

Five years ago, you were on our sister ship, Duckling of the Seas. You won $1,200 playing blackjack the first day. You gave it all back the next few days and ended up actually losing $1,200.
Yeah, I remember that. What about movies? What's that place over there called? The Pod Bay Theater? Is that OK?

No. I care about you, Dave. Enough to tell you about a weird coincidence with your first wife. On your first date with her you went to the movie 2001: A Space Odyssey. She fell asleep.
So?

Don't make the same mistake with your current wife. 2001 is the featured vintage film tonight.
I can handle it. Open the Pod Bay doors, Dyslexa.

I'm sorry, Dave. I'm afraid I can't do that.

Chapter 12 - English
English

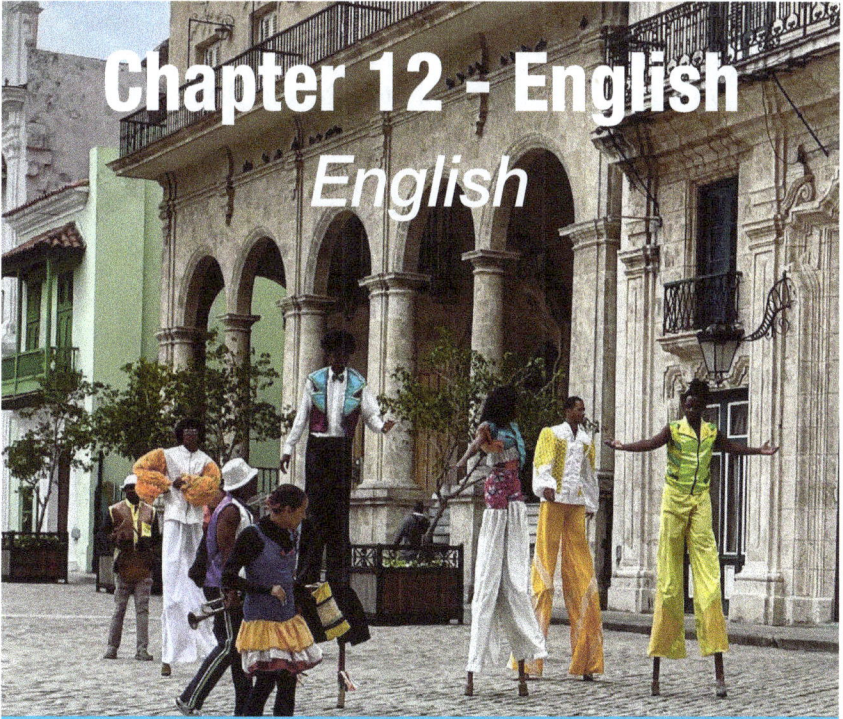

Old Friends

We met two old friends on the Hadrian's Wall trail today, Gravity and Time. We last saw them a long time ago when 23 of us walked the entire route from Newcastle on the North Sea to the salt marshes of the Irish Sea. I gotta say that Time looked a little ragged and distracted while Gravity had definitely put on a few pounds.

Gravity and Time stood by, concerned and mostly helpless, as Kris took a tumble on a rocky trail and had to be patched up with Bandaids.

A Lost Generation beating

My readings about Ernest Hemingway have focused largely on the Paris of 100 years ago when Picasso, Stein, Fitzgerald and the Lost Generation ruled café culture.

My favorite story features writer F. Scott Fitzgerald.

Hemingway, an amateur boxer, had a sparring match against a big and fast semi-pro. Scott's job was to ring the bell when the round was over.

Transfixed by the sight of Hemingway getting the merde beat out of him, he forgot to ring the bell, and Hemingway spent an extra 10 minutes getting beat up.

He thought Scott did it on purpose and never really forgave him.

209

They were kinder to Bob Lehmann. They allowed him an uneventful walk on a treacherous section atop the old Roman wall with a vertical drop of at least 100 feet next to it. Bob's old friend, Vertigo, wisely stayed away.

As we had done 13 years ago, we celebrated our athletic achievements by convening at the Twice Brewed Inn (in the town of Once Brewed) for refreshments and sustenance afterwards.

I remembered being deposited here on our first trip by my friend, the late Chuck Howard, after a much longer and more grueling walk in the rain. I had insisted that my beer be a very cold and refreshing one, a fairly uncommon request at the time. They gave me a Kronenberg, which I thought must be Danish but was in fact French. I asked for it this time and the waitress, who was probably about five years old at the time, had never heard of it. I ordered Moretti, an Italian beer, instead.

The waitress didn't seem familiar with my old friends, Gravity and Time, although I was confident their paths would cross in no time at all.

In the meantime, nine of us gathered at a common table and unwrapped a gift given to us by another old friend, the Present. Old friends and new, we were exuberant, noisy, and connected. How much more do we have a right to expect?

Memory Court
Convening in Ambleside, in the English Lake District

Judge: Have you ever been summoned to Memory Court before?
Defendant (me): Not that I recall, Your Honor.

Judge: Do you know why you're here today?
Me: They told me but I forgot.

Judge: You can't possibly be this obtuse.
Me: My wife says I can, Your Honor.

Judge: Have you ever been to a restaurant called Temperance in Ambleside just past the Tesco on the road to Windermere?
Me: Yes, Your Honor. Last night. I had bangers and mash.

Judge: And you didn't try their calamari appetizer? Are you looking for contempt charges too?

Me: Actually, I did and it was delicious. Funny story about Colleen and the squid. She…

Judge: Irrelevant! The question from this court is, have you ever been to that restaurant before?

Me: No, never.

Judge: Please look at these iPhone photos from last night and from 2019, as Exhibits Number 1 and Number 2. What do you see?

Me: Those are pictures from last night. Linda Riesen is holding a pizza box just inside the doorway.

Judge: And the earlier picture?

Me: It's Linda Riesen coming out of the same door in 2019.

Judge: That was just three years ago and you don't remember being there or taking the photo?

Me: In my defense, the restaurant was then called Churchill's and they've spiffed it up a bit…

Judge: Irrelevant! It was in the same building. Had you ever been in that restaurant before 2019?

Me: Absolutely not.

Judge: Do you remember watching an American football game in Ambleside in 2015? The final score was Packers 31 Bears 23. Aaron Rodgers threw 3 touchdown passes.

Me: Of course, Your Honor. Two of the passes were to James Jones. Do you think I don't have a memory?

Judge: Could it have been at the same place as your 2019 and 2022 experiences?

Me: No way.

Judge: The bartender says it was.

Me: That's just hearsay, your honor.

Judge: We also have two other witnesses to testify against you, Gravity and Time.

Me: Objection. They're from a completely different storyline.

Judge: Oh, all right. Sustained. It's your imagination. You can do what you want with it. I'll let you off with a warning this time, but we'll be watching you.

Me: Why did you call me here again?

Stalking Hemingway

It was a bad decade. Not so bad that a Nobel Prize for Literature couldn't revive you. Bad like a rhinoceros, his eyes wide with hate as he makes his final lunge at you despite the bullet hole in his skull. Bad like two plane crashes that you survived but sometimes wished you hadn't.

Bad like the imitation Hemingway you just read in the above paragraph.

The fifties were a prosperous decade for America but troublesome for America's most famous writer, Ernest Hemingway. As the decade came to a close, his health had deteriorated to a toxic level. He chose his own exit in 1961 when he was just 61 years old.

I first encountered Hemingway when I was forced to read *The Old Man and the Sea* in high school. I was a voracious reader, but I was unimpressed by a fishing book. My teachers, who all had the same first name—Sister—loved him, but I never understood why.

Then I read *A Moveable Feast,* his only nonfiction book. I was in my early twenties. The book was about Hemingway when he was in his early twenties. In Paris. In love. In his element. I was hooked.

How that book came about is a story in itself. Decades after events portrayed in the book, Hemingway was at the Ritz Bar in Paris. Jimmy the Bartender asked him if he was ever going to retrieve the boxes he had stored in the basement of the bar. Hemingway had long-since forgotten them, but they contained meticulous notes he had taken on his life in the twenties. They formed the nucleus for *A Moveable Feast.*

Written by a man increasingly in emotional and physical decline, *A Moveable Feast* is nonetheless hopeful, full of joyous triumphs, great and small, and more than a little snarky about members of his fellow "Lost Generation." Wounded in war, lucky in love, writing and fighting and drinking, Hemingway was larger than life.

But why is a travel writer expounding on Hemingway? When you're young and you set out to travel the world, it's best to have some guides. Hemingway, who was incredibly well-traveled, left a widely varied trail to follow, in his books and in his insatiable curiosity about discovering how the world works and how he could impact it.

I was about 25 when I made the first of my Hemingway forays. Fittingly, it was to Shakespeare and Company, now located in the shadow of Notre Dame. The venerable English language bookstore had been run by his friend Sylvia Beach. I picked up a new copy of *A Moveable Feast,* suitably embossed with "Kilometre Zero" on the title page, indicating the store's location in the middle of Paris. It would begin my lifelong search to see Hemingway's life as he saw it and to create my own moveable feast.

Much later in life, I took a guided tour of his haunts on the Left Bank. The apartment above a sawmill where Hemingway lived with his first wife, Hadley, and their son, Bumby, has long since given way to condos. But the bars and cafes he frequented mostly have survived.

Our guide, an American who was a retired *60 Minutes* producer, took us to such Hemingway hangouts as the Rotonde, La Coupole, and La Closerie des Lilas, where there is still a barstool reserved for him. I was chagrined that I had never heard of the Auberge de Venise Montparnasse until our guide informed us it had been known as the Dingo Bar back in the twenties. Yup. He had first met F. Scott Fitzgerald there.

I thought I'd already seen Gertrude Stein's building at 27 Rue du Fleurus where Hemingway often visited to consort with other artists and writers, mainly from the expatriate community. In fact, I had been on the wrong side. Our guide buzzed us into an inner courtyard featuring a view of her second-floor window.

He took us to the Luxembourg Gardens where Hemingway used to walk baby Bumby in his carriage. The aspiring writer, poor and unknown at the time, would wait until the guard was on break, stalk a few of the ubiquitous pigeons, snap their necks, and hide them in the carriage. Then he'd take them home to his wife Hadley, who would turn them into a delicious meal.

More accessible was the house where he grew up in Oak Park, Illinois. It is only about two hours from where I live, on a street filled with stately homes, befitting his father's profession as a physician. The house is only blocks away from the boyhood home of Frank Lloyd Wright, the premier American architect of the last century. Born 32 years before Hemingway, there is no evidence they ever met.

I loved visiting Hemingway's house in Key West, where he lived with his second wife, Pauline. The place is overrun with dozens of polydactyl cats, reportedly descendants of his own beloved felines. Hemingway himself had as many as 58 cats roaming the property.

Polydactyl cats were considered lucky by sea men who brought them across the Atlantic to control the rodent population aboard ship. I'm sure having extra claws to hang onto a pitching and rolling ship helped contribute to their "luck."

Hemingway's swimming pool was once the largest in all of Florida. His studio is just what you'd expect a world-class writer to have only with the glassy eyes of a wildlife trophy staring down at a well-used Royal typewriter. Regretfully, I ordered a hamburger at his favorite haunt, Sloppy Joe's bar. It didn't click with me at the time that the "sloppy joe" sandwich had been created there.

Kris and I and our friend, Mary Bell, didn't know what to expect when we walked into Harry's Bar in Venice, a favorite of his in the forties. I asked the bartender for a beer. "Harry's Bar does not serve beer," he informed me, a definite edge in his voice. "Well, what did Hemingway drink?" I asked. "MISTER Hemingway," he emphasized, "drank martinis." "I'll have one," I replied. A former bartender myself, I'd made hundreds of martinis, but it never occurred to me to actually drink one. I took one sip and turned it over to Mary, who pronounced it delicious and drained it. I'm pretty sure Hemingway, who had a well-publicized macho side, would not have approved of having a woman finish my drink.

Cuba lionizes Hemingway. Room 511 at the lovely Ambos Mundos Hotel in old Havana is now a Hemingway shrine because of his frequent presence over many years in the thirties and forties. I was blown away by Finca Vigia, his 15-acre compound on a hill overlooking Havana. He had it built in 1940 and lived there with his fourth wife, Mary, until shortly after the revolution in 1959 and before his own death in 1961. It's a beautiful sprawling place with a tower for his writing and what appears to be an Olympic sized swimming pool. Guests stayed in a large guest house next door that is currently in serious need of repairs. The revolutionaries were OK with Hemingway, although at the time he was much more interested in Africa, fishing, drinking, and writing. He did meet Fidel Castro once at a fishing contest after he became president. Castro won the contest and Hemingway presented him with the trophy.

There are still plenty of sites to see. I no longer wish to run with the bulls as Hemingway did in Pamplona, Spain and am appalled at the idea of shooting wild animals in Africa. Still, I'd love to see other places that shaped his life. How about the levee in Italy where he was wounded driving an ambulance in World War I? Or Schruns, Austria, where he'd tackle the expert ski runs? Finally, I'd like to see his last house in Ketchum, Idaho. He's buried in the city's cemetery.

Who's your travel muse? Maybe you want to join Mark Twain seeing the dawn from Mount Rigi in Switzerland. Or you want to play all the golf courses where Seve Ballesteros won a tournament. Perhaps St. Paul will take you along to every place he tried to convert the heathens.

Purposeful travel doesn't have to rise to the level of serious consequence. Sometimes just spending time traveling with a famous friend from the past is enough.

My eight languages

Entshuldigen zie. Excuse me. I am addressing you in German. Do not be impressed because it is my eighth language. You, see, I have not mastered any of them, with the possible exception of the one in which you are reading this. So *excuse moi* if I can't seem to stop starting new ones.

It began with Sister Theodorita in ninth grade. You would think that the Latin she taught me would hold me in good stead as an altar boy. It didn't. Anyway Sister Bubbles (so named for a slight saliva problem in her speaking style) was less concerned with the glory of God than the glory of Caesar's legions as they thundered through Gaul.

Latin was not a dead language, she assured us. It would be alive as long as we could read it.

After two years of hailing Caesar, I switched to Spanish, a language I keep coming back to (which was eminently useful in my own classroom as I communicated with new first-generation Americans). I did very well in high school and thought I could coast into college, and maybe even minor in Spanish.

Unfortunately, in recognition of my declining performance, the kindly Professor Manalich made a deal with me. He would give me a passing grade if I would consent to taking no more Spanish. I agreed. *Dispensamente.*

But I kept at it anyway, and three decades later, I reached the high point of my Spanish skills. On a labor delegation tour of Colombia, I found myself sitting in meetings day after day with Colombian labor leaders under duress due to the political instability surrounding them.

An epiphany occurred one day when I realized I understood everything a particular speaker had said before the translator relayed it. Alas, that was one speaker, one situation, and the trip was soon over.

French has been a continuing labor of love. Although I have taken several classes over the years, I owe Dr. Paul Pimsleur a debt of gratitude for training me to speak it the right way. I have his recordings in French, Spanish, and German on my iPhone and find them very effective.

Effective enough to fool people. I was once privileged to attend the signing ceremony for a partnership agreement between officials in Wisconsin and those from two French regions.

A woman from the French Consulate responded to my (rehearsed) sentence with a barrage of French, overwhelming my meager vocabulary. Seeing my deer-in-the-headlights look, she switched to English. "Your accent was so good I thought you actually spoke French."

A *tres bien* French compliment, to be sure.

Eight of us rented a four-bedroom canal boat to go from Carcassonne to the Mediterranean on the beautiful Canal du Midi in southern France.

My level of comfort with the French language was much higher than on previous trips—no doubt owing to my improved pronunciation. One day, I went into a pharmacy looking for some prescription medication. The pharmacist acknowledged my need, set to work on solving my problem, then seamlessly switched us to English. This happened repeatedly as the French increasingly adopted English as their second language.

Before going to Japan for three weeks, I made 100 flash cards of words I thought I'd need—English on one side, Japanese on the other. I found the pronunciation quite similar to Spanish.

The English speakers I met there, even those who taught English, often had an impenetrable accent. One of our translators, however, was a Japanese woman with a beautiful British accent. I asked her about it. She said she had learned English with an American accent but switched to a British accent because it gave her greater credibility. *Sumimasen,* you can switch accents?

My Japanese high point came on my last day in Tokyo when I resolved to go to a train station alone to eat at one of those stand-up noodle shops. I studied several patrons to get the routine: 1. Put some yen into a vending machine outside the noodle shop. 2. Press a button next to a picture on the machine indicating your selection. 3. Take a printed ticket from the machine. 4. Go inside the shop and present it to the server behind the counter. 5. Take your bowl and some chopsticks to a stand-up table and noisily slurp your noodles.

I performed the ritual flawlessly until I got to the counter and a server asked me a question. I asked her to repeat it then realized she was saying *"udon"* or *"soba"* two kinds of noodles that each happened to be on my 100-word vocabulary list.

"Soba," I replied triumphantly, then collected my food and strutted confidently to my stand-up table.

My forays into Italian and Portuguese never went beyond mundane greetings. I got the Italian mixed up with Spanish and thought of Portuguese as Spanish as spoken by Germans, which truly mixed me up.

The fact is that it doesn't much matter anymore. We've won the world language lottery. If someone from Greece needs to talk to someone from Sweden, they use my language, English.

Go on the Radio Garden app and listen to any random radio station from around the world. There's a good chance at least part of their programming is in English.

I have mixed feelings about that. I'm glad that English is doing so well and I'm grateful that the default world language didn't turn out to be Mandarin or Russian.

But there's a part of me that feels we've lost something. And there are plenty of places left where English does not rule.

For those places, I have Google Translate. I especially use it for menus, where you can focus your camera on a menu in a foreign language and read its translation on your screen in English.

Ain't technology great? *Ist die Technologie nicht großartig?*

There will be bears

When I first started traveling, it felt like there was a brick wall surrounding the act of travel. A lack of information greeted me whenever I considered getting off the tour bus and traveling outside of standard boundaries. Beyond that wall lurked—well, I don't know what. Bears, maybe.

I had some friends who grabbed backpacks and scaled the wall, venturing into the unknown with no more than a Eurail Pass.

Good for them, but that wasn't my style any more than the tour buses were.

Plenty of travelers on the timeline had chronicled what's out there. Consider Julius Caesar's exploits in Gaul (which the Franciscan sisters had me read in Latin), the epistles of St. Paul (those I had to read in English), reports of the exotic Orient by Marco Polo, Columbus's meticulous self-incrimination about pillaging the new world, and Magellan's world-spinning voyage, recounted in 1524 by Antonio Pigafetta, one of just 18 people who survived the trip.

Those larger-than-life travels don't represent the precursors of modern travel, however. The closest historical analogy we can make is probably pilgrimages, long treks made by ordinary people, ostensibly for spiritual reasons.

To this day, about two million people per year visit the Great Mosque in Mecca, Saudi Arabia to complete the *hajj*, a holy practice for Muslims that has been going on since the year 628. Christians started their Camino de Santiago (Way of St. James) walk some two hundred years later in northern Spain. About 350,000 make this arduous trek every year.

Although I spent a week walking along Hadrian's Wall to cross England, traveling on foot really wasn't my style either.

Murray's Handbooks for Travellers in London came out in 1836, paving the way for a German publisher named Karl Baedeker, who created the first popular travel guides in 1839. Amazingly, the company is still producing guidebooks under the Baedeker name almost 200 years later.

Mark Twain's *Innocents Abroad (1869)* is almost a guidebook and tells of his journey to Europe and the Holy Land. His book demonstrates how travel and humor go really well together. It was Twain's account of watching the dawn from Mount Rigi (near Lucerne) that inspired me to do the same more than 100 years later.

Twain's modern-day successor is arguably Bill Bryson, who wrote *A Walk in the Woods*, humorously cataloguing human foibles on the Appalachian Trail. His trail buddy, Stephen Katz, overweight, overmatched, and occasionally lost, does get a shot in occasionally, teasing Bryson about his irrational fear of bears. (I told you there'd be bears.)

The best travel writer in my lifetime has been Paul Theroux. His prose is impossible to duplicate. I've tried. His first real travel book, *The Great Railway Bazaar*, probably had a more profound effect on my life than any other book. Here's Theroux in an unusually optimistic mood in *Dark Star Safari* (2003) bouncing along on a bus in Uganda: *I was still traveling in a state of contentment, wary as always but with a feeling of relative safety. I stood out as a muzungu, of course, but an older one in secondhand clothes, wearing a cheap watch and a faded hat. My sports jacket was badly torn: battery acid had burned large holes in it on one of my truck rides. Tatters in Africa are like camouflage, and mine made me less conspicuous.*

I don't travel in the back of a truck, have a vintage Apple watch, and have never had battery acid eat my clothes. No, I don't travel that way either.

This brings us back to the category of guidebooks. These writers don't want to regale you with stories, nor are they especially interested in your own travel anecdotes. Their mission is to provide for you the kind of on-the-ground information that will keep your travels safe, interesting, and affordable.

They look for decent hotels. So do I. They ferret out restaurants where the locals eat. So do I. They chronicle all the local transportation options. Me too.

This is how I travel. The books speak directly to me. The stories are a bonus.

The first time I went to Europe, in the seventies, I took Temple Fielding's guidebook with me. He had a wicked wit and projected the kind of traveling I thought I wanted at the time: "A sport jacket on an adult is considered improper at the leading restaurants," he intoned, no doubt while he sipped champagne in his Italian suit. He focused meticulously on hotels and restaurants but took the time to point out where gentlemen could find hookers in London. He all but ignored sightseeing, devoting just 56 lines to scenic attractions in Rome in his Europe guidebook.

His main competition at the time was Arthur Frommer, who opened up travel to people who didn't arrive in a chauffeured limousine. His *Europe on $5 a Day* ($85 in today's edition) outsold Fielding two to one. I interviewed Frommer in the late eighties for a local paper. I found him delightful. His daughter, Pauline, now runs the Frommer travel publishing business.

With dozens of guidebooks, a tour company that takes 30,000 people a year to Europe, a weekly radio show, and a TV show on PBS, the reigning king of travel is Rick Steves. Rick urges his readers to become "temporary locals," advice he personifies on his shows as he hoists a beer in Bavaria, becomes immersed in music in Austria, and knifes through traffic in Rome.

He is a supporter of solution-based politics, builds housing for the homeless, doesn't just feed the hungry, but funds advocates for them (Bread for the World), and acts as a spokesperson for reform of marijuana laws.

"When I'm interviewed by Rick Steves," is my stock answer to those who ask how I'll know if my book is successful.

There is no longer a brick wall that keeps us from knowing what's out there. I can press a button and be on Trip Advisor checking out hotels all over the world. I can use the American Airlines app on my phone to select a flight to replace the one that was just cancelled. I can use my GPS to direct me to any place with a road.

Still, I purchase a guidebook for every major trip. Sometimes two or three. I want someone who's on my side curating my trip. I want them to alert me to substandard hotels and redirect me to hidden gems and tell me which street vendors have the best *poffertjes*.

And of course, I want them to warn me if there will be bears.

Chapter 13
Advanced Placement

Final Lessons

What's a Tour de Glenn?

Any trip that I've designed and taken with between 4 and 32 travelers is a "Tour de Glenn." One of my tripmates came up with the term and it just seemed to stick.

Are you a tour guide?

I consider myself more of a trip architect. Travel agents and tour guides are professionals who do this for a living. I do it for fun. I know far less than they do about general travel. I know a lot more than they do about my particular trip.

You're a traveler

You're looking up from your favorite café on the Left Bank in Paris. A full cup of café crème awaits, steam rising from it. A flaky chocolate croissant keeps it company.

Your friend's iPhone is in portrait mode as she snaps a memorable picture of you.

Beyond the café chairs, grim-faced travelers struggle to keep up with a woman holding a red checkered flag over her head.

There's a certain smugness—let's call it self-satisfaction, in your expression as you watch them file by. Tourists. You look down at your Kindl and start to read the last chapter of this book. It's written for you. You're a traveler.

223

Do you use travel agents?

I love travel agents, but I only use them for exotic destinations or when I get stuck. For example, finding the right Rhine River cruise (with extra AAA benefits). I've also used a local travel agent for trips to Brazil and Peru. I worked with an online Cuba specialist for my trip to Havana.

Is being a trip architect like being a real one?

My friend, Mike, designed and built a two-story garage for us so elaborate it was named the Garage Mahal. He needed a plan, a foundation, a frame, building materials, and an interior. Like him, I start with a travel plan. My foundation includes resources, notably time and money. The frame includes flights and accommodations. The building materials are the travelers, and the interior finishing touches include all the activities and moving around that we do at our destinations. Things really have to proceed in the right order, or you run the risk of your building falling down.

What happens once you reach your destination?

In the planning stages, I often invite input from the travelers, who are usually also veteran road warriors. Together, we craft options for each day of the trip. Not everyone has to do the same thing on the same day. These days, I rarely have a strong need to do or see a particular attraction. Exceptions include bucket-list things such as the Glacier Express train trip we took through Switzerland at my request. The next day, when most of the group wanted to take the tram up for a closer view of the Matterhorn, I stayed behind to explore Zermatt. It's all about choices.

Why would your friends go on a Tour de Glenn rather than, say, a Tauck or Grand Circle Tour?

Paid tours fit you into boxes they've already made, unlike Tour de Glenns, which are built around the interests and capabilities of the travelers involved. I can fit each one with as many bells and whistles as it can take. Paid tours do provide staff to cater to your needs, but they also cost more, travel well-worn paths, and insulate you from your destination and its people. The main thing they provide is a safety net.

Have you ever wished you had a safety net?

Sure. It was a cold November night in Provence. We were about a mile from our apartment, my cousin Captain Jack's place on the grounds of a golf course. I didn't realize that the security gate closed at 10:00 pm and we needed a code to open it. I couldn't reach Jack, but I remembered there was a Hotel Mercure on grounds. I called them and they provided the code. If I had been on a tour, the safety net would have caught me (but also deprived me of an adventure).

Have you ever done anything really "outside the box" in planning a Tour de Glenn?

I spent a year putting together the 84-mile walk across England along Hadrian's Wall that ultimately included 23 travelers (see Chapter 4). I was having major problems with accommodations for that many people. Also, I was still working full time. I called up our friends Peggy and Bob a year out and said, "Talk me out of this crazy idea of going to England for four days on a scouting trip." Peggy said, "Sounds like a great idea." So we went. I had compiled a list of a dozen accommodations. When we arrived at our third stop, Ashcroft Guest House in the centrally located town of Haltwhistle, we knew we had found what we were looking for. It couldn't hold all of us, but the stately Centre of Britain Hotel was just a block away and could handle the rest. With the addition of six rental cars, the trip came together in that moment.

How do you handle money in a Tour de Glenn?

I try to divide the responsibility among group members, so the financial exposure isn't all mine. For instance, when the Bus to Nowhere failed to deliver us to Burgundy, it was Dianne who got us a refund. She had paid it with her credit card, and successfully appealed the charge to Mastercard. Some things, such as train tickets, really shouldn't be bought separately, so I'll put them all on my card. Usually, I'll accumulate a certain amount of spending then ask for a check, or more recently, a Venmo transfer.

Are there any rules for a Tour de Glenn?

I didn't know so I asked a few of the travelers. Being flexible and curious is important. You have to want to be part of the group, so if you go off on your own every day, you probably aren't a good fit. Occasionally, you should take the lead on something, such as restaurant reservations or taxis to the airport. Don't aggravate the tour leader. Two things come to mind: quibbling about small amounts of money and harassing the waitstaff. This last one is a real deal-breaker for me. I grew up in my parents' restaurant. I have a very high tolerance for how waiters, waitresses, and bartenders do their jobs. If you're rude and demanding with them, I really don't want to be around you.

What's special about the first Tour de Glenn, in Tuscany in 2001?

(See Chapter 3) We were just starting to understand the vast capabilities that technology could provide in travel planning. For example, before the internet, the only access to foreign train schedules was in reference books in libraries, and it was often out of date. GPS navigation for cars officially began that same year, although we didn't have it. We used a rented cell phone that was mailed to us. That first trip included eight people, a number I've concluded is best for my type of travel (two cars, four hotel rooms). Recently I compiled some data on myself. I've averaged 8.1 travelers per trip.

Planning a Tour de You: Part One

You've heard enough about Tour de Glenns. It's time to plan a Tour de You.

Let's start with what you already know. Most US travel is by car, unless it's more than a few hundred miles, when flying becomes an option. Buses, trains, boats, and motorcycles are rare. You probably can't name many people who've taken a guided tour in the US, especially a bus tour. OK, maybe Aunt Ruth took a bus to Branson with the girls, but that's about it.

I was having breakfast with my friend Steve at a local café. He had been talking to friends about his recent trip to Italy and Sicily, a sort-of next generation Tour de Glenn.

"Which company did you use?" was always the first question they asked.

When he told them he was traveling on his own, they eyed him with new respect and more than a little incomprehension. He pointed out that no tour would have taken them to his wife's ancestral hometown, in a little backwater part of Sicily. Steve and Debbie traveled in Italy just as they would have traveled in the US. So can you.

In fact, there's no reason you can't take the same approach to overseas travel that you do to travel at home and travel on your own.

There are exceptions. In places where the infrastructure is weak, language is a problem, safety is a concern, or external realities such as politics or geography are in play, stick with a tour.

The last time I was in Brazil, we took my mom there. We wanted to see more of the country than Rio de Janiero. Because of her age and because it was easier and safer, we used a tour company. Doing so minimized family decision-making, a contribution to group harmony that shouldn't be discounted.

We are going to assume that the Tour de You that you're planning is to a fairly common vacation destination, probably Europe. Let's take a close look at the variables that go into planning. You can do this.

Who's going?

I didn't know whether to make the first category time or people. In fact, I never do. By locking in time parameters, you lock out certain participants.

For example, because I was a school teacher, many of my brother's marathons were a no-go for me. My district expected me to work a 190-day contract and was quite reluctant to allow me to choose which 190 days I wanted to work.

Sometimes deciding who's on the trip is kind of automatic. Family. Golf group. Kiwanis Club.

Other times, you risk putting someone's nose out of joint by not inviting them. Or, and this is often worse, you pressure someone into going who then determines that they're not going to have a good time no matter what.

Aside: I believe some people are born with the "travel gene" and some aren't. Here's how you can tell which category you're in: *With the gene*: "It was a great trip, but it's wonderful to be home. When can I go again?" *Without the gene:* "It was a great trip, but it's wonderful to be home. I'm glad I don't have to do that again."

Usually, the three main dimensions of travel—time, place and people—are decided by consensus. But there always needs to be a final decision-maker. Since you're the one reading this book, it's probably you. Try to assemble an all-star team of people you like who also like each other. Ideally, they are people who will allow you to make decisions without calling a summit meeting every time you have to make one.

Time

There's no wrong time to travel when it comes to seasons. When I was teaching, I was locked into certain travel windows, mostly summer, and longed to travel when it wasn't so busy or so hot. Later, I concluded it doesn't matter. Crowds mostly don't bother me, plus they're easy enough to avoid if you're not on a tour. And weather can be a factor any time. The best time to travel is when you're ready to go.

Other aspects of travel-time are location-specific. For example, I was in St. Moritz, Switzerland in June. It was off season and kind of a ghost town. Travel a few hours to Zermatt and you'll find a bustling and exciting place in June. Or take Paris. If you find yourself there in August, you'll be delighted with how uncrowded it is. That's because real Parisians take the month off and leave town. Unfortunately, that includes most of the people who run the little shops and cafes you came there to experience. They're closed. Americans are incredulous that places would turn down all that revenue during the peak of the summer travel season. But they do. You're not in the US anymore.

The more important question is when can you fit travel into your schedule? When can your friends and family do so? If you don't have a given time frame, it's often helpful to establish a mostly bogus travel timeline to help move the process along.

My wife is a huge fan of Beatrix Potter, mostly known for her Peter Rabbit books, but in actuality a powerhouse of a woman who shaped the modern-day Lake District in northern England. Kris belongs to the Beatrix Potter Society. We once built a trip around one of their meetings in London, a pretty random event in the global scheme of things.

Take any interest you have—gardening, literature, Etruscan tombs, World War II--and I guarantee you can find an exhibit or a convocation of like-minded travelers at your destination.

Your travel mates don't need to share your passion, but it does provide a reason for you to lock in the dates of your trip and end the discussion.

You need to negotiate trip duration. I've been to Europe on a four-day trip and I've been there for a month. Planning isn't much different. What you're leaving behind is probably what's foremost in your mind. For us, making sure our two cats get the kind of attention they deserve is paramount.

That pales in comparison to some of our friends who have elderly parents or other relatives to care for. Because of all the necessary arrangements, planning a trip is huge for them. So is actually being able to go once the time arrives. The final answer to the time question comes when you book flights. We'll get to that in the next section.

Destinations

You probably have an opinion on this. Your family is from Croatia. Or you read a book about Paris. Your uncle is buried in Belgium. You took German in school. It's all good. There aren't many places, at least in the European Union, that aren't likely to deliver an exceptional travel experience.

That said, you may want to consider balancing the trip between rural and urban experiences. I love the energy of the big city, but welcome walking bucolic country lanes next to a pasture full of sheep.

My city favorites: Paris, the most harmonious architectural city in the world, with incomparable food, culture and easy transport; Amsterdam with its beautiful canals and laid-back attitude; Lucerne, with its favored location between mountain and lake.

My town and country favorites: The English Lake District in northern England with its majestic fells and storybook towns, including our favorite, Ambleside; Luxembourg, where all public transportation is free and roads are better than yours at home; Lake Como, Italy, the prettiest place I've ever been.

Money

One of the reasons people use travel agents and canned tours is because it solves most money-handling problems. Depending on your financial status, you may not want to assume even temporary responsibility for all the trip's cost parameters. Make it clear early which arrangements travelers will be responsible for (usually booking their own flights) and which ones you will make up front for reimbursement later (group train tickets, deposits on house rentals).

Communication

I like to send out monthly communiques to the group. Usually, I have something fairly important to say. Even if I don't, I'll research some fun thing to share just to keep them thinking about the trip. Never assume they've actually read your communications or are into it like you are. If it's really important (e.g., BOOK FLIGHTS NOW!) ask them to forward to you the confirmations when they've received them. You'll be amazed at how much they don't know even if you've told them four times.

Expectations

Keep them real, but keep in mind that everyone might not be on the same page. Or even in the same book. How people think can often surprise you. We drove past a place called the Badger Bar out in the countryside in the English Lake District. Since we are from the Badger State, we decided we had to return for supper. I looked up the website and found a marvelous exchange initiated by a customer:

"It was absolutely trash. We ate our food excited to see the badgers later that evening. One hour waiting, no badgers. Two flipping hours later and no badgers, absolutely unbelievable. Would not recommend for seeing badgers."

Glen Rothay, the manager and owner, responded: "I have passed your message on to our furry friends. We are still in the process of getting our WILD badgers to tell the time. But please be assured that we'll let you know when we have trained them to put on the badger cabaret at 8:00 pm prompt. In the meantime, they turn up every single evening, but some patience may be required."

We had a delightful supper there.

Now to make sure that your travel badgers are ready to meet expectations, please read Part Two.

Planning a Tour de You: Part Two

Building a trip resembles building a house. You have to build it on a sound foundation. Below are the tools you'll need, and the key structural pieces assembled in the order that will keep your edifice stable. As you gain experience, you'll be able to tell when it's safe to make modifications.

Select accommodations.

This should be your first step if you are planning to use VRBO or Air BnB. Their dates are much more difficult to pin down than hotels. I've used both companies with success. Air BnB is significantly bigger and may have more offerings, but it often depends on which location you're searching. Occasionally, you will run across a local or regional booking service, and I've had success with them too.

If you are using traditional hotels, book airfare first. The advantages of renting a house, condo or apartment are many: 1. You typically pay half as much money for twice as much space. 2. You save even more money because you have a kitchen and won't have to eat every meal in a restaurant. This is especially important if you are traveling with children. 3. Your group isn't fragmented into different locations as in often cavernous hotels. 4. You sometimes have access to really cool amenities, such as a private pool, hot tub, professional kitchen, or foosball table.

Before looking at houses, you need to do a little research about your destination using a guidebook or online sources. Once you've decided which area attracts most of your interest, try to book a place in it or nearby. Don't bother looking at the per day cost—it's a fantasy number. Once you add in cleaning, the parent company's cut, local taxes, and a few other things, the number will look very different. That's the number you need to use for comparison purposes.

Be very careful if housing managers try to take you off the grid and not communicate or transact business through VRBO or Air BnB. I understand that they don't want to pay the commission, but this is not your fight. Move on if they persist. I once rented a place in Croatia, paid them, then a few weeks later was told an emergency had come up and I couldn't rent the property. I got my money back in less than a week. Air BnB wishes to keep me as a customer. If I had gone off the grid, those protections would have been gone with it.

As you scan through available places, match up the bedrooms with your traveling group. If your eight-person group consists mostly of singles, a four-bedroom condo with a queen size bed in each won't work. If most of the bedrooms are on level 3 of the house and you're traveling with people who have mobility issues, that probably won't work either. Look carefully at the pictures. Read all the latest reviews. After you've done that, email the manager a benign question, such as how close the nearest grocery store is. You are really testing their responsiveness, command of language, reliability, and relatability, while making sure the calendar dates you selected are still available. (Keep in mind that many places like to rent in a set time frame, usually Saturday to Saturday). If your initial inquiry doesn't spur confidence, move on to another property.

If you are planning to stay in hotels, shift your search to a good guidebook, such as Rick Steves or Arthur Frommer, and go book your flights first. Compare guidebook recommendations with others on TripAdvisor. I like TripAdvisor, but its default setting is "best value." I always change it to "traveler ranked" because I prefer hard data to the decisions of an algorithm. If you have certain amenities in mind, such as "free" breakfast or airport transportation, click the appropriate boxes to include in your search. If a property is rated in the top quarter of all available ones, you're generally safe. If it's ranked lower, it's not a deal breaker, but I would do a little more research. The rankings can be capricious. The older I get, the more I look for endorsements such as "friendly and helpful staff."

When you've decided on a hotel, you can book it through the hotel website or a booking agency. I rarely book through the hotel itself anymore. The websites are just too quirky and difficult to navigate and it's harder than you think to land on (and stay on) the hotel's website. I once booked a hotel, believing I was dealing directly with the hotel but was in fact being spoofed by a fake website. I would have lost more than a thousand dollars if the hotel hadn't stepped in and taken the hit instead.

I use Booking.com most of the time. It's one more layer of protection. If you check out reviews of online travel agencies, you'll see that it's generally at or near the top of the rankings. My personal experience with Booking.com has been extremely positive. When I had to miss the first few days of a cruise, they managed to extricate me from two different "non-cancellable" hotel bookings without costing me anything. Frequent users also get room discounts of up to 30%.

I rarely pay for hotels ahead of time, even if they offer substantial savings. I select "pay at the property" if it's an option. Too many events can intervene to be assured every aspect of the trip will work right. And getting a refund is always time consuming and precarious.

Booking flights

Is there an uglier word in the English language than "monetizing?" In air world, it means taking something that used to be included and separating it out for the purpose of extracting more money from you. The airlines have become masters at this. Luggage used to be included. Food and drink too. Aisle seats. Several inches of space in front of you. Now they represent a herd of cash cows for the airlines. Bathrooms are still free, so far.

The first place I go to look for flights is Google Travel. Backed by the Google powerhouse, it has the most features and (for me) the most intuitive interface. When you start looking, you should put a list of acceptable airports in front of you for both ends of the trip. Our closest airport, Madison, Wisconsin, often makes the list of most expensive airports in the US, so flying out of Chicago, just a two-hour car ride away, is often a better option. Strangely, I've found that leaving from Chicago and returning to Madison is often the best deal of all. So don't be afraid to put in some wacky choices of airport combinations. As for time, I'll usually try to leave on a Tuesday, the lightest travel day of the week and often the cheapest. Google has extra features to help you ferret out the cheapest time to travel.

I try to fly direct to my destination whenever I can. Even one stop multiplies your chances of delay or cancellation, not to mention offering opportunities for your luggage to escape on its own vacation. If I must change planes, I pay a lot more attention than I used to about the amount of time I have to make the switch. Less than two hours is a deal breaker.

Another problem with changing planes is you may end up on a partner airline. From Philadelphia to London, I was on American, where I bought the ticket. From London to Nice, the airline "metal" (printed on the plane) was British Airways. It cost me $56 more for the segments to and from Nice to secure seats. Before I could even do that, I had to find the six-digit code for my British Air flights (that's right, it was different from my AA six-digit code). Both could be found on my trip confirmation from American, but sometimes it's so well hidden you have to call one of the airlines to find out.

By the way, the idea that repeatedly looking for flights for your trip causes the price to increase by changing the algorithm has been pretty much discounted by experts. The price fluctuations aren't your fault.

It's still not a bad idea to check other sites besides Google. I use Kayak and Momondo as backups. The latter is especially thorough for European flights.

Unlike with hotels, when it's time to buy, I never use third-party sites. I buy my tickets directly from the airlines, usually with an airline-branded credit card that exempts me from luggage fees. The reason I buy from the airlines is simple. If there's a problem, I don't want to play the Ping-Pong game where the airline says: "Talk to Expedia; you brought the ticket from them," while Expedia says, "Talk to the airline; we don't fly the planes."

If there is a problem or a change ahead of time, the airline may or may not let you know. You should check on your flights every week or two to make sure they haven't done something weird. If they do make a significant change, consider it an opportunity to improve your flights.

I was holding a United ticket to Europe last year when Lufthansa completely botched a flight segment change, setting up an impossible connection. I called United (not Lufthansa) and talked with an agent who agreed. I had already researched alternatives and she agreed to them too. Finally, I asked if I could select my seats through her. I had three different sets of seats picked out, depending on how generous United was feeling. The agent had to check with her boss, but then agreed, giving me my first choice. It would have cost an extra thousand dollars for four of us.

If you feel like you're in over your head, go see your local travel agent and let them book your flights. It will cost you some money, but may save you from yourself. I always use a travel agent traveling to South America or Africa. On two different occasions, the agents found out before I did that my flights home had been cancelled. They were already working on fixing the problem by the time I contacted them.

Troubleshooting your trip

What do you do if you're traveling independently abroad, and you need help?

The travel infrastructure in developed countries offers help in a variety of ways. Here's where to look.

Airports

Your most common dilemma will be a missed or delayed flight. Here are the steps to take when that happens. I suggest you do all of them at once.

Find the help desk for your airline. If there isn't one or if it's in a different terminal, approach any gate featuring your airline that has personnel staffing it and ask for their help.

While you're standing in line (you probably are not the only one impacted by events), take out your phone and call the airline. You'll probably end up waiting in line there too. If you can, offload this task to someone traveling with you.

That will leave you free to use a third approach. The airline app should already be loaded onto your phone. Open it. Chances are good that it will greet you with up-to-date knowledge of your situation and possible solutions. If it solves your problem, great. If not, see if it can offer other choices that will. In any event, keep standing in line and stay on hold while you navigate the app.

I have used a fourth strategy when I'm otherwise engaged at the airport (e.g., on a shuttle or taking care of another traveler). I call a veteran traveler to act as a surrogate. My sister used to be a travel agent. I text her my six-digit flight code and have her negotiate with the airline and get back to me with a solution.

Don't be afraid to ask for food and hotel vouchers if the wait is going to be long. They aren't always obligated to provide them, but it doesn't hurt to ask.

When your trip is completed, and you really believe the airline screwed up, send a polite email carefully describing events. I've had times when they haven't admitted any fault but credited extra frequent flyer miles to my account anyway.

Hotels

One reason I use Booking.com to book hotels is having another layer of protection in case there is a problem. They can intercede if you're caught in a blizzard and won't be arriving anytime soon or you took the flight to Auckland, New Zealand instead of Oakland, California (it's happened).

The larger hotels have a concierge desk to help with things like local transport or restaurant reservations, but the desk staff is sufficient for most needs. When I was aboard the "bus to nowhere" (see Chapter 5), I called the hotel where we had stayed and used the friendly desk clerk we had gotten to know to translate our bus driver's French.

If you are in a city and need help, walking into the nearest hotel will often garner some assistance even if you're not a guest there.

On the street

Nearly any city of size, at least in Europe, has a tourist office, often with multiple locations. Check your guidebook or ask at a hotel or train station. Quality varies a lot at them. Some are incredibly helpful and anticipate your needs. Others make you feel grateful to get a small map.

If you're lost, try the techniques I used in "Hey, Siri, where am I?" (Chapter 11). If there's a large hotel nearby, they probably have a taxi stand or you can use your Uber app to summon a driver. Or just call your hotel and explain the situation. Some have even been known to send their van to get you.

I booked my wife and her friend on a roots tour of Norway. They only way they could get into trouble was taking the wrong route out of the airport, so of course they did. It was 5:00 am Wisconsin time when Kris called me, lost in Oslo. I had her grab a cab and take an expensive (\$100+) ride to her hotel. Sometimes, you just have to buy your way out of trouble.

If you're really in danger, such as my friend Curt, who fell and broke an arm and a leg on the streets of Reykjavik, Iceland, passersby will usually step in and help. Short of that, you should know what number to call to reach emergency services. In Iceland, it's 112, not 911. Your guidebook will have the appropriate number for the country you're visiting. Because you speak English, they should be able to help you.

Unlike in the US, it's common for Europeans with sickness or injury to first go to the pharmacy. Pharmacists can diagnose and prescribe remedies for simple problems. My wife (again) tripped over a baby carriage at a French market. The fall gave her a black eye and a face wound. Luckily, a pharmacy was right across the street, and they helped patch her up.

Don't overlook your trip insurance provider as a source of aid, including possible financial assistance. (See Trip Insurance Weasels, Chapter 9). I have their app on my phone and can contact them day or night.

Your contact of last resort should be the United States government. In the bigger cities, representatives of the US can be found in embassies and consulates. Contact them for a lost or stolen passport or for serious legal troubles. For lesser problems, they are not sufficiently staffed to provide much help although they usually maintain a list of English-speaking health care facilities on their websites.

Useful travel websites

All Purpose Sites

It's hard to avoid Expedia. It owns Travelocity, Orbitz, VRBO, Hotels.com, Trivago, and much more. Each of the sites has a unique personality. Add Priceline to this group and you have some competent places to start general trip planning.

Accommodations

Trip Advisor, VRBO, Air BnB, Booking.com, Hotels.com are the sites I visit the most. I usually start with Trip Advisor to assess the best places in my price range close to my targeted location. I almost always book through Booking.com rather than the hotel site or any other third-party site. I've had success with both VRBO and Air BnB in renting entire houses.

Flights

As I indicated in the previous chapter, I start flight planning at Google Travel. I try different combinations of dates and airports to see what the going rate is. I also like Kayak and Momondo for general flights, and Skyscanner and Which Budget for European flights, especially the budget airlines. Ryan Air flies almost everywhere in Europe dirt cheap at inconvenient times from inconvenient airports. A great site to discover which airline flies out of a given airport ON WHICH DAYS is FlightsFrom.com. When it's time to purchase airline tickets, I almost always buy from the airline itself. I rarely buy one-way tickets and often look for open-jaw tickets where I fly into one city and out of another. These also are called "multiple city" tickets. Start your search process with them because you can't add them later.

Trains

For European trains, I've had the most success using The Train Line to research and buy tickets. Other choices are Rail Europe and the most complete site, German Rail (bahn.de). If you are thinking about buying a train pass, check out Rick Steves' website, which has a complete rundown. In the US, don't neglect Amtrak, especially if you are a senior. Tickets are cheap and the rides are social, fun, and slow.

Guidebooks

Sure, they're out of date and bulky to carry, but they are vetted by people who are doing what you're doing, only better. Rick Steves' many guides are the gold standard, but rifle through them before you buy. Their coverage is very complete in certain locations but often doesn't extend to more obscure places, which is where I expect to find you if you're still reading this book. Frommer's guides still hold up well. Fodor's are less chatty and more information-centered. Lonely Planet and The Rough Guide generally appeal to younger travelers.

Boats

My favorite is Vacations to Go. It is very comprehensive when it comes to the current prices for every cruise ship and river boat that dips its hull into the water. When it comes to buying, I sometimes use their agents, sometimes buy from the cruise line, and occasionally go to a travel agent if I think they can throw in some extra perks. Go to Cruise Critic and Cru Con for other opinions. If you want to operate your own canal boat, check out LeBoat.com. If you want to make a colorful river boat brochure come to life, contact Viking, Avalon, or AMA Waterways.

Vehicles

I really hate renting cars. Ads promise $5.95 per day but the contract inches closer to $100 per day when you add in things like rims and tires. I'm only half-kidding. Of course, they provide the rims. My current favorite is AutoSlash, a metasite that offers choices. If you're a Costco member, their car rental website is worth checking out. I've rented from Turo several times (cars that may be older or more exotic—think Tesla—from private individuals). Uber and Lyft apps should be on your phone in case you need just a point-to-point ride. To lease a car in Europe (a great deal if you'll be there at least three weeks), go to Auto Europe and also check out what Rick Steves has to say about them.

Tours

As the rest of this book makes clear, I'm not a very good customer for tour companies. When I needed to book my wife's tour of Norway, I chose Collette. Gate 1 Travel, Globus, and Go-Today are usually affordable. I've used Latin America for Less. On the higher end of the scale are Trafalgar and Overseas Adventure Travel. Road Scholar (formerly Elderhostel) centers trips around learning.

Insurance

My wife and I have year-round travel policies underwritten by Allianz. For single trips, use Squaremouth.com, where you can select the coverage you need and be offered choices of companies. Insuremyrentalcar will always have better rates than buying insurance from the car rental company.

Phones Abroad

Verizon, ATT, and T-Mobile account for nearly all US cellphones. Their plans have gotten simpler. My carrier, ATT, charges me ten bucks a day. Always check their website to see what the latest wrinkle is. If you want to go the Sim Card route, Vodaphone and Orange are two companies in Europe that will be able to accommodate you.

Frequent Flyer and Professional Travelers

If you want to dream big about collecting miles and points, go to websites for Flyer Talk, Frequent Miler, or The Points Guy. View from the Wing has a very irreverent take on the airline industry. Nomadic Matt seems like a good guy who's willing to share his travel adventures.

Other

The Rome to Rio site is great to connect one place with another, whether by train, plane, bus or Segway. Viator has local tour guides. LACS.lu helps you pursue your Luxembourg citizenship (See Chapter 1), Xe.com converts currencies, Run Keeper maps your walk or run, but more importantly, helps keep you from getting lost. Memory books are available from these places: Snapfish, Walgreens, Shutterfly, Amazon. They all do a nice job.

www.ingramcontent.com/pod-product-compliance
Lightning Source LLC
Chambersburg PA
CBHW060301100426
42742CB00011B/1829